DEMOCRACY, SECURITY, AND DEVELOPMENT IN INDIA

DEMOCRACY, SECURITY, AND DEVELOPMENT IN INDIA

Raju G. C. Thomas

St. Martin's Press
New York

JQ
281
T56
1996

DEMOCRACY, SECURITY, AND DEVELOPMENT IN INDIA
Copyright © 1996 by Raju G. C. Thomas

ISBN 0-312-06607-4

Library of Congress Cataloging-in-Publication Data

Thomas, Raju G. C.
    Democracy, security, and development in India / Raju G.C. Thomas.
        p. cm.
    Includes index.
    ISBN 0-312-06607-4
    1. Democracy—India. 2. National security—India. 3. Civil
-military relations—India. 4. India—Economic policy. I. Title.
JQ281.T56 1996
320.954—dc20   95-26193
                                                                CIP

Book design by Acme Art, Inc.

First Edition: March 1996
10 9 8 7 6 5 4 3 2 1

CONTENTS

Preface vii

Map of India ix

List of Abbreviations x

1. DEMOCRACY, STABILITY, AND THE ECONOMY 1

The Scope of the Problem

Democratic Movements and Democratic Maintenance

The Democratic Experience in South Asia

Authoritarianism, Democracy, and Development Elsewhere

The British Experience and Other Cases

Democracy, Ethnic Nationalism, and Secessionist Violence

The Importance of India as a Case Study

The Analytical Dimensions

2. THE CONCEPTUAL DIMENSION 25

The Relationship between Democracy, Security, and Development

Normative Choices and Policy Priorities

The Question of "Appropriate" Democracy

The Instability of Centralized Democracies

The Inefficiency of Public-Sector Capitalism

The Issue of Equitable Income Distribution

Secularism and Democracy

State Sovereignty versus Ethnic Self-Determination

3. THE SECURITY-POLITICAL DIMENSION 51

Security Threats and the Erosion of Democracy

The Sources of External Threats

The Sources of Internal Threats

The Effects of Civil-Military Relations on the Policy Process

Secularism, Hindu Nationalism, and Domestic Stability

The Use of Force and Human Rights Violations

4. THE CONSTITUTIONAL DIMENSION 73
    The Constitution and State Security
    National Security Emergency
    The Debate in the Constituent Assembly
    New Acts and Constitutional Amendments
    The Constitution and Fundamental Rights
    The Suspension of Democracy in the States
    The Adequacy of the Indian Political System

5. THE MILITARY DIMENSION 99
    The Military and Politics
    The Military and National Integration
    The Ethnic Factor in Recruitment Policy
    The Role of the Military in External Defense
    The Military and Internal Security
    Civilian Rule, the Military, and Internal Security
    Internal Security and the Rise of Paramilitary Forces
    The Consequences of Military Involvement in Internal Security

6. THE ECONOMIC DIMENSION 121
    Democracy and the Development First Thesis
    Indo-U.S. Security and Economic Cooperation
    Defense and Development
    Domestic Criticism of Economic Liberalization
    The Nature and Prospect of Economic Reform
    Initial Results and Consequences of Reform
    The Effects of Security Problems on the Economy

7. OPTIMIZING DEMOCRACY, SECURITY, AND DEVELOPMENT 145
    The Future of India's Democracy
    Federalism and Internal Security
    Confederalism and External Security
    Prospects for Stability in India

Notes 161
About the Author 177
Index 178

PREFACE

This book grew out of several lectures I gave between 1990 and 1995 in India, Pakistan and Sri Lanka under the auspices of the United States Information Agency (USIA) and its local United States Information Service (USIS) offices in South Asia. Apart from lectures and discussions organized at the American Centers of USIS in New Delhi, Bombay, Madras, Karachi, Islamabad, Lahore, and Colombo, USIA in Washington, D.C., also arranged for several speaking arrangements at universities, and interviews and press conferences with journalists in the region.

Among the several universities I spoke at under USIA sponsorship were Jawaharlal Nehru University, Allahabad University, Benares Hindu University, Aligarh Muslim University, Bombay University, University of Hyderabad, Madras University, and Poona University in India; Qaid-e-Azam University in Islamabad, University of Hyderabad-Jamshoro, and the University of Balochistan in Pakistan; and Colombo University and the University of Peredinya in Sri Lanka. Lectures were also delivered at the Institute for Defense Studies and Analyses, the United Services Institution of India, the Center for Policy Research, and the India International Center in New Delhi; the Institute for Strategic Studies and the Institute for Regional Studies in Islamabad; and the Bandarnaike Center for International Affairs in Colombo. Not all of these lectures at the institutes were sponsored by USIA. My thoughts about the Indian constitution and issues regarding individual rights and state rights were provoked by a USIS-sponsored lecture that I delivered at the Allahabad High Court in 1992 to some 200 lawyers and judges. This court, one of the oldest in India, has the largest membership of lawyers and judges in Asia.

Over the last decade, I have also had the privilege of delivering several lectures at the U.S. Army War College, the Foreign Service Institute of the U.S. State Department, the Defense Intelligence College of the U.S. Department of Defense, and the Royal College of Defense Studies and the Royal Naval College of the British Ministry of Defense in London.

My lectures covered themes such as "Security Versus Democracy in South Asia," "Nationalism, Secession and the State," "Defense Versus Development," "The Constitution and Indian Security," "Strategic Overview of South Asia,"

"South Asian Security in the 1990s," "The Growth of Indian Military Power," "The Sources of Indian Naval Expansion," and "The Kashmir Question."

These lectures, discussions, and feedbacks provoked me into collecting my notes and the many comments that were offered and developing them into some of the chapters that now constitute part of this book. This book is a reorganization of those lectures and my reflections on the subject of Democracy, Security, and Development in India. I looked back at my past writings and asked whether my old views and analyses still made any sense, especially following the sudden end of the Cold War in 1991. While many of the regional issues remained the same, it was clear to me that much else had changed. To begin with, the concept of security had taken on less military implications and more political and economic significance. I saw political security measured in terms of individual rights and democratic values, and economic security defined in terms of economic and social well-being for all the people of India. External military issues had become less urgent but the use of the military for internal security had become more critical. I now perceive the three essential pillars of India's stability to be political democracy, military security, and economic development. All three have to be addressed at the same time but the desired priorities and the balance between these three conditions will be subjective and controversial. This book provides the reader with alternative views regarding the essential priorities and balance that should be maintained by India while concurrently pursuing all three goals.

Funding to pursue this book project was provided by the Marquette University's Committee on Research and Bradley Institute for the Study of Democracy and Public Values. My research assistant at Marquette, Amrita Shetty, assisted me in collecting some of the data and in the final preparation of the book. Caroline Herrick was the copyeditor and Jessica Olin the editorial assistant on the manuscript.

—*Raju G. C. Thomas*
November 1995

INDIA
States and Union Territories

AFGHANISTAN

JAMMU AND KASHMIR

Line of control between India and Pakistan

CHINA

TIBET

HIMACHAL PRADESH

ARUNACHAL PRADESH

PUNJAB

Chandigarth (U.T.)

SIKKIM

BHUTAN

PAKISTAN

HARYANA

Delhi (U.T.)

NEPAL

ASSAM

NAGALAND

RAJASTHAN

UTTAR PRADESH

MEGHALAYA

MANIPUR

BIHAR

BANGLA-DESH

TRIPURA

MIZORAM

GUJARAT

WEST BENGAL

Diu (U.T.)

MADHYA PRADESH

Calcutta

BURMA

Daman (U.T.)

DADRA AND NAGAR HAVELI (Union Territories)

MAHARASHTRA

ORISSA

Bombay

BAY OF BENGAL

ANDHRA PRADESH

GOA

LAKSHADWEEP ISLANDS (Union Territories)

KARNATAKA

Madras

ANDAMAN AND NICOBAR ISLANDS (Union Territories)

Pondicherry (U.T.)

TAMIL NADU

KERALA

SRI LANKA

LIST OF ABBREVIATIONS

BJP	Bharatiya Janata Party		MQM	Mohajir Qaumi Movement
BSF	Border Security Force		NAM	Non-Alignment Movement
CCPA	Cabinet Committee on Political Affairs		NDG	National Security Guards
CDS	Chief of Defense Staff		NPT	Nuclear Non-Proliferation Treaty
CENTO	Central Treaty Organization		NSA	National Security Act
CPM	Communist Party—Marxist		OAU	Organization of African Unity
CRPF	Central Reserve Police Force		PAC	Provisional Armed Constabulary
CSC	Chiefs of Staff Committee		PPP	Pakistan People Party
DCC	Defense Committee of the Cabinet		RCD	Regional Cooperation for Development
DIR	Defense of India Rules		RIAF	Royal Indian Air Force
DMC	Defense Minister's Committee		RR	Rashtriya Rifles
DPC	Defense Planning Committee		RSS	Rashtriya Swayamsevak Sangh
ECO	Economic Cooperation Organization		SAARC	South Asian Association for Regional Cooperation
GNP	Gross National Product		SEATO	South-East Asian Treaty Organization
IJI	Islami Jamhoori Ittehad		TADA	Terrorist and Disruptive Activities Preventive Act
IMF	International Monetary Fund		ULFA	United Liberation Front of Assam
IPKF	Indian Peace-Keeping Forces		VHP	Vishwa Hindu Parishad
IRA	Irish Republican Army			
JVP	Janatha Vimukthi Peramuma			
LTTE	Liberation Tigers of Tamil Ealam			
MISA	Maintenance of Internal Security Act			
MP	member of parliament			

1

Democracy, Stability, and the Economy

THE SCOPE OF THE PROBLEM

Security analysts often separate or overlook the effects of various security policy measures on the democratic process.[1] It is no secret that the formulation and carrying out of defense policies are more difficult in open democratic political systems than they are in closed political systems controlled by authoritarian or totalitarian regimes. Especially during times of sudden and acute crises, the implementation of security policies may be hampered if various legislative and consultative procedures must always be followed by the government. Under these circumstances, the executive branch of government in a democracy may try to bypass the legislature, or to amend the constitution through legislation.

Even democratic governments sometimes feel that policies and actions must be conducted outside of public scrutiny and review. The often sudden occurrence of security crises and the need for secrecy to avoid enemy observation may make some of these actions inevitable. However, as such practices become frequent or prolonged, a political leader may become tempted to manipulate or avoid the democratic process—even in instances in which there may be little justification for doing so. Just as the pressures of security may place stress on the maintenance of democratic processes in existing democracies, such pressures may forestall democratic movements in nondemocratic countries. The need for, and the perpetuation of, authoritarian and, especially, military regimes have been justified on the grounds of maintaining the security and stability of the state. Movements for greater individual freedom and fair elections are suppressed in the name of the greater national good.

In retrospect, it should be apparent that the Cold War was not primarily a struggle to promote or maintain democracy. The Cold War was an ideological encounter between the capitalist West, led by the United States, and the Communist East, led by the Soviet Union. Although this struggle was sometimes also characterized as one between the free world and totalitarian states, there were a number of states in the first group, especially in East Asia and Latin America, that were not democratic. Thus, periodic struggles within the "free world" to overthrow ruling dictatorships surfaced occasionally as the Cold War continued, but they were given less attention or support by the democratic West. The attitude of the Western industrialized democracies, especially the United States, was that totalitarian Communist systems were more oppressive and a greater threat to the rest of the world than other types of authoritarian political systems. Non-Communist dictatorships at least maintained a private capitalist economy and open international markets, and they appeared as anxious as the Western democracies to prevent the spread of Communism. Whereas authoritarian regimes may have deprived the majority of their citizens of political representation and fair economic opportunities, they did not go as far as Communist systems in dictating and controlling the lives of their people. A free-market economy under a dictatorship was considered significantly more free than a Communist system.

As a consequence, a country like Pakistan, which was under military dictatorships for long spells but was willing to join the West's military strategy against the Communist bloc, was considered more acceptable to the West than an Indian democracy that saw military and economic benefits in maintaining close ties with totalitarian Communist states. Moreover, there was less socialism in Pakistan under its military dictators than there was in India under its democratic governments.

In the post–Cold War era following the collapse or modification of Communist systems in Europe and Asia, arguments for pushing democracy have revolved around the hypothesis that more democracies mean fewer wars and therefore fewer problems of security for most states and regions.[2] The collapse of Communism in the Soviet-bloc countries supposedly meant not only that there would be greater security for the Western democracies, including the United States and Japan, but also that the prospect of war in Europe among the old and new democracies would greatly diminish. There are, of course, several arguments that may be advanced against this hypothesis. For example, democracies have been largely confined to the affluent regions of Western Europe and North America, and the absence of wars in these regions may be attributable to their cultures and affluence rather than their political systems. And there are some questions as to whether the spread of democratic governments in the Middle East, where radical Islamists are elected to power, is likely to reduce the chances of war between them and emerging moderate secular democracies.[3] However, Bruce Russett of Yale University pointed out the following:

> Over the past 50 years, pairs of democratic states have been only one-eighth as likely as other kinds of states to threaten to use force against one another, and only one-tenth as likely to carry out these threats. Democracies have also been less likely to escalate disputes with one another, and more likely to avail themselves of third-party mediation. Moreover, the fact of peaceful relations between democracies cannot be attributed solely to other influences, such as their distance from each other, wealth or common alliances. These influences do matter; but in quantitative analyses that compensate for their effect, democracy still exerts a powerful, independent pacifying influence. There are many cases of distant authoritarian states fighting each other. The two World Wars pitted several wealthy industrialised states against one another; the Soviet Union invaded its ally Hungary in 1956. [And we may add Communist China attacked Communist Vietnam in 1988.] There are no such examples of war between democracies however.[4]

Thus, the empirical fact remains that with some exceptions, the spread of democracies within particular regions, including South Asia since 1989, has eliminated or reduced the prospect of war.

DEMOCRATIC MOVEMENTS AND DEMOCRATIC MAINTENANCE

This struggle for democracy intensified in the post–Cold War era as the threat from Communist states diminished. In Europe, Communist states have crumbled and disappeared. In Asia, they have undergone considerable liberalization and modification and may soon go the way of the European Communist countries. With Communist totalitarian regimes now mainly gone, the focus has shifted to the promotion of democracy in capitalist authoritarian states. The issue in the early 1990s was how best to displace authoritarianism with democracy in existing capitalist states. Meanwhile, new democracies that have taken root remain fragile. Old and, especially, newly established democracies are sometimes faced with the prospect of either authoritarian encroachments or collapse as they attempt to address severe internal and external security problems. The problem of "democracy under stress" is especially true of newly established democracies in the former Communist world and of states that were ruled for decades by military dictatorships. But this stress is also faced by more established democracies, such as India and Sri Lanka, that face violent ethnic secessionist movements.

In the first case—that is, in which a democracy does not exist, but in which persistent movements to establish a democracy occur—suppression by authoritarian or totalitarian regimes is usually justified on the grounds that a developing or industrializing country cannot afford the "luxury" of a democracy. According to this argument, external and, more often, internal threats to the state and the need for rapid economic development necessitate tight control and limitations on individual freedom. The struggle for democracy in such dictatorships then becomes acute, often taking the form of organized armed violence or spontaneous street demonstrations and rioting by dissident groups.

When resistance by the state provides no hope for the introduction or restoration of democracy, the violent overthrow of the existing undemocratic order may appear to be justified. However, the adoption of such violent means would seem to contradict the underlying basis and purpose of a democracy. Can those who push for democracy by using violent methods against dictatorships be sincerely democratic themselves? Chairman Mao Zedong of Communist China once proclaimed that "Political power grows from the barrel of a gun."[5] Under oppressive and repressive conditions, if democracy is to gain power, must it also come from "the barrel of a gun"? The struggle for democracy against military and civilian authoritarian regimes has occurred on many occasions since the 1970s in countries such as South Korea, China, the Philippines, Thailand, Burma, Nigeria, Algeria, Argentina, Brazil, Guatemala, and Haiti.

In the second case—that is, in which democracies already exist, but are faced with severe external or internal security threats—official representatives of democratic governments sometimes resort to "excessive" military force or other violent means, such as search and seizure, police beatings, or torture, in order to maintain what they perceive as law and order. Such actions may violate basic democratic norms, but are declared to be justifiable and necessary to preserve democracy in the long run. Indeed, the democratic constitution—often through ad hoc legislative amendments—may allow such violent actions by the state under special circumstances. However, such actions may lead to civilian riots, terrorism, and armed insurgencies that may threaten to overthrow the prevailing democratic system. Undemocratic methods adopted by democracies, ostensibly to preserve the democracies against internal and external threats to their territorial integrity and political unity, may destroy democracy in the long run and add new security problems.

How should existing democracies deal with severe internal and external threats? Questions have been raised periodically about British policies in Northern Ireland and Israeli policies in the West Bank. The British have passed legislation that appeared to limit democracy in troubled Northern Ireland, and both British and Israeli forces have been accused of excessive use of force. Following the establishment of democracy in the Philippines in 1987, questions were raised about some of President Corazon Aquino's tactics against her domestic political opponents. In pursuit of national security against the global Communist threat, various American presidents have sought to bypass or suppress Congressional scrutiny to achieve global strategic objectives. The controversy between Congress and the president on the "War Powers" to be retained by either illustrates one aspect of the dilemma in the security versus democracy debate.

Then there is the development question. Less democracy has been justified for the sake of more rapid economic development.[6] More development will presumably allow for more resources to be channeled to the defense effort and thereby provide greater national security. Authoritarian regimes and their supporters consider "too much democracy" unsuitable for developing countries because democracy handicaps the ability of political leaders to implement harsh but necessary economic measures in the short run in order to achieve high rates of economic growth in the long run. Thus, the right to vote does not necessarily guarantee people the right to food, shelter, and the basic necessities of life. The presumption that elected political leaders are responsive to the needs of the people is not always borne out in practice, at least in delivering the economic necessities of life. India's democracy did not produce economic prosperity during the first four decades after independence. On the other hand, the spectacular economic successes of the East Asian countries under authoritarian regimes gave them the ability to make sophisticated weapons for defense or to buy them from overseas. Both "economic democracy" and defense capabilities were enhanced in these countries. However, authoritarian regimes have not produced economic miracles in Africa and Latin America, nor have they reduced or eliminated armed insurgencies and the periodic threat of coups and countercoups. The East Asian experience has been unique.

Various regional conditions that are discussed in the rest of this chapter and the book will suggest the following general propositions:

1. In developing countries, the military usually justifies its intervention in and control of government by claiming that it is in the interest of maintaining internal law and order, advancing the country's security interests, and promoting economic stability and growth.

2. In the transition from authoritarianism to democracy, the formulation of new constitutions and the institution of the electoral process almost always lead to initial problems of corruption, malfunctions, and the intermittent failure of democracy.

3. In developing countries that have adopted the democratic system, the democratic process is sometimes limited, restricted, bypassed, or suspended in the name of national security and economic stability.

4. In both developing and industrialized democracies, legislation restricting freedom is sometimes adopted to address specific internal security problems that are judged to be either localized and prolonged, or nationwide but temporary.

5. Developing countries are faced with greater difficulties in maintaining national security and sustaining economic growth under democratic systems than are the Western industrialized states.

6. Rising nationalism and ethnic conflict make transition to democracy or the maintenance of an existing democracy difficult and tenuous.

7. There are greater levels of human rights violations in a developing democracy than in industrialized democracies as the state attempts to cope with the concurrent pressures of security and development.

8. Where there have been long-standing disputes or conflicts between states, successful democratization of a particular region tends to reduce or eliminate interstate wars, though not necessarily the clandestine contribution of guerrilla fighters and weapons in support of insurgency wars across national boundaries.

THE DEMOCRATIC EXPERIENCE IN SOUTH ASIA

The seven member states of the South Asian Association for Regional Cooperation (SAARC), India, Pakistan, Bangladesh, Nepal, Sri Lanka, Bhutan, and Maldives, presented a mixed picture until the late 1980s. Of the five states that were at one time under military regimes or authoritarian monarchies, three—Pakistan, Bangladesh, and Nepal—were able to establish democracies between 1989 and 1993. In the fourth, Bhutan, the king was under pressure to liberalize and democratize as he faced the possibility of being overthrown by ethnic

Nepalese citizens of Bhutan in the early 1990s. There was no movement toward democracy in Maldives, a sparsely populated cluster of islands in the Indian Ocean. Meanwhile, a struggle was going on in neighboring Burma, where the military regime had put under house arrest the leader of the democracy movement, Aung Sang Suu Kyi. Ironically, the military regime had allowed a free and fair election in Burma in 1990. The Burmese electorate seized the opportunity to sweep aside the candidates of the military regime and vote in the candidates of the prodemocratic forces of Suu Kyi; however, the military refused to accept the verdict and the elections were nullified. In 1995, Suu Kyi was released from her house arrest but the military retained power.

A similar situation had occurred in the formerly united Pakistan in December 1969, when the military regime of General Yahya Khan held a national election.[7] The election was won by Sheikh Mujibur Rahman's Awami League because of the nearly unanimous support from the Bengali population of East Pakistan who outnumbered the other ethnic groups in West Pakistan. The Awami League won all but two seats contested in East Pakistan, but it did not contest any seats in West Pakistan. Of the 300 seats in the national parliament of Pakistan, Mujibur Rahman's Awami League won 160 seats with two more going to other candidates in East Pakistan.[8] The Pakistan People's Party (PPP) won 81 seats, and 57 seats went to other West Pakistan–based parties and independents. East Pakistan had acquired a clear majority in the national parliament of Pakistan. The election was rejected by Pakistan's Punjabi-dominated military regime under pressure from the leader of the PPP, Zulfiqar Ali Bhutto, whose support came almost exclusively from West Pakistan. The ultimate result of denial of the election results was civil war in East Pakistan and yet another Indo-Pakistani war which led to the creation of Bangladesh.

Some seventeen years later, a variety of factors have contributed to the instability of the democratically elected governments of the PPP led by Benazir Bhutto and later that of the Islami Jamhoori Ittehad (IJI) led by Mian Nawaz Sharif. These include ethnic strife between Sindhi nationalists (who are demanding a separate state of Sindhudesh) and Mohajirs (Muslims who emigrated to Pakistan from areas that remained part of India after partition in 1947); sporadic violence between Balochis and Pashtuns in Balochistan; the continued presence of millions of refugees from Afghanistan in the North-West Frontier Province; black marketeering in American and Chinese weapons left behind in Pakistan following the withdrawal of Soviet military forces in March 1988; and the illicit growth of heroin by Afghan refugees and the growing international drug trade emanating from Pakistan.

Amid rivalry between Sindhis and Punjabis for political control and allegations of corruption against the Bhutto government, President Ghulam

Ishaq Khan, who is a Pashtun, declared a nationwide state of emergency in August 1990. He dissolved the National Assembly and handed over power to an interim government composed of members of opposition groups headed by Ghulam Mustafa Jatoi. Although these actions were in accordance with Pakistan's democratic constitution, which was adopted in 1973, the relevant clauses that permitted the dismissal of the Benazir Bhutto government in 1990 and that of the Nawaz Sharif government in 1993 without a vote of no confidence in parliament were introduced in 1985 by the military dictator, General Zia-ul Haq.[9] This Eighth Amendment, which was passed in 1985 by an assembly controlled by the military, gave the president of Pakistan, who is voted in by members of the National and Provincial Assemblies, the right to dismiss the prime minister, who is elected directly by the people and who carries a majority in the popularly elected National Assembly.

Under the declaration of emergency powers in 1990, Benazir Bhutto's news conference was blacked out by the state-run television; the chairman of the state-owned National Press Trust, which also owned a string of newspapers, was sacked; and only official statements by the newly set up government of Jatoi were published by the two domestic news agencies.[10] The military, under Chief of Army Staff General Mirza Aslam Beg, had taken control of key installations and communications. The democratic government of Pakistan had lasted only 20 months.[11] However, elections were held again in Pakistan in October 1990, this time bringing to power the IJI led by Mian Nawaz Sharif. Prime Minister Sharif's IJI government met a similar fate in early 1993 when it was dismissed by President Ghulam Ishaq Khan. This time Pakistan's Supreme Court invalidated the dismissal and there was no military seizure of power. However, under a mutual agreement between Ishaq Khan and Nawaz Sharif, both agreed to resign and new elections were scheduled for later that year. Elections held in October 1993 returned Benazir Bhutto's PPP to power.

The democratic system and process did not develop readily in Pakistan, as it did in both India and Sri Lanka despite some occasional setbacks in these two countries. Democracies allow for periodic elections and freedom of expression, which in turn provide an outlet for political frustrations. Indeed, violent ethnic separatism in India and Sri Lanka has occurred largely in areas where the democratic process has broken down. At least one of the reasons for the breakdown of the democratic process in Punjab and Kashmir has been the centralization of economic and political powers in New Delhi and the manipulation of electoral politics in these two states by Congress Party governments, especially under Prime Minister Indira Gandhi. In Sri Lanka, the existence of a Sinhalese-controlled unitary system of government during the first few decades after independence contributed to the separatist sentiments in the

Tamil-dominated areas of the northeast and east-central regions. With these exceptions, democracy has prevailed in India and Sri Lanka. In contrast, Pakistan has been under the rule of the military from 1958 to 1971 and then from 1977 to 1988. The military was more than 80 percent Punjabi in composition, but it also included powerful groups of Pashtuns. The first two military leaders, Ayub Khan and Yahya Khan, were both Pashtuns; the third, Zia-ul Haq, was a Punjabi. The Punjabi-Pashtun domination of the Bengalis (before the creation of Bangladesh in 1971), Sindhis, and Balochis—whether real or imagined—is an issue that may not be easily resolved through a system of adult franchise and periodic national elections.

The separatist movement among significant segments of the Sindhis tends to rise and dissipate periodically depending on the nature of the regime in power in Pakistan. Sindhi grievances and nationalism have risen when the Punjabi and Pashtun-dominated military controlled the reins of government and have dissipated when the Bhuttos, Zulfikar and his daughter Benazir, gained power of the central government. Rising Sindhi nationalism threatens to undermine Pakistan's unity—and the prospect for sustaining democracy—for a variety of reasons. Sindhis constitute only 13 percent of the total population, but they are the second largest ethnic community of Pakistan. (Punjabis form 66 percent of the population, Pashtuns 9.5 percent, Mohajirs 7.6 percent, and Balochis 2.5 percent.[12]) Sindh is a large province through which the Indus River flows and in which Pakistan's largest city, Karachi, is located. Sindhi violence is also directed against the economically powerful Mohajir community, which was primarily responsible for the creation of Pakistan out of British India in 1947. In response, the faction of the Mohajir Qaumi Movement (MQM) led by Altaf Hussain wants a separate province for the Mohajirs to be carved out of Sindh within Pakistan. Since Mohajirs control the main cities of Karachi, Hyderabad, and Sukkur, which are all located in Sindh, the separate province presumably would consist of those cities, linked by Mohajir-controlled corridors, or, as demanded by the MQM, much of Sindh south of the twenty-sixth parallel. The remnant Sindh province for the Sindhis would be reduced to a unit that would not be economically viable.[13] On the other hand, an independent Sindh locked in a civil war between Sindhis and Mohajirs would probably end the rationale for the existence of Pakistan since what would be left of Pakistan would essentially be a Punjabi Muslim state.

Is Pakistani democracy here to stay? Despite the restoration of democracy in Pakistan after two prolonged spells of military rule, elected civilian representatives function under the shadow of the Punjabi-Pashtun dominated military.[14] The relationship among the presidency, the prime minister's executive branch of government, and the army is tenuous. All three parts carry considerable but uncertain political power. In this rule by troika, each side does not necessarily balance the others to prevent the abuse of power, but instead tends to act as a threat to the others, thus undermining their authority. In particular, the institutional relationship between the president and the prime minister under the Eighth Amendment did not work under either the prime ministership of Benazir Bhutto during her first term or under Nawaz Sharif subsequently. The presence of the military in the background and, especially, the unusual power held by the army chief, complicate the picture. In struggles between the president and the prime minister, it is the support of the military that tends to tip the scales and determine who will come out on top. Even under civilian democratic rule since 1990, a "martial law culture" (as former army chief General Mirza Aslam Beg phrased it) remains below the surface. The expectation is that if elected civilian leaders cannot maintain law, order, and stability in Pakistan, the military will step in and do the job.

When Bangladesh emerged as an independent state, there were great expectations that a new era of democracy and freedom would prevail in the new state. Shaikh Mujibur Rahman, the hero of the independence struggle and Bangladesh's first prime minister, immediately introduced three basic principles of governance in imitation of India: democracy, socialism, and secularism.[15] In the 1973 elections for a new parliament, Mujib's party won 307 out of 315 seats. In spite of the party's overwhelming majority in parliament, within a year law and order had deteriorated. A state of emergency was declared in 1974, and by 1975 Mujib had assumed absolute power. Mujibur Rahman was assassinated in August 1975 in a coup led by Bangladeshi army officers. Like Pakistan, Bangladesh fell under a military authoritarian regime, first under General Ziaur Rahman, from 1976 until his assassination in 1981, and then under the more repressive General H. M. Ershad, until 1991, when he was deposed by civilian leaders. The elections of 1991 returned the Bangladesh National Party to power under the leadership of Begum Khaleda Zia, wife of the assassinated military leader Ziaur Rahman. However, the military and the rising radical Islamic groups, while still a minority in the early 1990s, threaten to undermine the democratic process in Bangladesh.

Until the late 1980s there were only two democracies in South Asia: India and Sri Lanka. Both have been under severe stress arising mainly from violent separatist movements occurring among Kashmiris, Sikhs, and Assamese in India, and Tamils in Sri Lanka. There have been partial or temporary breakdowns of the democratic process in several Indian states as the central government has responded to separatist violence with counterviolence and through new acts and amendments in parliament that have restricted or bypassed the democratic process. In 1975, faced with national agitation calling for her removal, Prime Minister Indira Gandhi suspended the democratic constitution of India by invoking the clauses pertaining to national emergency. Democracy collapsed briefly in India between June 1975 and March 1977 under the pressures of internal security. Since then there have been allegations by critics that India's democracy was less than adequate since legislation directed against terrorism and domestic violence continued to curb the rights of Indian citizens.[16]

In Sri Lanka, the democratic process was abandoned in the Tamil separatist areas and stopped functioning in the rest of the country during the counter-Sinhalese extremist activity of the Janatha Vimukthi Peramuna (JVP) between 1987 and 1990. The tactics of escalating terrorism and guerrilla warfare by the Liberation Tigers of Tamil Ealam (LTTE), a separatist Tamil faction, the fierce military response by the Sinhalese-dominated Sri Lankan government, and the brief rise and fall of the JVP shook the foundations of Sri Lankan democracy. These experiences led to the steady corrosion of democratic norms in Sri Lanka in the 1980s and the end of democratic practices in the war-torn, Tamil-controlled areas of the northeast.

The resurgence of democratic regimes in Pakistan and Bangladesh and the perseverance of democracies in India and Sri Lanka suggest that the South Asian picture, with all its flaws, is not entirely dismal. In 1991, Nepal too reverted to a democratic constitutional monarchy although it had elected a Communist government under Giriga Prasad Koirala to power. Intermittent failure of the democratic process and continuing problems of internal security have not slackened the struggle for democracy and the struggle to maintain democracy. In the early 1990s, the states of South Asia, all of which were democracies except Bhutan and Maldives, represented the largest single regional bloc of democratic states outside of Western Europe. In terms of sheer numbers, South Asia certainly has the largest group of people in a single region experiencing democracy—more than one billion people compared to less than 400 million each in Western Europe and North America. Since the spread of democracy throughout South Asia began in 1988, no interstate wars have occurred there. Although it may be noted also that no wars have occurred since the 1971 Indo-Pakistani war, the most intense and prolonged Kashmir crisis, which began in 1989, had until 1995 not led to war between democratic India and Pakistan.

AUTHORITARIANISM, DEMOCRACY, AND DEVELOPMENT ELSEWHERE

Just as security pressures tend to erode the democratic process in existing democracies, such pressures are often presented as the justification for thwarting the establishment of democracies in authoritarian and totalitarian states.

Democracies are perceived as being weak and ineffective in dealing with various perceived threats from external enemies and domestic dissidents that are likely to destabilize the country. Attempts to establish democracies in Asia—in Pakistan, Bangladesh, Nepal, Myanmar, Thailand, Indonesia, Singapore, the Philippines, Taiwan, and South Korea—have been stymied at various times over the last few decades, usually in the name of national security or political and economic stability. In many cases, the military, having established themselves as rulers for prolonged periods of time, were unwilling to give up political control, either because they had acquired too many privileges that they could not give up, or because they feared being held accountable and punishable for crimes committed against the nation during their rule.

The political experience in the Philippines has been similar to that of Pakistan. Ferdinand Marcos, who had ruled through dictatorial powers since 1965, held an election in 1986. Although he declared himself the winner over his rival, candidate Corazon Aquino, the election was widely seen to have been rigged. Faced with prodemocracy demonstrations, Marcos fled and Corazon Aquino assumed the presidency. But parallel Communist and Muslim insurgencies, together with efforts by forces loyal to Marcos to regain power through an armed coup, continued to place Filipino democracy in peril. In 1995, the nascent Filipino democracy continues to survive under Aquino's elected successor, Fidel Ramos, an army general turned civilian.

In Myanmar, after decades of military rule that had crushed political opposition and fought the rebellious Kachin and Shan separatists movements in the north, a free and fair election was held in May 1990. The election produced an overwhelming victory for the party that opposed the military dictatorship, despite the arrest of thousands of opposition-party workers and the exclusion of nearly a million voters from pro-opposition constituencies. The main opposition party, the National League, won 396 out of 492 seats.[17] However, the military regime claimed that this was not a real election and simply refused to give up power.

In Nigeria, a similar set of events occurred in July 1993. Africa's most populous state had been ruled by military dictators for all but nine years since its independence from Britain in 1960.[18] The country had experienced seven successful coups and several unsuccessful coups. In 1993, Nigeria's military dictator, Major General Ibrahim Babangida, allowed elections to take place. The Social Democratic Party, led by Moshood Abiola, won a clear lead over the National Republican Convention, led by Bashir Tofa. General Ibrahim nullified the election results on the grounds that both party leaders had violated election laws. He then called for an interim government of both parties, but excluded the participation of Moshood Abiola, the leader of the successful party.

This arrangement did not last long. In November 1993, General Sani Abachi seized power and became the sixth military dictator of Nigeria since the country obtained its independence from Britain in 1960.

According to Zubair Kazaure, Abachi's ambassador in Washington, "General Abachi's emergence as a leader in November 1993 was the outcome of pressure from well-meaning politicians who felt they had no choice but to invite the military to stop the country from drifting into chaos when it became clear that the interim government set up in August could not end the slide."[19] These remarks endorse the standard explanation of dictatorial regimes in developing countries everywhere, namely, that the military must intervene to restore or ensure political stability and order.

There was a more fortuitous outcome in Haiti under similar circumstances. Much of that outcome was due to U.S. political intervention and the threat of military intervention. In December 1990, Reverend Jean-Bertrand Aristide became the first democratically elected president of Haiti; however, Aristide's democratic government did not last. It was overthrown by the Haitian military, led by Lieutenant General Raoul Cedras, the following year. However, by 1993, under pressure from the Organization of American States, led by the United States, and the United Nations, which imposed economic sanctions on Haiti, Cedras agreed to restore Aristide's presidency.[20] Cedras abdicated in 1994, under an agreement negotiated by former U.S. president Jimmy Carter, and Aristide was installed as president in an unusual "democratic" arrangement in Haiti that was enforced by the presence of U.S. military forces.

In the Middle East, as in Pakistan, the military and radical Islam are obstacles to the implementation or maintenance of democracy.[21] Whereas extremist Islamic groups and their demands were largely co-opted in Pakistan through the enforcement of Islamic laws under the military dictatorship of General Zia-ul Haq, radical Islam, in attempting to seek power through the democratic process, has come into violent confrontations with secular military dictatorships in the Middle East.[22] In Egypt, this confrontation has been between secular authoritarianism under the successive military leaderships of Gamel Abdel Nasser, Anwar Sadat, and Muhammed Hosni Mubarak, on the one hand, and Islamic radicalism spearheaded by a transnational movement, the Muslim Brotherhood, on the other. Algeria sank into civil war because its secular military dictatorship stole a democratic election from the Islamic Salvation Front in 1992 on the grounds that this alleged Islamic radical organization had no intention of maintaining democracy once it took over the government.[23] In Tunisia, the growing struggle is between civilian democracy and radical Islam.[24]

In this struggle between radical concepts of the Islamic state and Western concepts of the democratic state, there is a similarity to the earlier fear that

Communist parties seeking to achieve power through the democratic process, as in France and Italy in the 1950s and 1960s, would eventually destroy democracy if they proved successful in their election bids. Controversy revolves around the alleged irreconcilable differences between Islamic and Communist concepts of freedom and democracy and the liberal, secular Western concepts of these terms.

In all of the above cases, authoritarian regimes have attempted to justify their hold on power for reasons of security, law, and order; however, in East and Southeast Asia, authoritarian regimes have justified their existence for reasons of economic growth and prosperity. China, South Korea, Taiwan, Indonesia, Thailand, Malaysia, and Singapore have experienced very high rates of economic growth, usually between 8 and 14 percent of GNP annually, under authoritarian or quasi-authoritarian governments. Although Malaysia and Singapore are formally democracies, they have strong authoritarian characteristics. While both states have experienced spectacular rates of economic growth, draconian laws exist to maintain law and order, exemplified by the death penalty on those convicted of drug smuggling. Likewise, in Latin America, military rule in Chile has produced relatively high levels of economic success. However, military rule in Argentina, Brazil, Uruguay, and some Central American republics has not produced similar economic successes or even domestic political stability.

THE BRITISH EXPERIENCE AND OTHER CASES

Even established Western democracies are not entirely immune to security pressures that threaten to undermine the democratic system. In the United States, the internment without cause and without trial of about 120,000 Japanese Americans during the Second World War was undertaken on the grounds of national security; the basic rights of the individual were flouted, and democratic norms were discarded.[25] The McCarthyism of the 1950s, which arose from the ideological struggle against the Communist bloc, and the domestic strife that arose from the American military intervention in Vietnam from 1964 to 1974, threatened to corrupt democratic values and attitudes within the intelligence bureaucracies and the higher levels of the Johnson and Nixon administrations. The bombing of the World Trade Center in New York in 1993 and the Federal building in Oklahoma City in 1995 again raised debate in the United States about the need to enact measures restricting the freedoms of individuals and groups to protect society at large.

The terrorist tactics of the more extreme factions of the Palestine Liberation Organization and related groups against the state of Israel following the 1967 Arab-Israeli War resulted in Israeli military retaliation against Palestinian refugee camps in Lebanon and the exclusion of Palestinians living within the state of Israel from the Israeli democratic process. Similarly, the White minority regime of South Africa under the system of Apartheid, perceiving an internal political and military threat to its security and economic well-being, suppressed and excluded the Black majority from its "Whites Only" democratic process. Although the security conditions and the nature of the threats perceived in all of these cases varied greatly, they all adversely affected the workings of established and nascent democracies.

The dilemmas in dealing with terrorism facing the Indian state are probably best reflected in miniature form in Britain. The British situation is unique because the British constitution is unwritten. There are no parallels between Britain's unwritten constitution and the U.S. Constitution's First Amendment, which forbids laws that abridge freedom of speech or freedom of the press, or the Fifth Amendment, which guarantees that a person accused of a crime cannot be compelled to be a witness against himself. In Britain, as in India, a government with a comfortable majority in Parliament possesses considerably more power and can enact more far-reaching legal and social changes than can an American president whose party may control the House and the Senate. For example, in 1988, there were moves by Prime Minister Margaret Thatcher's Conservative Party government to resort to special parliamentary powers to deal with the terrorism of the Irish Republican Army (IRA). In November 1988, the Thatcher government barred British radio and television from broadcasting live or recorded interviews with the IRA or its affiliated legal political organizations in Northern Ireland.[26] Judges would also be allowed to draw negative inferences if accused IRA suspects chose to invoke the right to remain silent to avoid self-incrimination.[27]

The terrorist tactics of the IRA and the Ulster Protestants also have undermined the workings of democracy in Northern Ireland. In 1991, after more than 20 years of IRA terrorism coupled with terrorism by the Ulster Loyalists, the question of whether to reintroduce the internment law of the early 1970s was raised. The internment law, which was introduced in mid-1971 in Britain, was similar to the various laws passed in India that allow preventive detention to deal with threats to security, especially internal security.

Various security chiefs in Britain argued that the only way they could begin to win the war against the Irish terrorists would be to take such preventive detention measures. In 1991, one senior British security chief told a London newspaper, the *Independent*, the following: "The IRA terrorists are better equipped, better resourced, better led, bolder and more secure against our penetration than at any time before. They are absolutely a formidable enemy. The essential attributes of their leaders are better than ever before. Some of their operations are brilliant, in terrorist terms. If we don't intern, it's a long haul."[28] These are all familiar arguments in India.

British security chiefs who advanced arguments for internment point out that the terrorists who are caught and convicted under the current laws almost always are the "minnows," while the leaders and the brains of the organization remain at bay. Moreover, the leaders are able to move freely across the porous border between Northern Ireland and the Republic of Ireland to escape capture. The deployment of over 30,000 British troops and the security forces of the Royal Ulster Constabulary is not sufficient to control and contain the situation because these forces are handicapped in their operations. The choice may boil down to either giving up Northern Ireland or introducing draconian laws that may violate democratic sensibilities but offer the hope of decapitating the IRA brains and organization. Again, these are conditions and arguments that are applicable to India's problems in Kashmir and Punjab.

Reginald Maudling, one of the British ministers who was instrumental in introducing the internment law in 1971, expressed the dilemma of that time: "No one could be certain what would be the consequences, yet the question was simply this: what other measure could be taken?"[29] Opponents of reintroducing internment in the early 1990s pointed out that the death toll rose dramatically—often more than tenfold—during the years after internment was introduced in 1971. Opponents to internment also claimed that such a law might cause Britain's relations with Ireland to deteriorate. It might further activate Irish expatriates in North America and could invite condemnation from human-rights organizations. Thus, although Britain considered bypassing democratic processes and restricting individual rights, it decided to reject such moves because they were perceived as aggravating the problem rather than resolving it. Such a curtailment of democratic rights was not expected to advance security interests in Northern Ireland. On the other hand, the Indian government, which had made the same arguments, went ahead and curtailed individual rights in order to deal with problems of internal security.

All the arguments for and against bypassing the democratic process in order to deal with the IRA problem in Britain applied to the situation in India. The similar, if not common, experience in dealing with terrorism enabled India to persuade Britain to enter into an extradition treaty in July 1993 so that India could extradite Sikh and Kashmiri terrorists who may have sought refuge in Britain.[30] The extradition treaty was, however, severely criticized in the British Parliament before its passage. Many British members of Parliament (MPs) condemned India for its poor human rights record in dealing with the separatists in Kashmir and Punjab and expressed concerns about the possible misuse of the treaty. Labour MP Graham Allen cited a report from Amnesty International stating that 25,000 people were held in India without trial, that torture was widespread and systematic, and that extrajudicial killings were common. Some MPs pointed out that this would be the first extradition treaty signed by Britain with a country outside of Western Europe and the United States. They felt that there were not enough safeguards against human rights violations in India. Nevertheless, even those British MPs who were critical of India during the debates eventually voted in favor of the Indo-British extradition treaty.

While the essence of the dilemma appears to be the same for both Britain and India, there are differences in scope and intensity. The problems of India are more extensive and severe. While "extrajudicial" measures to address the problems of internal security have been avoided in Britain, they have been enacted in India, especially since the National Emergency was declared by Indira Gandhi in June 1975. But in India preventive detention had been used earlier, under the 1962 Defense of India Rules and the 1971 Maintenance of Internal Security Act. Both legislations were intended to address the external threats from China in 1962 and Pakistan in 1971 by suspending or curtailing the democratic rights of individuals and groups within India that were perceived (but not proven) to constitute a danger to national security. The constitutional basis of such measures and their political consequences in India are discussed in subsequent chapters.

DEMOCRACY, ETHNIC NATIONALISM, AND SECESSIONIST VIOLENCE

Amid post–Cold War demands for freedom and democracy throughout the world, there are new or renewed demands for national self-determination by various ethnic groups.[31] This has been especially true in South Asia, which is a multi-ethnic region. According to a more liberal interpretation of freedom, ethnic groups within a state are believed to have the right to hold referendums to determine whether they wish to remain part of the state or secede from it. However, the right of ethnic self-determination is mentioned only obliquely and in passing reference in Article 1 (2) of the UN Charter, and its intended meaning appears directed at ending colonialism.[32]

Thus, while the end of the Cold War eliminated many security concerns based on the ideological conflict between the West and the Communist countries, it has generated security problems based on ethnic rivalries. As these security issues intensify, the stability of existing democracies has come under greater stress, and democratic movements in nondemocratic states are increasingly thwarted.

There are similarities between the ethnic nationalism and separatism that tore the former Soviet Union and Yugoslavia apart and the ethnic nationalism and violence in India, Pakistan, and Sri Lanka that threaten to tear those states apart.[33] The democracy movements (together with demands for free-market economic systems) that swept through the former Communist states of Europe had parallels in the democracy movements in Pakistan, Bangladesh, and Nepal. All of these movements proved successful as the Cold War wound and disappeared. But they have been supplanted by destabilizing ethnic nationalist movements.

The growing intensity of "old-fashioned" conflict issues in the 1990s, based on racial, linguistic, and religious nationalism, may turn out to be more acute in the developing region of South Asia than in the more developed region of Eastern Europe. Indeed, rebellious Sikhs and Kashmiris have pointed to the European experience as reasons for the creation of new states and the reunification of divided ethnic groups on either side of international boundaries. Similarly, potential Bengali, Tamil, Balochi, and Pashtu nationalism may gain inspiration from successful and unsuccessful demands by Germans in Europe, Kashmiris in South Asia, and Koreans in East Asia for reunification across existing international frontiers. This could generate newer conflict issues between India and Bangladesh, India and Sri Lanka, Pakistan and Afghanistan, and Pakistan and Iran. What makes the European and South Asian conditions complex is the uncertain and fluid nature of conflict issues and the types of wars that are likely to be fought in the future.

While ethnic nationalism threatens existing democracies or prevents democracies from taking root, the prevalence of democratic regimes in antagonistic states also tends to minimize the chances of war. It may be useful to observe that Western-type democracies have not been engaged in any direct wars with each other since the Second World War. Although a variety of other factors also may have contributed to preventing wars between democracies (e.g., between Greece and Turkey over Cyprus in the 1960s and 1970s, and between India and Pakistan over Kashmir in the early 1990s), the promotion and maintenance of democratic systems and free-market economies in antagonistic states serves as a useful tool for conflict management. However, as the Indo-Pakistani crisis over Kashmir in the early 1990s indicates, democratic systems may alleviate but not necessarily resolve conflict issues between rival states. And it should be apparent from the military actions of the United States, India, and

Israel that democracies are not necessarily less belligerent in their external behavior than nondemocratic states such as the Soviet Union, Pakistan under military dictators, or Iran under the Shah.

Although India is a democracy with unrestricted adult franchise, the right to vote may be perceived as an inadequate expression of freedom among minority groups since it does not necessarily ensure effective self-government. In democracies that are more centralized and in which voting takes place along ethnic lines, the majority ethnic group will always rule the minority ethnic group. Minorities may then believe that "real freedom" may be obtained only through territorial secession. Secession enables the ethnic minority to become the majority in the new state and thus allows for self-rule.

However, secessions generate new problems of ethnic majorities and minorities.[34] Multiple secessions from the former Soviet Union and Yugoslavia altered the pluralist majorities that Russians and Serbs carried in the former states and created Russian and Serb minorities in the newly created independent states. The question that then arises is whether the new minorities also have the right to self-determination, as the old minorities did. Following the recognition of Croatia and Bosnia as independent states in 1991 and 1992, Serb minorities in those two states declared independent Serbian republics.[35] Neither have been recognized by the international community. If they are recognized, then the right to secession of the Albanians, who are a majority in the Serbian province of Kosovo will arise.

Two other "unilateral declarations of independence" have not been recognized. These are that of the Turkish Republic of Northern Cyprus, which was carved out with the help of invading Turkish forces for the Turkish Cypriot minority in 1974; and that of the de facto republic of Abkhazia, which was carved out from the former Soviet republic of Georgia by Abkhazian rebels in 1993. Fear of discrimination among the newly generated Russian minorities in the former Soviet republics of Latvia, Moldova, Georgia, Ukraine, and some of the central Asian republics suggests the possibility of further secessions in the future in that part of the world.

Similar problems and dilemmas prevail in South Asia, but no new states have emerged since Bangladesh seceded from Pakistan in 1971. Secessionist demands among minorities—and even an ethnic majority—have been endemic in South Asia since the countries of this region received their independence from Britain after the Second World War. Indeed, the breakup of the Soviet Union, Yugoslavia, and Czechoslovakia, as well as other ethnic conflicts and separatist demands elsewhere in the world, have added fuel to similar differences and demands in South Asia and thereby exacerbated conflict conditions within these multiethnic states. Past and present separatist movements include those in Kashmir, Punjab, Assam, and the tribal areas of northeast India; in the Tamil areas of India and Sri Lanka; and in Sindh, Balochistan, and the North-West Frontier Province of Pakistan. Such movements may spread to other groups in South Asia, with potentially disastrous consequences.

Sikh and Kashmiri separatists in South Asia have, for instance, specifically pointed to conditions in the former Yugoslavia and the Soviet Union to justify their own demands. A dissident Sikh group in exile, the Sikh Council of Khalistan, based in Washington, D.C., moved swiftly to recognize Slovenia and Croatia when they declared their independence in July 1991—long before any other state in the world had done so. Similarly, Kashmiri "councils" based in London and Washington have pointed to the independence of the Baltic states. They have justified their own independence on the grounds that the Indian absorption of Kashmir in 1947, following partition, has not been recognized by the United Nations, a status of nonrecognition that is perceived to be similar to, if not the same as, that of the Soviet annexations of the Baltic states.

In many parts of the world, such demands for self-determination inevitably have led to the central government's insistence on the sovereignty and territorial integrity of the state. In rejecting the right to self-determination of Kashmiris, Sikhs, Nagas, and other minorities, India has argued that the democratic rights of individuals and groups cannot be extended so that the result is the self-destruction of the state itself. According to what amounts to an implicit Indian internal "doctrine," all resolutions of ethnic grievances must be resolved within the boundaries of the Indian state.

THE IMPORTANCE OF INDIA AS A CASE STUDY

India is one of the few states of the postcolonial developing world in which democracy was installed at the time of independence and in which it has survived.[36] However, pressures arising from external and internal threats have usually shown a tendency to compromise and erode the democratic process in India. These tendencies have been evident on various occasions: during and after the Sino-Indian war of 1962 and the Indo-Pakistani wars of 1965 and 1971; during the period of the 1975-77 National Emergency declaration following violent and widespread demonstrations against Prime Minister Indira Gandhi's Congress government; and during the violent separatist movements in Punjab and Kashmir.

Faced with threats of varying severity from within or without, the government of India has resorted to special legislation and constitutional amendments intended to increase its powers in dealing with such crises.[37] They include the Defence of India Rules (1962); the Maintenance of Internal Security Act (1971); the 42nd Amendment to Article 352 of the Indian Constitution (1975), passed during the National Emergency; the National Security Act (1984); the Terrorist Affected Areas Special Courts Act (1984); the Terrorist and Disruptive Activities Prevention Act (1987); and the 59th Amendment to Article 352 (1988). Moreover, the Official Secrets Act of 1923, a legacy of British rule, allows the Indian government not to reveal the information and basis for actions undertaken in the name of national security. Of related concern is the passage of the Defamation Bill of 1988, which has restricted freedom of the press by preventing the publication of charges of misconduct against government officials without documentary evidence. These measures have led to a series of political crises in India that have raised doubts among the country's more extreme critics at home and abroad as to whether India has remained a legitimate functioning democracy according to Western definitions and standards.

This study is concerned, first, with the erosion of the democratic process and its periodic recoveries in India in the face of external and, especially, internal security pressures; and, second, with the impact of democracy and security on development. This stress on Indian democracy has become critical with the growth of violent separatist movements in Indian Kashmir and Punjab and the threat of war with Pakistan. Other separatist movements and violent struggles in Assam, Nagaland, Tripura, "Bodoland," and "Gurkhaland" continue to place a burden on the Indian government, which has to function within the slow and restricted procedures provided by the Indian parliament and the courts. (India has refused to grant internal statehood for the Bodos and Gurkhas.) However, going back to the wars with China in 1962 and Pakistan in 1971 and the declaration of the National Emergency between 1975 and 1977, a series of laws were passed in the Indian parliament that provide the government with sweeping powers to deal with problems of external and internal security.

Democratic and authoritarian states in both the developed and the developing world have undergone some aspects of the above security pressures and legislative responses at various times. However, the experience of India is particularly significant. India, the world's most populous democracy, has faced several external security problems. Since independence in 1947, India has fought three wars with Pakistan and one with China. India has had to deal with severe problems of internal security that have tended to undermine the stability of the state in Kashmir, Punjab, Assam, Nagaland, Mizoram, Meghalaya, Manipur, and Tripura. India has the fourth largest military force in the world, consisting of approximately 1.3 million men to deal with external security, and almost another 1.5 million paramilitary forces and reserves to deal with problems of internal security. The size of the military in itself could pose a potential threat to Indian democracy.

India is also a nation in which 18 distinct major languages are officially recognized by its constitution and over 180 minor languages and a thousand dialects are spoken. Almost all the major religions of the world are represented. The largest religious groups (those with more than 5 million followers) are the Hindus, Muslims, Christians, Sikhs, Buddhists, and Jains. Additionally, Zoroastrians and Jews exist in small but influential numbers. There are four major castes *(varnas)*, the former untouchable caste, now known as *Harijans*, and over a thousand subcastes *(jatis)*. As is the case elsewhere in the world, substantial economic differences exist between the upper, middle, and lower economic classes. All of this provides the potential for extensive internal conflict and for the possible breakdown of society and the disintegration of the state. These security stresses are compounded by development pressures and the ongoing "revolution of rising expectations." Can India's democracy survive the various external and internal threats that it faces when other developing nations with much less pronounced social and economic divisions have failed?

Giuseppe Di Palma noted that influential scholars in the 1950s and 1960s generally pointed to three qualities that are necessary if democracy is to take root: "(1) economic prosperity and equality; (2) a modern and diversified social structure in which independent middle classes occupy center stage; and (3) a national culture that, by tolerating diversity and preferring accommodation, is already implicitly democratic."[38] India does not fulfill the first precondition and may only partially meet the second. It is the third condition that India meets and on which India's democracy hinges. Similarly, Robert A. Dahl provided four "ideal standards" for evaluating a democracy: (1) equal opportunity and effective participation; (2) voting equality at the decisive stage; (3) an enlightened understanding of the issues affecting the citizen; and (4) control of the agenda that is subject to the democratic process.[39] India may roughly fulfill all of these criteria although not to the extent that Western democracies do.

In the developing world, where efforts to establish or preserve democracies have been dismal, India has remained from the time of its independence an important test case. If India can manage to maintain its democratic character in the face of several external and internal threats and domestic social and economic odds, then the survival of old and new democracies elsewhere in Asia and the world that face similar problems would appear to be more promising.

THE ANALYTICAL DIMENSIONS

The various issues raised by the problem of security pressures on democracy and development are examined in the following chapters on five levels: the conceptual, the security-political, the constitutional, the military, and the economic.

The conceptual dimension explores the relationship between democracy, security, and development and the significance of that relationship in understanding the various crises of instability in South Asia. The security-political level of analysis concerns the underlying causes of the problem and the nature of the political debate in India on the maintenance of national security, especially on the question of how far democratic processes may be bent, suspended, or even abrogated for the sake of security. Constitutional issues include the historical background and, in particular, the intent of the framers of the Indian constitution when they introduced authoritarian emergency powers to deal with problems of security. Military issues include questions about the authority and role of the regular armed forces and paramilitary forces in the maintenance of external and internal security and the degree to which their increasing size and authority tend to corrupt or threaten the democratic process in India. The economic debate raises the question of whether authoritarian systems are more conducive to economic reform and development than democratic systems. A weak and declining economy also implies a weak and declining military capability; however, economic instability may be the justification for military coups and military dictatorships.

The book concludes by examining alternative structural and procedural changes that need to be made to balance the demands of democracy, security, and development in India. To deal with the problems of internal security, for instance, proposals for economic and political decentralization, or perhaps even for installing an alternative constitutional and political system, are assessed. To deal with the problems of external security, for instance, the prospect for promoting confidence-building measures and of establishing confederal arrangements in South Asia are considered.

2

The Conceptual Dimension

THE RELATIONSHIP BETWEEN
DEMOCRACY, SECURITY, AND DEVELOPMENT

National security is an ambiguous and nebulous concept. Governments often call upon their citizens to make sacrifices in order to preserve the security, sovereignty, and stability of the state. When the state is threatened, its citizens are expected and often willing to contribute even greater resources and effort to national defense. Whether these contributions entail the military draft, higher taxes, or longer working hours, individuals and groups are expected to give up benefits and rights for the sake of national security. The state's demand for personal and financial sacrifices often leads to the denial of the individual's basic rights and freedoms. For example, the Second World War led to the curtailment of the individual rights of Japanese Americans in the United States. During the 1962 Sino-Indian war and the 1965 Indo-Pakistani war, large numbers of Communists and Muslims in India were temporarily incarcerated without due process. Claiming that there was a potential major internal threat to the state, Prime Minister Indira Gandhi suspended the fundamental rights of the citizen by proclaiming the National Emergency between 1975 and 1977.

The exigencies of national security thus constitute a powerful psychological and political tool that can be used to obtain individual political and economic sacrifices. The degree to which such sacrifices may be obtained from citizens will vary depending on the perceptions of the level of threat and the ability of the political system to exact such sacrifices from the individual. Threats may be "low" or "high"; sacrifices obtained may be "volunteered" or "imposed"; and the ability of the state to derive the maximum effort and contribution from its citizens will depend on the "persuasive" or "coercive" powers held by the state.

Totalitarian and authoritarian systems have more powers to marshall resources to carry out national security objectives than do democratic systems. While a totalitarian state may resort to coercive powers to promote national security, a democratic state is expected to rely on persuasive powers. No doubt, persuasive powers may often be a powerful and effective means for marshalling resources and effort for national defense, especially where the threat is clear and the stakes are high. Those living in a democracy may be argued to have a greater commitment to the survival of the state than those living in a totalitarian state. However, such conditions are rare. Perceptions of the level of threat may vary among citizens, and especially between average citizens and the ruling elites. As the Vietnam War progressed, many Americans became convinced that U.S. national security was not at stake and were no longer willing to sacrifice their lives. The major legacy of the Vietnam war was that Americans would no longer allow their decision makers to rush to war over regional crises that did not directly affect U.S. security. However, while the inclination to go to war may have diminished in the United States following the Vietnam experience and the end of the Cold War, it remains in countries in which security problems show no signs of letting up, that is, the states of the Korean Peninsula, South Asia, the Middle East, the Balkans, and the former Soviet republics.

Thus, objective evidence of a "clear and present danger" may not always exist for every threat to security that is claimed by foreign policy decision makers. Threats to national security are always conjectural until an actual attack takes place. Some threats may be perceived to be greater than others, especially in countries where past wars, insurgencies, or terrorist attacks have taken place, or the capabilities to launch such attacks exist. In a democracy, even if it can be demonstrated that such dangers might occur in the future, sustaining national security commitments over a prolonged period of time may be difficult without having to address growing public dissatisfaction. Where such uncertainty and ambiguity occurs, there may be civilian resistance to the national security policies of democratic governments. Under such circumstances, those in positions of power in democratic societies may increasingly resort to more authoritarian measures to maximize the state's security. Such tendencies have been evident in India at various times since the Sino-Indian war of 1962.

In authoritarian regimes, however, coercive power to enforce national security policies, especially those that are costly and unpopular, also suffers from severe limitations. Eventually, public dissatisfaction can lead to the fall of the regime itself. This was the case in Pakistan: the disastrous military policies of President Yahya Khan in East Pakistan eventually led to war with India in 1971, the breakup of Pakistan, and the brief return of civilian democratic rule.

Even more ambiguous and controversial are perceived internal threats to the state. Whereas the external enemy may be clearly identified, the internal enemy is less clearly identifiable. And again, whereas the destructive capabilities of the external enemy (combat ships and aircraft, bombs, missiles, tanks, and artillery) may be clearly discerned, the destructive capabilities of the internal enemies of the state (violent demonstrations, armed insurgencies, and acts of terrorism) are less clearly defined.

Since "the enemy within our midst," whether real or imagined, cannot always be identified, there may be a tendency to curtail the individual liberties of many or all citizens in order to restrict the movements and potential dangers that may arise from the few. A government, whether authoritarian or democratic, may resort to a series of preventive measures in order to combat the enemy within and to advance the security of the state. These measures may include surveillance, wiretapping, widespread arrests based on suspicion rather than evidence, frequent search and seizure, and the killing of suspects in armed encounters. Indeed, an erosion of democratic values and an increase in human rights violations are likely to occur when a nation responds to internal rather than external threats. Such allegations have been made against the Pakistani government in its fight against the Bengali separatists in 1971, against the Sri Lankan government in its fight against the Tamil separatists since 1982, and against the Indian government in its fight against the Sikh separatists since 1984 and the Kashmiri separatists since 1989.

There are linkages, latent or overt, between the degree of freedom of the individual and the degree of threats perceived by the state. Individual sacrifices for the military effort, or the need for patience and understanding as the government resorts to widespread arrests and seizures, are demanded by the state for the common good. Thus, in democracies, as in authoritarian systems, the relative degree of freedom that the individual enjoys may increase or decrease depending on the level of threat perceived by the state. The greater the threat, the greater the "sacrifice" demanded and the fewer the freedoms that may be enjoyed by the individual, whether these restrictions are obtained by voluntary or imposed means. There would appear to be an inverse relationship between security and democracy.

Underlying the various issues that India faces in the 1990s is the relationship between economic priorities and political means—between resource allocations for defense and development and between the level of democratic or authoritarian means that should be adopted to achieve security and economic objectives. More security through an arms buildup may mean less economic development. Less economic development may lead to more problems of internal security. Widespread economic deprivation and frustration may provoke violent protest movements among the lower middle class and the impoverished masses, or it may lead to interethnic and intercaste strife over territories and scarce resources. More internal violence may lead to less democracy and perhaps even an end to democracy. Domestic strife may also scare investors away, especially foreign investors.

On the other hand, in India, less democracy (or even no democracy) may mean more development as wasteful public-sector undertakings are dismantled, trade union activities are curtailed, and national economic and social disciplinary regulations introduced. More development may mean more available resources for India's arms buildup, thereby leading to an arms race and heightening political tensions in the region. The nature of the relationship between democracy, security, and development is varied and complex, and, therefore, policy choices become difficult and controversial.

NORMATIVE CHOICES AND POLICY PRIORITIES

The central question of this book is the following: should the urgency or intensity of national security issues or development pressures restrict or override democratic institutions and processes? In India, the political debate may be seen—at least conceptually—as a debate between those who believe that the democratic process must be preserved whatever the intensity of security and development pressures and those who believe that the security of the state and development priorities must take precedence over democratic processes.

The primacy of democracy over security (the *democracy first* argument) may be justified on the grounds that the curtailment or suppression of freedoms adds to or aggravates the security problems of the state. Such actions become self-defeating and would eventually destroy the democratic system in India irretrievably. The choice is therefore between an open society that guarantees individual liberties, on the one hand, and a police state characterized by oppression and fear, on the other.[1] Thus, a democracy cannot solve its security problems by restricting, bypassing, or suspending democracy. According to this perspective, the cause of the violent upheaval in Kashmir and Punjab was the failure to implement equitable policies and fair democratic procedures. While such a view applies to problems of internal security, it also applies to external security in the sense that foreign policy and security policy made without much public scrutiny can lead to more aggressive and uncompromising decisions against one's adversaries and to costly military campaigns. Rulers without responsibility and accountability are unlikely to act in the best interests of the people although they may claim to do so. Similar arguments may also be made about the relationship between democracy and development. Rapid rates of economic growth achieved through oppressive political measures may defeat the overall purpose of development. Economic development without political development, meaning a free and open society, may satisfy those in power and their beneficiaries but not the nation as a whole.

The primacy of security over democracy (the *security first* argument) may be justified broadly on the grounds that there will be no democracy to preserve if the security of the state is compromised.[2] Fighting subversive antidemocratic forces through democratic means can mean the death of democracy because using democratic methods alone might be a handicap when fighting against agents who place no restrictions on their methods. If the state cannot preserve itself from its external and internal enemies, there will be no democracy to defend. The choice, therefore, is between maintaining the sovereignty and territorial integrity of the state and internal law and order, on one hand, and the likelihood of external subjugation, domestic political instability, and even anarchy, on the other. In the long-term interests of democracy, the state must at times curtail, suspend, or bypass democracy. The military dictators of Pakistan, Ayub Khan and Zia-ul Haq, have often used this line of reasoning to rationalize their martial rule. They did not really consider themselves to be against democracy in Pakistan, but when democracy was not working well and when there was a major threat from India to Pakistan's sovereignty, then discipline and order at home took precedence over the maintenance of democracy. Arguments such as these were also made to rationalize the National Emergency proclaimed by Indian Prime Minister Indira Gandhi from 1975 to 1977 and, later, the suspension of democracy in strife-torn states such as Punjab, Assam, and Kashmir.

A third possible perspective emphasizes the primacy of development over democracy (the *development first* argument). Here, the ultimate purpose of maximizing economic growth rates is to promote internal political stability and national security. The choice is between economic prosperity, which is perceived as leading to greater levels of security, on the one hand, and individual rights and political freedom, which are perceived as not necessarily providing decent living standards, on the other. Authoritarian regimes such as those in

South Korea, Taiwan, and Thailand have achieved rapid rates of economic growth while also promoting strong defense and disciplined militaries. Authoritarianism (or totalitarianism as in Communist China) may have been largely responsible for the various Asian economic miracles. Unhindered by opposition groups, trade unions, and a free press, and unfettered by restrictive and time-consuming democratic procedures, the state is able to implement economic policies that may be unpopular in the short run but that carry long-term benefits. A fast-growing economy enables a greater diversion of resources to defense programs and the military than does a slow and stagnant economy, which can lead to an increase in domestic security problems. Thus, a country can become economically and militarily strong by emphasizing development priorities. Following this line of reasoning, freedom for the majority in an underdeveloped country may be defined as the absence of economic deprivation. Voting rights mean nothing when the masses of people have inadequate food, clothing, and shelter. (Of course, in places such as Burma, North Korea, Haiti, and Cuba, there has been no development, security, or democracy.)

The three basic perspectives—democracy first, security first, and development first—are put forward here as analytical reference points only. The choices to be made are not necessarily clear-cut, but rather are questions of emphasis and feasibility. State interests may indicate that combining all three approaches in different forms and proportions may provide a comfortable optimum for promoting democracy, security, and development.

THE QUESTION OF "APPROPRIATE" DEMOCRACY

If democracy of whatever kind is supposed to ensure freedom for the inhabitants of a state, then this is a very elusive goal. There is no political system that can guarantee pure or perfect freedom for all its people. Moreover, concepts of political freedom (e.g., self-government, the right to freely associate or practice one's beliefs, the right to free speech) may vary from concepts of economic freedom (e.g., a free market, the right to own property and capital, the right to the basic necessities of life). In developing countries, both democracies and dictatorships serve as a means to implement elite political, economic, and social agendas. These agendas may be the same in both democracies and dictatorships, except that in democracies periodic elections serve to legitimate these agendas whether or not they prove to be in the interests of most of the people.[3] There may be other prescriptions for constituting democracy. Many Communist countries have considered themselves to be "democratic republics" or "people's democracies" in the belief that Communist systems existed for the benefit of the workers. Many Muslim countries have called for democracies based on Islamic beliefs and practices that are different from Western concepts of democracy. The problem with such alternative concepts of democracy is that they do not guarantee freedom of thought or individual rights.

The question that also arises is whether too much democracy is a good thing for any state or society, developing or industrialized. Have democracies in the West gone too far and given their citizens so much freedom that stable social structures have begun to break down? This problem may be considered self-evident by conservatives who see traditional values being replaced by the license to do anything so long as it is within the law or is protected by laws that have become too liberal. Freedom may prove socially counterproductive. Thus, for example, a high-ranking diplomat from Singapore, Kishore Mahbubani, declared in 1995 that America was falling apart from too much freedom, which has led to increasing levels of murder, rape, and other violent crime, illegitimate births, high divorce rates, single-parent homes, and the lowering of national standards in high schools.[4]

With obvious justification, Robert L. Rothstein noted:

> Democracy seems especially difficult to define because it is not a given or a thing in itself but rather a form of government and a process of governance that changes and adapts in response to circumstances. Any "universal" definition is likely to ignore differences in detail or to need constant redefinition and adjustment. Moreover, since all democracies are more or less imperfect, finding a single definition that indicates precisely where "more or less" becomes "either/or" (a democracy or not a democracy) seems impossible.[5]

Assuming that the promotion of democracy in South Asia is an important objective, what are the appropriate, if not ideal, principles and conditions that should underlie the practice of democracy in these states? I would like to put forward conditions I consider necessary for the establishment of appropriate and stable democracies in the states of South Asia. They are based largely on Western concepts of democracy.

1. A highly decentralized political system instead of a centralized federal system or even a unitary form of government with tight central control.
2. A mainly private-sector-oriented economic system functioning in an open, free-market economy, instead of a centrally controlled socialist or planned economy.

3. A political and economic system that ensures a minimum standard of living and generates a fair distribution of wealth and resources, as opposed to a system that favors the few.

4. A secular political system in which the government treats all religions equally and, as far as possible, separates governmental functions from religious functions, as opposed to a system in which one religion is declared to be the official religion of the state, even if basic rights are guaranteed to the practitioners of other religions.

5. A system of democratic rights of people that stops short of the right to national self-determination where this may lead to territorial secession and the disintegration of the state itself. Such an extended version of freedom would violate the territorial integrity and security of the state, which is considered here as the essence of state security and political stability.

These conditions may seem especially appropriate for secular, multiethnic, and multireligious states such as India and Sri Lanka. However, they should also be applied in the Islamic republics of Pakistan and Bangladesh. Although Muslims constitute 98 percent of the population of Pakistan, the country is composed of several ethnic and linguistic groups, including Punjabis, Sindhis, Balochis, Pashtuns, Hazaras, Siraikis, Mohajirs, and Kashmiris. And although Muslims constitute 80 percent of the population of Bangladesh, more than 15 percent of the population is Hindu, and there are sizeable numbers of Buddhists and Christians.

The first two conditions are related. A decentralized political system cannot incorporate a centralized, planned, socialist economy, although it is quite feasible to have a centralized political system (including a dictatorship) and private-sector capitalism. In general, the more political power and decision-making authority held by provinces, districts, villages, and municipalities, the greater the political democracy. More people have a greater say and control over their own lives. When ethnic minorities are scattered throughout a society, this devolution of power becomes particularly important. By the same token, economic decentralization can occur only where the state does not control all the means of production and essential services. Ideologically rooted socialism tends to be less democratic than competitive capitalism, although there have been many democratic socialist countries such as Sweden and authoritarian capitalist countries such as South Korea. If private capitalism is more closely tied to democracy than is centralized socialism, then Nehru's socialist democracy was an insufficient or imperfect democracy. Gandhi's economic emphasis on village *panchayats* (councils of local leaders) and small-scale village industries was much more democratic, although the Gandhian approach was not necessarily a guarantee of rapid economic growth.

Capitalism also has its flaws and does not ensure complete freedom. Where capitalism tends toward monopolies in many sectors of the economy, workers and employees do not always have a freedom of choice. The problem with competitive capitalism is maintaining the competition and ensuring that there is an equitable distribution of wealth. This is where private capitalism and the Indian constitution would appear to be in conflict. Article 39 of the Indian constitution, which falls under the heading "Directive Principles of State Policy," prescribes the following:

> 39. *Certain principles of policy to be followed by the State:* The State shall, in particular, direct its policy toward securing (a) that the citizens, men and women equally, have the right to an adequate means of livelihood; (b) that the ownership and control of the material resources of the community are so distributed as best to subserve the common good; (c) that the operation of the economic system does not result in the concentration of wealth and means of production to the common detriment; (d) that there is equal pay for equal work for both men and women.[6]

While these directives do not specifically prescribe a socialist state, socialism appeared to be the preferred choice of the members of the Constituent Assembly (who belonged mainly to the Congress and Socialist parties) who drew up the constitution between 1947 and 1949. To the majority of the constitution makers, a capitalist economy was perceived to be socially unjust. In this, they seemed to concur with Karl Marx, who pointed out more than a century ago that competitive capitalism leads to monopoly capitalism since the purpose of private economic competition is to beat out or eliminate the competitor. It was the fear of economic power being held by industrial giants owned by a few extended families, who often came from minority ethnic and caste groups such as the Parsees, Marwaris, and Gujerati Banias, that motivated India's Congress Party to adopt the mainly state-owned socialist economic system.

THE INSTABILITY OF CENTRALIZED DEMOCRACIES

Three examples on the subcontinent perhaps best exemplify the problems underlying demands for a centralized state in the hope of preserving the unity of the state. In each case, such demands produced instead the reverse result: the disintegration of the state. In 1946, the British put forward the Cabinet Mission Plan to preserve the unity of India as it moved toward independence. According to the plan, a confederation of three parts that approximately followed the lines of the existing states of India, Pakistan (including all of Punjab), and Bangladesh (including all of Bengal and Assam) was proposed. The plan was accepted by Mohammed Ali Jinnah, the leader of the All-India Muslim League who led the struggle for Pakistan, but rejected by Jawaharlal Nehru, leader of the Indian National Congress. Failure to agree to what would have been a confederal India led to the partition of India in 1947. Although Nehru's rejection had much to do with his rivalry with Jinnah and his unwillingness to accept what was perceived to be a British plan, it had also to do with his unwillingness to accept a state that was so decentralized that it amounted to de facto partition. A similar failure on the part of West Pakistan to accept a decentralized constitution that would have given East Pakistan considerable autonomy eventually led to the disintegration of Pakistan in 1971 and the emergence of Bangladesh. And it was the Sinhalese-dominated Sri Lankan government's insistence in the 1950s on a Sinhalese-dominated centralized state that eventually brought about the Tamil-Sinhalese civil war from the early 1980s onward and the demand for an independent Tamil state.

Thus, the disintegration or threat of disintegration of the states in South Asia can be traced to the centralization of power in these states. One of the initial efforts to centralize power and consolidate unity in the newly independent states of India, Pakistan, and Sri Lanka was through a single "official language" policy. However, efforts to impose Hindi in the non-Hindi-speaking areas of the south and east of India, Urdu in East Pakistan, and Sinhalese in the Tamil areas of Sri Lanka, were all resisted. Ironically, when a multiethnic nation feels that it is threatened by territorial disintegration, the instinctive tendency on the part of the government is to centralize power rather than to decentralize power to accommodate the provinces seeking to break away. Such policies aggravate the problem rather than resolve it. For example, after assuming the prime ministership of India in the newly elected Congress government in 1991, P. V. Narasimha Rao declared that the central government would assume greater powers in order to deal with secessionist violence in Kashmir, Punjab, and Assam.

However, there is always the danger that decentralization intended to be a step toward a new confederation may be the first step toward the eventual dissolution of the state. Indeed, the objective of ethnic groups that make demands for decentralization may in fact be eventual outright secession. While the European Community is a case in which several independent and sovereign states have attempted to become a single confederation, the Commonwealth of

Independent States is a case in which a largely centralized federation—the former Soviet Union—attempted to change itself into a confederation. The movement from a single state to a confederation of several states may be riddled with strife, and the new confederation may find itself likely to collapse. Such a confederation will not solve the fears of ethnic groups who were a majority in the old state but find themselves a minority in the new states. This was one of Nehru's fears in deciding whether to accept the British Cabinet Mission Plan for a three-part confederation. If that plan had been accepted in 1946 and Pakistan had subsequently seceded, then India would have lost all of Punjab, Bengal, and Assam. A similar problem existed in the former Yugoslavia. The internal republics of Croatia and Slovenia proposed a confederation as a compromise between a strong, centralized federation and total independence for themselves. However, Serbia perceived the confederation as a first step toward secession that did not address the fears of newly created Serb minorities in what would become the independent states of Croatia and Bosnia-Herzegovina.

In the last century, after Italy was united by force, an Italian statesman, Massimo D'Azelio, declared: "Having made Italy, now we must make Italians."[7] His suggestion implied that uniting Italy was relatively easy, but molding the Italian nation was difficult. Similarly, for India, Pakistan, and Sri Lanka, gaining independence from Britain was relatively easy, but uniting and consolidating these multiethnic states have proved to be trying and laborious. What system is right for these multiethnic countries—centralism, federalism, decentralization, or confederalism—has not yet been satisfactorily resolved.

If a highly decentralized state were not feasible, would a system of proportional representation in parliament for minorities be desirable? Proportional representation would have advantages and drawbacks. Muslims have complained that they are underrepresented in the central and state legislatures. This may be because in every constituency, even those in which they may exist in sizable numbers, Muslims may still remain a numerical minority. Muslim and other non-Hindu candidates may stand a chance of winning an election only if there are multiple candidates and the votes are spread out over two or more Hindu candidates, or if many Hindus vote for Muslim or other non-Hindu candidates. In a multiple-candidate election, even if all the candidates in a constituency are Hindu, the successful candidate may not be the preferred choice of the majority community anyway, unless he receives more than half the votes cast. Any candidate who wins by a plurality rather than a majority of the votes cast may not be truly representative. Thus, a Muslim or other non-Hindu candidate who wins an election with a plurality of votes in a Hindu-majority constituency may not be truly representative at the constituent level and may be resented. But he could serve as the representative of that particular minority community at the national and state levels. The application of the "majority principle" in a pluralist system where people are fragmented by religion, language, and caste, is inadequate.

It is significant to note that the Congress Party has never won the majority of all votes cast in a national election, even when it won nearly 80 percent of the seats in the Lok Sabha (the lower house of India's central parliament) in 1986. Total votes cast for the Congress Party have always been under 50 percent. Thus, Congress representation at the national level has not always been truly representative. Why then is there no similar representation for Muslims based on a plurality of votes cast? If Muslims are a minority in most electoral constituencies and non-Muslims do not vote for Muslim candidates, even in multiple-candidate electoral races, Muslims may never be represented in the central and state legislatures in proportion to their numbers.

Proportional representation would clearly be unacceptable in India since it could accentuate communal distinctions and lead to social polarization. The Indian National Congress has alleged that proportional representation under the British was one of the main factors that led to the partition of India. So-called communal representation based on the proportional system amounted to a British policy of "divide and rule." Moreover, such representation along religious lines alone would make no sense. Why not along linguistic and caste lines as well? But combined proportional religious and linguistic representations—Gujerati-speaking Muslims for instance—could overlap and distort the representation of the electorate in the legislature. Proportional representation will continue to be resisted by the Hindu majority in India because it accentuates religious divisions and exacerbates communal conflict.

Even if proportional representation was introduced in India, it might not lead to the best form of representation for minorities. In Pakistan, where less than 2 percent of the population is non-Muslim, proportional representation has not served the minorities well. Hindus, Christians, and Parsees in Pakistan feel that this form of representation gives them little political clout. Their representation tends to be symbolic and insignificant. It may be better for minorities to elect a candidate from the majority Muslim community who is sympathetic to their grievances than to elect one of their own kind who may have no political influence in high places. Until his death in 1964, Jawaharlal Nehru, the high-caste Brahmin Hindu prime minister, was the best representative of the Indian Muslims. He was sensitive to their needs and constituted their main protector and benefactor. In later years, Hindu nationalists claimed that Nehru pampered the Muslims to the detriment of Hindu interests. Similarly, Prime Minister V. P. Singh, a Hindu from a high-caste princely family, was strongly supportive and protective of the rights of the lower castes, who are also mainly the underprivileged. Although he was unsuccessful, Singh sought to introduce new quotas for the so-called "Backward Classes" in addition to those already granted to the Harijans, formerly known as the "Untouchables." The "fair" representation of minority interests—in whatever way "fair" is defined and achieved—may be preferable to proportional representation. In a complex, multiethnic society, extensive decentralization down to the village level may provide the better representation for minorities than proportional representation.

THE INEFFICIENCY OF PUBLIC-SECTOR CAPITALISM

The conventional wisdom in the West is that socialist systems based on centralized economic planning imply a lack of economic freedom. In such systems, consumers do not make the decisions on what will be produced, how much will be produced, and where it will be produced. In capitalist systems, on the other hand, such decisions are made through the exercise of "consumer sovereignty" and "purchasing power." In theory, a competitive capitalist system allows for the entry into the production sector of all individuals and groups capable of making investments. It also allows for consumer choice that directly or indirectly determines what goods will be produced, how much will be produced, and where it will be produced. Competitive capitalism, therefore, results in a decentralized economic system and greater economic freedom.

The choice of economic systems carries implications for India's internal and external security. A strong and equitable economy contributes to domestic political stability and to the state's ability to procure weapons for external defense. Although in the first three decades after independence socialism was perceived as the best choice for reaching such objectives, it has recently become more controversial. One of the major causes underlying some of India's separatist movements may be traced to India's heavy socialist planning. The location of industries through centralized planning is often perceived to be discriminatory, emphasizing political rewards to pro–Congress Party states without reference to economic efficiency. Other economic grievances have been that the more productive and prosperous states are taxed more heavily to subsidize the less productive states. This has been one of the major Sikh grievances in Punjab. In contrast, private-sector investments are based mainly on competition, cost of production, labor productivity, and general economic efficiency. The location of private-sector investments is not usually based on political and bureaucratic interests that may emphasize electoral considerations and political influence in the location of industries, excessive labor recruitment to absorb the work force, and large bureaucracies that become obstacles to productivity and efficiency.

Socialism and Stalinist-type planning were the brainchild of Prime Minister Jawaharlal Nehru, who sought to implement such programs within a liberal Western-style parliamentary democracy. Nehru believed that only central planning would lift the country from backwardness and poverty toward rapid, self-sustaining economic growth. Although Nehru's strategy emphasized a development first approach, the results were anything but spectacular. During Nehru's time, India's annual GNP growth rate averaged about 4 percent. In the late 1960s and the 1970s, under his daughter, Indira Gandhi, annual GNP growth rate dropped to about 3 percent; and because of high population growth rates, the per capita economic growth rate was a dismal 1.5 to 2 percent. However, not all of this dismal economic performance was due to centralized planning; it was also due to the vagaries of the monsoon rains, which continue to afflict post-reform India.

Nehru's economic and political system was a combination of socialism and centralized planning with a parliamentary democracy. This formula, which included Stalinist-type five-year plans, proved to be a recipe for economic failure. Democracies raise levels of economic expectation dramatically. But where there is no profit motive or incentive and people hold secure jobs in government bureaucracies and public-sector corporations, and without the undemocratic Stalinist form of enforcement of economic policies, not much productive work gets done. The Chinese totalitarian Communist model did much better than the Indian democratic socialist model because China could ban industrial strikes and political dissent and thus enforce its planned economic programs, while India had to carry out its economic plans through democratic persuasion and consent.

One example of the differences between the Chinese and Indian political systems is the way they approach population control. Population control is one of the keys to generating greater savings for investment and rapid economic expansion. By the early 1990s, China, through its rigorously enforced "one child per family" policy, had reduced its population growth rate to less than 1 percent and was expected to bring its annual population growth rate to zero before the year 2000. Meanwhile, in India, which has half-hearted voluntary family planning programs, per capita income growth continues to be hampered by an annual 2.2 percent population growth rate, with no breakthrough in sight. Thus, between 1980 and 1991, the annual per capita GNP growth rate in China was 7.8 percent, compared to 3.2 percent in India, and reflected both a faster growing economy and a declining birthrate.[8]

China's spectacular economic success since the early 1980s is due to the gradual introduction of a capitalist, free-market economy while maintaining a totalitarian Marxist-Leninist political system. While Chinese capitalist entrepreneurs are free to operate, especially in certain designated regions, the basic trappings of democracy—adult franchise and freedom of speech—are denied. One writer, Nicholas Kristof, has called the new Chinese political-economic hybrid "Market-Leninisim."[9] According to Kristof, "in the 1990s, the business of the [Communist] party is business." Indeed, Deng Xiaoping's model of economic development appears increasingly to resemble that of the Chinese states of Taiwan and Singapore. The Chinese approach has been substantially different from that of Russia, in which political and economic liberalization were attempted simultaneously. The results by the mid-1990s have been political order and economic success in China and political and economic chaos in Russia.

Clearly, the greatest economic miracles occurred in those Asian countries that were governed by authoritarian regimes that maintained a private capitalist economy: South Korea and Taiwan, and, later, Thailand, Malaysia, and Indonesia. Japan, despite its formal democratic system and procedures, functions like a disciplined autocracy, which explains much of Japan's economic success. A similar situation prevails in Malaysia, which has a formal democracy based on adult franchise and a bicameral legislature but functions in a disciplined manner under the watchful eye of a constitutional monarchy. The "paramount ruler," Sultan Azian Muhibuddin Shah, appears to have more influence and power in Malaysia than Queen Elizabeth does in Britain. Malaysia's annual GNP growth rate has been averaging 8 to 10 percent since 1985.[10] Similarly, in Singapore's "democracy," the ballot box kept Lee Kuan Yew, an authoritarian-type leader, in power for more than a decade. In November 1990, Prime Minister Lee stepped down from office, but his influence on the government and his style of leadership continue. How "democratic" Singapore is remains controversial at best.

It is difficult to imagine disciplined democracies of the Japanese, Malaysian, or Singaporean type functioning in India. India's democracy resembles the Western democracies, especially in its allowance of free-wheeling dissent, confrontations, and opposition to policies adopted by the government in power. On the other hand, India's democracy is not about to be replaced by an authoritarian political system of the South Korean, Taiwanese, Indonesian, or Thai type either. No doubt, authoritarianism and private-sector capitalism alone cannot explain the economic miracles of East Asia since dictatorships elsewhere, in Africa, the Middle East, and Latin America, have not achieved similar results. In the Philippines, both under the dictatorship of Ferdinand

Marcos and under the democratic governance of Corazon Aquino, economic growth and prosperity have remained relatively low compared to other East Asian countries. But in general, authoritarian political systems or leaderships have not hurt the East and Southeast Asian economies. Significantly, Pakistan's highest rates of economic growth—an annual average of about 6 percent of the GNP—occurred in the 1960s under the military dictatorship of President Ayub Khan, and between 1977 and 1987 under the military dictatorship of President Zia-ul Haq. During this time, India's annual GNP growth rate averaged only about 3 percent.

Is economic development without political freedom worthwhile? The impoverished masses of South Asia would surely prefer to live in the authoritarian boom economies of East Asia than in the wretched misery of their "democratic" villages. Indeed, there can be no "real" freedom until the basic necessities and perhaps even comforts of life are first attained. Freedom from want may be more important for the poor than the freedom to vote. Thus, if the objective is development first, then authoritarian regimes, especially benevolent ones, may be more desirable than liberal democracies.

Yet, it is not at all clear that poor states need to make a choice between development and democracy on the belief that less democracy means more development. Corazon Aquino's husband, Benigno Aquino, who was an opponent of the Marcos dictatorship and who was killed at the Manila airport in August 1983, declared earlier that year in a speech in New York that poor countries do not have to exchange freedom for bread. After all, the Marcos dictatorship in the Philippines did not generate the high economic growth rates and levels of prosperity experienced by Taiwan, South Korea, Thailand, and Indonesia. Indeed, both democracy and development may be possible if the right economic policies are pursued, and if the size of bureaucracies and the level of corruption are minimized. And perhaps some exchange of high-development growth rates for more freedom may be desirable to maintain overall economic and political stability.

THE ISSUE OF EQUITABLE INCOME DISTRIBUTION

Opponents of free-market economies and private-sector capitalist development may argue that these systems do not ensure an equitable distribution of wealth. For example, the income gap between the top and bottom 20 percent of society in the United States is wide. On the other hand, in theory, socialism promises economic equality and a classless society. The average per capita income in India and China is similar; it is about $400 to $500 in both countries. But there is far less poverty in China than in India, and the gap between rich and poor is much less there than in India. This observation, however, cannot justify the choice of a totalitarian Communist system over a democratic capitalist system. The Indian failure thus far has been due to the strangulation of private-sector capitalist enterprise combined with the implementation of a half-hearted socialist economy on a voluntary basis. As a consequence, India could not match the economic success of Communist China and the even greater successes of the East Asian "Tigers." The combination of democracy and socialism has given India some undesirable handicaps and results. The rich few in India have become richer, and the poor masses have increased in number and remain poor. However, the limited and handicapped private sector that was allowed to operate in India during the socialist era did generate a modest middle class.

Although considerations of equality of economic justice lay at the heart of Nehru's choice of socialism over capitalism, his choice also carried a political rationale. In an economically underdeveloped democracy, a socialist political party platform has a greater chance of winning elections. Conversely, a capitalist party platform is unlikely to win many votes among the impoverished masses. Poor voters are unlikely to buy the claim that if the rich get richer, all will eventually benefit because wealth created at the top of the social-economic pyramid will ultimately trickle down to the society's poor. In earlier decades, political parties in India were unlikely to gain power by promoting big business in their election campaigns. This is quite unlike the United States, where the poor are a small minority and neglecting them may not be crucial in winning elections. Thus, the Republican Party may ignore the very small minority of poor Americans and still win handsomely if it addresses the needs of the middle- and upper-class electorate. By contrast, the poor are the overwhelming majority in India and hold the key to winning elections. Hence, parties like Congress and Janata have constantly appealed to the economic demands of the lower castes of Hindu society, the Shudras and Harijans, who are also overwhelmingly the lower economic classes of India. They constitute almost 70 percent of the Hindu electorate.

There is yet another problem. In developing countries like India, the rich few stand out visibly in stark contrast to the poor masses. Moreover, the deliberate display of financial opulence by the rich, which is often coupled with personal arrogance and mistreatment of the poor, does little to alleviate the tensions between rich and poor. The rich in poor countries, including India, have generally shown a notorious lack of compassion, sensitivity, and understanding for the less fortunate. Such conditions make the transition from state socialism to private-sector capitalism in poor countries complicated, and difficult to sustain once established.

However, the argument that private capitalist development does not ensure an equitable distribution of wealth is misleading because it overlooks the objectives of promoting economic freedom and advancing private enterprise and investment, which are to create general wealth that will eventually provide all or most of the population with a higher standard of living. The purpose of economic freedom is not to promote economic equality. Indeed, "freedom" and "equality" do not necessarily mean the same thing, one being political in its meaning and the other being social and economic. Whether they provide equality or not, clearly the Western free-market democracies and Japan have provided nearly all of their citizens much better living standards than have the earlier Communist or formerly Communist states of the Soviet Union, Eastern Europe, China, North Korea, and Vietnam.

One of the problems with Nehru's socialist philosophy, and indeed with the Congress Party's broad economic platform adopted just after independence, was the tendency to focus on the distributive aspect of development rather than on economic growth. Nehru appeared to believe that failure to establish a fair measure of economic equality would imply lack of political equality and, therefore, less democracy. But Nehru's search for greater economic equality was successful only in the sense that over half the population remained below the poverty line by India's standards of poverty, and much of the rest of the people remained exceedingly poor by Western standards. Economic equality in India under socialism appeared to mean equal poverty. One private Indian industrialist and businessman in Bombay informed me some years ago that the Congress Party's obsession with distribution made no sense when "we only have poverty to distribute." According to him, India had to generate wealth first before it worried about distribution, something he felt would happen automatically if productivity increased. He concluded with approximately the following words: "We businessmen and industrialists in India must either reinvest our profits or spend our profits. What else can we do with our money? Either way, our actions can only generate more demand, more production, more employment, and more income for more people."

The above observations are not intended to suggest that free-market, private-sector capitalism is a perfect system or a magic cure for the economic ills of a nation. Extremes of wealth and poverty are a form of social injustice. Corporate arrogance and mistreatment of employees, especially under monopolistic conditions, as well as perpetual fear of job loss even after a long period of dedicated service to the company, may generate high levels of psychological and social insecurity. General economic prosperity does not address such problems in affluent capitalist societies.

SECULARISM AND DEMOCRACY

Perhaps a contentious argument of this thesis is that a policy that embraces and promotes an official religion for the state cannot be truly democratic, even within a monoreligious society.[11] In a multireligious state, a theocratic state by its very nature does not provide equal status for people of other religions, irrespective of whether it allows freedom of worship. Religious minorities will always be less than equal and will not feel a total sense of loyalty and commitment to such a state. Moreover, in principle, a theocratic state does not respect the beliefs of secularists, agnostics, and atheists, who may not wish to participate in religious ceremonies at official functions. On the other hand, in a secular state, the right to practice religion at the private level is guaranteed in principle. Even for those who adhere to the official religion in a theocratic state, complete freedom of worship and expression may not always exist since dissent, deviations, and alternative interpretations of scriptures may not be acceptable. Once religious leaders enter the political arena to enforce what they consider correct religious thought and practice, freedom of expression and democratic rights become diminished. These observations apply to all religions including Christianity, Islam, Hinduism, Buddhism, and Sikhism. Alternative concepts of the democratic state advanced by Muslim, Hindu, Buddhist, and Sikh fundamentalists and nationalists tend to be less than democratic—if they are at all democratic—according to Western secular standards. Such concepts can lead to political instability in multireligious societies.[12]

Muslim advocates of an Islamic state may argue that Islam stands for equality and brotherhood among Muslims and guarantees the protection of religious minorities and that, therefore, an Islamic state and a democratic state are not mutually incompatible. A variation of this argument is that an Islamic democracy does not have to be the same as a Western secular democracy.[13] Shukri B. Abed has noted that Islamic fundamentalists or traditionalists believe that "Western concepts such as democracy, secularization, and the nation-state represent a direct contradiction of Islamic religious and political thought since they rely for their authority on human rather than divine legislation and are formulated through secular rather than God-given laws."[14] However, even if a religion-based democracy is possible in theory, there is always a difference between the philosophy and practice of religions. States that promote an official religion invariably turn out to be intolerant states and usually reduce members of their religious minorities to second-class status. The examples of post-Shah revolutionary Iran and medieval Christian Europe illustrate the dangers of religious states. Despite claims by Hindus and Muslims in India that they are basically tolerant of other religions, in practice Hindu and Muslim nationalists on the subcontinent have not been tolerant. Millions have died in South Asia over the centuries in the name of religion.

Muslim and other critics of a Hindu state in India may point to the traditional Hindu social code, the caste system, that promotes social inequality. They may claim that a Hindu state therefore cannot be a democratic state. However, democracy does not mean, nor necessarily guarantee, equality of status and power. As long as the Hindu caste structure is confined mainly to finding marriage partners and other private individual and group functions, and provided Hinduism does not unduly restrict political and economic mobility for all castes and religions, democracy may flourish in a Hindu society. Indeed, the emphasis on individual worship and salvation in Hinduism and Buddhism may make these religions conducive to the promotion and retention of democracy. It may be more than a coincidence that Western democracy has been relatively more successful in Hindu-majority India and Buddhist-majority Sri Lanka than in the overwhelmingly Muslim Pakistan and Muslim-majority Bangladesh. However, if both Pakistan and Bangladesh, which are officially Islamic republics, continue to remain democratic, as they have since 1990, this hypothesis would be negated. This scenario would demonstrate that an Islamic republic and a Western democratic system may be compatible.

In its essence, Hinduism tends to be secular and non-fundamentalist despite efforts by contemporary Hindu nationalists to make it appear otherwise. Hinduism has sometimes been defined as a way of life, one that is also found among the followers of other religions on the subcontinent.[15] A Hindu who is an atheist or agnostic remains as much a Hindu as does a devotee of one or more of the Hindu gods. And many Hindus tend to consider the followers of other religions in India, especially the followers of religions founded in India—Buddhism, Sikhism, and Jainism—but also the followers of Islam, Christianity, and Zoroastrianism, as essentially Hindus because they are part of "Mother India" or "Akhand Bharat" (One India), which encompasses the geographical Indian subcontinent.

Thus, both the agnostic Nehru and the saintly Gandhi were considered equally Hindu. Both professed a secular state for India, but each had his own vision of the type of secular state. Nehru's secular state was in the Western tradition of the separation of "church and state." Gandhi's secular state implied the promotion of all religions in India as equal.[16] Following Nehru's death in 1964, his concept of secularism was replaced by Gandhi's concept, which led first to multiple religious ceremonies at official functions, and then mainly to Hindu religious ceremonies. Eventually, the situation descended into the demand for a Hindu state in India. In the 1990s, Hindu nationalists claimed that all the peoples of the Indian subcontinent of any religion belonged to a larger Hindu weltanschauung. As strange as it may seem to many India-watchers, Hindu nationalists believe that the declaration of a Hindu state may actually produce a greater unity among all the peoples of India, whatever their religion.

In contrast to Hindu philosophy (but not necessarily practice), which emphasizes the individual, Islam tends to emphasize the community and does not provide for the separation of "church and state." Maulana Abul Ala Mawdudi, who founded the Jamaat-i-Islami in prepartition India in 1941, believed that an Islamic polity should be God-centered rather than human-centered. Therefore, the kind of British parliamentary democracy that India was moving toward would be unsuitable for Muslims.[17] For Muslims, popular will had to be subordinated to God's will as embodied in the Shariat. This did not mean that a Muslim state had to be an authoritarian theocracy, but that it should be an Islamic democracy, in which freedom was based on Muslim societal rights rather than on individual political rights. Needless to say, a strict interpretation of Maulana Mawdudi's Islamic democracy, or "theodemocracy," based on enforcement of the Shariat would amount to Islamic totalitarianism. The place of minorities in such a political order would be ambiguous, despite the Shariat's directives on the fair treatment of religious minorities. However, an Islamic state like Pakistan, in which nearly all of the population is Muslim, and a secular state like Italy, in which nearly all of the population is Catholic, may not be substantially different since in both, citizens may feel themselves subject to a spiritual authority that is higher than any secular authority.

The separation between "church and state" may be still possible in Muslim societies, as is exemplified by the case of post-Ottoman Turkey, although the Turkish secular democratic model has come under stress in the 1990s. The Pakistan that Mohammed Ali Jinnah envisaged was in all probability a secular democratic state—a Muslim majority counterpart to Nehru's Hindu-majority, secular, democratic India. Jinnah's All-India Muslim League was concerned about the political rights of Muslims in a democracy based on adult franchise in which, if all Hindus voted for Hindu candidates and Muslims for Muslim candidates, the democratic system would perpetuate permanent Hindu rule over Muslims. After the death of Jinnah, which occurred within a year of the creation of Pakistan, a Pakistani secular state was reconceived as an Islamic state rather a secular Muslim state along the Turkish model.

This later emphasis on the Islamic basis of the Pakistani state was symbolized by the shifting of the nation's capital from Karachi, in Sindh, to the newly built city in northwestern Punjab that was deliberately named Islamabad. The desire to couple a functioning Islamic state with Western democratic norms has been one of the underlying difficulties in the establishment of a democracy in Pakistan. The marriage between the two different systems will continue to be filled with tension and may eventually lead to the breakdown of democracy in Pakistan. Indeed, the greatest threat to Pakistan's democracy in the 1990s arises not so much from the Pakistani military but from Islamic fundamentalists.

If religion is separated from public life can moral values be sustained? Would democratic freedoms be less democratic if the values of society were eroded? Would a nonreligious democratic state be an ethical state? May secular freedom go too far and corrupt the values of civil society? Such questions have been raised in all religious societies, even within Western democratic states. Demands by right-wing Christian fundamentalists in the United States to allow prayer in schools and to allow religious practices to become part of government-supported or government-sponsored activity has been rejected thus far as violating the American constitutional principle of the separation of church and state. In the United States, this separation also implies the separation of religion and ethics: religion is part of the private domain, and ethics part of the public domain. While all citizens are free to practice religion privately, democratic participation and state functions are to be essentially secular. Right-wing religious groups in the United States have questioned whether ethics in the public sphere can be maintained without the moral values instilled through religion.

Similar arguments have been made in Islamic societies in which the separation of religion from public life and ethics is theologically difficult. Right-wing Muslim reactions against the secular authorities in Algeria and Egypt arise from dissatisfaction with what the Muslims see as the erosion of ethical values in civil society. According to them, only an Islamic state can ensure an ethical state, which could hardly be incompatible with a democratic state. However, religious interpretations and ethical values are subjective and controversial in any society. Once such issues become part of democratic debate, reason and tolerance can break down.

Although there are other concepts of democracy—an Islamic democracy, a socialist democracy, a workers' democracy, and the like—the Western concept of democracy remains the most practical and equitable. The fact that democracy emerged and evolved in the West does not necessarily deny its universalism. As in science, questions that need to be asked about what promotes the greatest freedom for the most people are objective ones. Obviously, majority rule can also prove despotic for minorities, especially where voting takes place along ethnic lines. However, the idea that a democracy that is highly decentralized, promotes competitive private capitalism, and separates "church and state" is the approximate ideal for ensuring the general security and political stability of the states of South Asia will be advanced in this book.

STATE SOVEREIGNTY VERSUS
ETHNIC SELF-DETERMINATION

One of the major dilemmas faced by multiethnic democracies is the demand for self-determination by various ethnic groups. Individual and group rights are often expressed in the right to hold referendums to determine the wish of ethnic minorities to remain part of the state or to secede from it. In a democracy, the right to vote may be an inadequate expression of freedom among minority groups since it does not necessarily ensure the right to self-government. Especially in centralized democracies in which voting takes place along ethnic lines, the majority ethnic group will always rule the minority ethnic group. Real freedom then may be obtained only through ethnic and territorial secession so that the ethnic minority group can become the majority ethnic group in the new state. As noted above, one of the major arguments put forward by Mohammed Ali Jinnah for Muslim secession from India was the prospect of Hindu-majority rule in a united India. Jinnah feared that Hindus would always vote for Hindu candidates, Muslims for Muslims and, therefore, the Hindus would always rule the Muslims. That may be democracy for Hindus but not freedom for Muslims.

The essential question here is whether the democratic rights of citizens can be extended to the point that the state may disintegrate. In many parts of the world, demands for self-determination with the objective of seceding from the state have inevitably led to the central government's insistence on the sovereignty and territorial integrity of the state. In rejecting the rights of Kashmiris, Sikhs, Nagas, and other minorities to self-determination, India has frequently argued that the democratic rights of individuals and groups cannot be allowed to lead to the self-destruction of the state.

There have been several bloody secessionist movements in various parts of the world, and nearly all of them have been crushed by military force. For example, in the early 1970s, the Muslim majority of Nigeria, consisting mainly of the Yoruba and Hauser tribes, crushed the secessionist movement of the Roman Catholic Ibo tribe of Biafra in a four-year-long bloody civil war. About 1 million Ibos died in that war. There are other examples of violent but unsuccessful secessionist movements: the Kurds from Iraq and Turkey; the Basques from Spain; the Balochis, Pashtuns, and Sindhis from Pakistan; the Muslim Kashmiris, Sikh Punjabis, Hindu Tamils and Assamese, and Christian Nagas from India; the Buddhist Tibetans and Muslim Uigyurs of Xinjiang from China; the Catholic East Timorese from Muslim Indonesia; the tribal Shans and Kachins from Burma; the Hindu and Catholic Tamils from Buddhist Sri

Lanka; and the Muslim Moros from the Catholic Philippines. It should not be forgotten that the United States fought a bloody civil war at the cost of a million lives to prevent the secession of the South. In general, the standard response, throughout the world, of the state to separatist movements has been brutal military suppression by the federal authorities no matter how long it takes to crush the separatists.

This problem has become more sensitive and problematic with the disintegration of the multiethnic states of the former Yugoslavia and the former Soviet Union. Once self-determination is conceded to one "nation," where will it stop? If Croatians and Muslims had the right to hold referendums and secede from Yugoslavia, then why should the Serb minorities not have the right to secede from the new states of Croatia and Bosnia? If the Serbs from these states could secede, then why not Albanians and Hungarians from Kosovo and Vojvodina? If Slovenia, Croatia, Macedonia, Ukraine, Georgia, the Baltic states, and the Central Asian states had the right to become free from Yugoslavia and the Soviet Union, then why should Kashmir, Punjab, Assam, Nagaland, and Mizoram not also have the right to freedom from India? The arguments for self-determination could then be extended to the Balochis and Sindhis in Pakistan, the Tibetans in China, the Kurds in Iraq and Turkey, the East Timorese of Indonesia, the Basques of Spain, the French-speaking Quebecois of Canada, and the Russians caught on the wrong side of the borders of the former Soviet republics.

However, the separation of Pakistan from India in 1947 demonstrated that secessionism did not solve the original problem of Hindu domination of Muslims. The demand for Pakistan was most acute in those regions of India where Muslims were a minority, so that after the creation of Pakistan, these Muslims found themselves to be in an even smaller minority in a more dominant and hostile Hindu-majority state. The partition of India merely introduced more Hindu-Muslim strife, territorial disputes, wars, conventional and nuclear arms races between India and Pakistan, and the sapping of productive energy for alleviating the misery of the poor in both countries. These long-term problems were in addition to the immediate massacre of about half a million civilians in interreligious communal strife and the uprooting and refugee flows of about 15 million people. The secessionist struggle in East Pakistan in 1971 resulted in the massacre of about a quarter million Bengalis by the Pakistan Army and the flow of 10 million Bengali refugees (mainly Hindu) to India. Although these refugees were returned after Bangladesh was created, through armed military intervention by India, a new minority and refugee problem was generated. Half a million Urdu-speaking Bihari Muslims who had supported the Pakistan Army were reduced to second-class citizens or driven out to

Pakistan. Similarly, the recognition of Croatia and Bosnia as independent states has created more problems than it has resolved. Indeed, if what was done in Yugoslavia were done in India, several new states would emerge, and there would be millions of refugees and communal massacres on a scale that would be completely out of control. Any decision to grant self-determination to ethnic minorities in India conjures up the image of such a massive catastrophe that makes the partition of India in 1947 look tame.

The creation of new states usually generates new problems of majorities and minorities and greater ethnic strife than ever before. The Indian position on this question of ethnic self-determination conforms to that of the Organization of African Unity (OAU). The OAU adopted the policy of not undoing colonial boundaries drawn by the European powers between 1870 and 1900, however unjust and illogical these boundaries may have been. Indeed, the OAU was unhappy when Eritrea broke free from Ethiopia in 1993 after a decade-long bloody secessionist struggle. Strangely, while most European countries were quick to recognize the independence of Slovenia, Croatia, and Bosnia in 1991-92, they were unwilling to recognize an independent state of Biafra despite the three-year bloody civil war from 1967 to 1970 between the Catholic Ibos of the Biafran province of Nigeria and the majority Muslim Hausers who inhabited much of the rest of the country. Considerations of security and stability would appear to dictate decisions made in choosing between ethnic self-determination and maintaining the international frontiers of a sovereign state during the Nigerian civil war. The aftermath of the disintegration of Yugoslavia and the Soviet Union between 1991 and 1993, the breakup of Pakistan in 1971, and the partition of India in 1947, would appear to demonstrate that, on balance, the maintenance the territorial integrity of a state generates fewer human tragedies and promotes greater good than does the breakup of a state.

Although Pakistan failed to crush the Bangladesh separatist movement in 1971 because of Indian military intervention, most secessionist movements in India, Pakistan, and Sri Lanka have been suppressed or crushed. This has been the worldwide standard response to secessionism, justified on the basis of the territorial integrity and sovereignty of the state. In the 1990s, this policy of crushing separatism through sustained military force has become a matter of controversy. The question of whether democracy should be extended to include the right of national self-determination will not be easily resolved.

Perhaps international pressure should focus on pushing for decentralization, democratization, and the prevention of human-rights violations in areas where violent secessionist movements prevail—and not on granting recognition to new states. In choosing between ethnic self-determination and the territorial integrity of the state, there is a need to maintain the territorial status quo. It is important to recognize that freedom and democracy are derived from appropriate political institutions and processes, not from breaking away from an existing state. After all, ethnic nationalists who succeed in creating a new independent state could then well set up an authoritarian or fascist state. The new majority could oppress members of the old majority now turned minority. On the other hand, political decentralization and free-market economies can do more for the political freedom and economic well-being of all citizens, including minorities, than the creation of new states.

3

The Security-Political Dimension

SECURITY THREATS AND THE EROSION OF DEMOCRACY

The political dilemma is whether to curtail, modify, suspend, or even dispose of democracy for the sake of national security. Three broad opposing viewpoints were delineated earlier for analytical purposes: democracy first, which is espoused by those who advocate the maintenance of democracy over security as the best way of advancing the interests of both democracy and security; security first, which is espoused by those who advocate promotion of national security over adherence to democratic principles, even perhaps at the cost of dissolving democracy itself; and development first, which is espoused by those who advocate economic growth as a means of stabilizing democracy and enhancing security. Chapter 2 discussed some of the pros and cons underlying the first two perspectives, while chapter 4 will examine some of the constitutional aspects of the debate. Chapter 6 will examine development first arguments.

The preoccupation with security, especially with internal threats to the state, has led to a certain amount of erosion of the Indian democratic process. This is reflected not only by the passage of several legislative acts and constitutional amendments, but also by the increasing powers of the central government over the state governments and by the rise of paramilitary forces. These trends do not imply that democracy no longer operates in India or that democracy is in serious danger. Sikh and Kashmiri secessionists, backed by Western supporters in the U.S. Congress, the British Parliament, and other institutions in Europe, allege that India's democracy is phony and that it is only a democracy for the Hindu majority. Such extreme allegations are simply wrong and unfair. No doubt, the Indian democracy has not operated well at all times and has sometimes failed in some states. These failures have affected both the majority and minority religious communities. Such deficiencies and occasional failures would be considered unavoidable or even inevitable by security first proponents because of the size and diversity of India and the magnitude of the security problems it faces. Maintaining the unity and territorial integrity of the state remains the primary and fundamental task of the state. On the other hand, democracy first proponents may consider the present trends deeply disturbing and may believe that if these trends are left unchecked, democracy could prove to be in danger. Indeed, this danger is not so much the threat of a sudden military takeover as the creeping authoritarianism along the fringes of the state that makes the transition away from democracy less noticeable.

This chapter will examine the underlying causes of the concerns of security first and democracy first proponents. Such issues include the nature of the external and internal threats faced by India; relations between civilians and the military that may affect or undermine the democratic process; the security consequences of moving from a secular Indian state to a formal Hindu state; and political and moral issues arising from the use of armed force by the state and from allegations of human rights violations.

THE SOURCES OF EXTERNAL THREATS

The policies of the great powers on issues such as Kashmir, other separatist insurgencies, nuclear proliferation, and human rights violations have changed substantively since the end of the Cold War, and India has therefore been compelled to re-examine and readjust its traditional positions.[1] In September 1993, the Sino-Indian border dispute was settled, thus eliminating—at least for the time being—a major traditional threat to India from the north. Except for concerns mainly about nuclear proliferation, the rise of Islamic fundamentalism, and the international narcotics trade, American strategic interests in South Asia, and Indo-Pakistani issues in particular, have been reduced. While nuclear proliferation may affect the security of all the states in the region, it does not increase pressure on the Indian government to invoke internal emergency measures to address the problem. Russian interests in the region are now almost exclusively in the area of commercial arms sales to any side that can pay in hard currency. In general, strategic great-power rivalry in South Asia, which was relatively weak even during the Cold War, has dissipated and almost disappeared. Because of these changes, security pressures on the Indian democratic process arising from external threats have considerably lessened.

A major external security concern for India in the 1990s is the potential of greater interaction between South Asia and Muslim Central and West Asia. Pakistan is seeking new alliances and economic ties with the newly emerged Central Asian republics. These strategic developments are not a major threat to India in the short run. However, instability in Central and West Asia due to civil wars or the spread of Islamic fundamentalism could spill over into India and increase the threat of war between India and Pakistan or aggravate India's internal security threats. This may be seen in the Kashmir crisis, for instance, in which the insurgency has drawn its ideological inspiration from the Ayatollah Khomeini's Iranian revolution, its tactical style from the Palestinian "intifadeh" of the 1980s, and its guerrilla strategy from the Afghan mujahideen. The Muslim factor may also be seen in the 1991 Gulf War, which aroused and angered much of the Muslim population of South Asia against the West. The rise of Islamic fundamentalism, even in the once more secular countries such as Indonesia and Malaysia, encourages similar movements in South Asia and aggravates Hindu-Muslim tensions in India.[2] And the emergence of the new Central Asian republics has added a new dimension to the Indo-Pakistani rivalry in the context of politics in the Muslim world.

The loss of the United States as an ally since the end of the Cold War has prompted Pakistan to step up its efforts in promoting Islamic solidarity in West and Central Asia.[3] This has been, no doubt, a consistent and continuing Pakistani policy since the early 1950s. Pakistan's membership in the United States–sponsored Central Treaty Organization (CENTO) in 1955 (it was then known as the Baghdad Pact) had brought it military links with CENTO's other two members, Turkey and Iran. The economic offshoot of CENTO was the Regional Cooperation for Development (RCD). Both collapsed following the overthrow of the Shah in 1979 and the rise of Islamic fundamentalism in Iran under the Ayatollah Khomeini. Pakistan's attempt to initiate and promote an Islamic Defense Pact in the 1970s was not successful. Its efforts to rally the *ummah* (the unity of the faithful as preached by the Prophet Muhammed) of Muslim nations to resolve the Iran-Iraq war in the 1980s also failed. In addition, Pakistan made various efforts to promote Islamic cooperation in trade and investments, and in 1991 Prime Minister Nawaz Sharif called for the creation of an Islamic Common Market.[4] All of these Pakistani efforts carried the dual purpose of promoting Islamic solidarity and confronting a much larger Hindu-dominant India.

Another arrangement called the Economic Cooperation Organization (ECO) was set up in 1986 by the same three Muslim states that had been members of the old RCD. However, the ECO remained relatively unknown, carried little economic or political power, and undertook few cooperative development programs. The ECO was expanded and rejuvenated when the five Central Asian Muslim republics (Kazakhstan, Tajikistan, Uzbekistan, Turkmenistan, and Kyrgyzstan) and Azerbaijan joined the organization in 1991, either as full members or as observers. Pakistan then proposed membership for Afghanistan, which was achieved. Pakistan has been one of the prime movers in attempting to consolidate the ECO[5] so that it can become a large Muslim trading bloc of territorially contiguous states. The expanded ECO was formally declared in the fall of 1992. However, the ECO has shown little progress since then because of the continuing civil war in Afghanistan, political instability in Tajikistan, and Turkish-Iranian rivalry, including Sunni-Shia rivalry, in the region.

According to an assessment in the Russian newsweekly *Novoye Vremya* (as reported in an Indian newspaper), Pakistan is advancing "Napoleonic plans for new Muslim alliances."[6] Pakistan envisages "rallying together" Iran, Turkey, Pakistan, the five Central Asian republics, Azerbaijan, and postwar Afghanistan. One Pakistani analyst has projected the eventual formation of a "United States of Hilal," a large Muslim confederation that would stretch from Pakistan to Turkey.[7] In a sense, this would be the logical extension of the concept of "Pakistan" beyond the subcontinent, Pakistan itself having been created as the homeland for Indian Muslims within the subcontinent.

Although the prospects seem to recede in the mid-1990s, the possible upgrading of the ECO into a loose confederation, stretching from Pakistan to Turkey with some military cooperation and arms transfers, could undo India's contemporary military preponderance in South Asia.[8] As a consequence, India has sought to counter Pakistani moves by pursuing cordial relations with the successor Muslim states of the former Soviet Union. Nearly all the heads of state of the Muslim republics of the former Soviet Union visited India within a period of six months following the breakup of the Soviet Union in August 1991. Such high-level exchange visits have continued. However, the continuation of secularism in Muslim Central Asia may be in question; and Islamic governments could rise in those states as they have elsewhere in the Muslim arc from Morocco to Pakistan. On the other hand, Pakistan's strategy of linking itself with the states of West and Central Asia also carries some weaknesses. Afghanistan needs to be stabilized so that road and rail communications with the Central Asian states can be established, a prospect that remains uncertain despite the over-throw of President Najibullah and the victory of the various factions of the Afghan mujahideen in April 1992.[9] Pashtuns, Tajiks, and Uzbeks now battle each other for control of Afghanistan. Perhaps, Pakistan could take over the short and narrow Wakhan corridor in Afghanistan that separates Tajikistan from Pakistan in order to acquire a direct land link with the Central Asian republics. This corridor was deliberately created as part of Britain's imperial strategy in the nineteenth century so that no part of the Indian empire touched the Russian empire. Politically, Pakistan could not take over the Wakhan corridor without arousing anger in Kabul, and the terrain in the corridor would make the construction of road and rail links difficult.

The stability of Tajikistan, like that of Afghanistan, remained uncertain at the end of 1995. The partial coup against President Rakhmon Nabiyev in May 1992, which demoted him to figurehead, had created a power vacuum and provoked a leadership struggle and civil strife. The Islamicists may rise to provide a national ethos and direction in Tajikistan.[10] However, at the end of 1993, former Communist leaders appeared to be gaining control, with the help of the Russian armed forces. More problems may be expected in the region as Tajik nationalism spreads among the Tajiks in Afghanistan. No doubt, the territorial contiguity with all the ECO countries already exists through Iran, but this connection has not produced substantive results for Pakistan in the past. Iran is foremostly a Shiite and Persian state, and it continues to maintain good ties with India.

While these developments in West and Central Asia may be worrisome, they do not call for emergency policy measures in India that may restrict individual rights and the democratic process. The circumstances that were present before and after the Sino-Indian and Indo-Pakistani wars that prompted the 1962 Defence of India Rules and the 1971 Maintenance of Internal Security Act did not exist in the early 1990s. Some concerns are periodically expressed about the growth of Chinese military power. These concerns are addressed through quiet Indian diplomacy and the development of missile capabilities and clandestine nuclear weapons technology in India.

THE SOURCES OF INTERNAL THREATS

What is worrisome for India are the increasing threats from within and the prospect of the disintegration of the state. Not only are these threats greater than they were in earlier decades, but also they are more directly threatening to

India's democracy. The former chief-of-staff of the Indian Army, General V. N. Sharma, noted:

> India's greatest weakness is not its economy but internal dissensions. Perhaps the most dangerous threat the nation faces is not so much from its enemies on the borders as from internal political struggle causing growing violence between ethnic groups, castes and creeds; the political scramble for votes at any cost, and the struggle which makes sworn enemies of those in power and those who wish to wrest this power by all available means fair or foul. In our so-called democratic polity, the question of even a fair election is in doubt as criminalised politics uses money and "goonda" muscle power to sway the voters.[11]

Violent struggles for independence by the Muslims of Kashmir, the Sikhs of Punjab, and the Assamese-speaking Hindus of Assam—three major states in politically sensitive and strategic locations—were of a far greater magnitude and importance than past struggles for independence among the Christian Naga, Mizo, and Gharo tribes in the northeast of India.

There is also a regional dimension to ethnic conflict in South Asia. Almost perennially, communal and separatist violence in one country has been aided from across national boundaries. Separatist movements receive, or have received, encouragement and material support from across national boundaries in Indian Kashmir and Punjab, in the tribal districts and states of India in the northeast, in the Tamil areas of Sri Lanka, in the former East Pakistan (now Bangladesh), and in the provinces of Sindh and Balochistan in Pakistan. When such support is sustained, as in the case of Pakistan's support for Kashmiri separatists, it takes on the dimensions of a war by proxy. The danger exists that proxy wars can turn into full-scale wars.

Finally, the frequent use of the armed forces for the maintenance of internal security tends to politicize them, often aggravates the conflict, and increases the danger of military takeovers. Prolonged and extensive use of the armed services to deal with internal conflicts lowers military professionalism and makes the military less prepared for the task of defending the country against external aggression. The year-long Bangladesh crisis in 1971 and the Pakistani military defeat, which was partly due to the collapse of military professionalism and morale, are illustrative of this phenomenon.

The demand by the Tamils in India for an independent Dravidastan (or Dravida Nadu) ended when the separatist party, the Dravida Munnetra Kazhagham, gained power in Tamil Nadu through the electoral process in 1967. After years of guerrilla warfare, India resolved the Naga, Mizo, and Gharo separatist movements by granting greater autonomy and internal statehood to these tribes, which had been converted to Christianity by Western missionaries. Meanwhile, new independence movements replaced old ones, especially among the Sikhs, Kashmiris, and Assamese of India. The intensity of violence of these separatist movements has varied considerably from each other and from that of similar movements in Sri Lanka and Pakistan. In the 1990s, India, Sri Lanka, and Pakistan faced severe ethnic violence. The Kashmiri, Sikh, and Assamese insurgencies in India and the Tamil insurgency in Sri Lanka have been prolonged, intense, and bloody. In comparison, the ethnic violence in Sindh, despite its lower level of intensity, appears to threaten the disintegration of the country only because Pakistan cannot afford another partition after the separation of Bangladesh. This does not mean that India is in less danger. If any part of India, such as Kashmir, Punjab, or Assam, were to gain independence, India might unravel faster than Pakistan. As in the former Soviet Union and Yugoslavia, in India the independence of one state might generate a chain reaction in other states that had hitherto not considered demanding independence. This explains India's paranoia and its determination not to concede independence to any separatist group, irrespective of the justification of the cause and the intensity of the violence. The implicit internal security doctrine, which has been followed by successive Indian governments, is that all ethnic grievances must be resolved within the boundaries of the Indian state.

Relative to the total number of ethnic divisions that are conceivable in India and the size of the country's territory and population, the dangers of separatism and territorial disintegration have not yet reached critical proportions. Nationalism and violence have emerged only among a small percentage of the total number of ethnic groups that exist in India and, at their worst, affect less than 10 percent of the total Indian population. Size is an advantage that India possesses over the smaller states of South Asia, and ironically, diversity has proved to be a positive rather than a negative factor. Apart from the Hindus, who are broadly defined to include all castes, including the Harijans, there is no single majority group in India. The Hindi-speaking Hindus of North India constitute only 30 percent of the total population of India.[12] No other linguistic group exceeds 9 percent of the total population, and therefore, domination and exploitation by one group over another becomes difficult. Even the high-caste Brahmins of Tamil Nadu and the Brahmin Pandits of Kashmir, both of whom have been driven out of their own states, consider themselves to be persecuted minorities.

When separatist or nonseparatist territorial violence surfaces in one or more regions, the Indian government is able to cope with the problem while maintaining normal conditions elsewhere in the country. The economies of

Punjab and Assam have continued to prosper despite the violence and counterviolence among armed separatists and government security forces in these regions. Punjab's agricultural economy has continued to feed much of India, while Assam's tea, timber, and oil industries have continued to boost the economies of the state and the nation. Indeed, the economy of Punjab grew by 7.5 percent in 1990-91, compared to the national average of 5.5 percent. Even in Kashmir, only the state's tourism industry has ground to a halt. The central government has continued to assist Kashmir in finding markets and outlets in India for the products of its timber, horticulture, and handicrafts industries in the hope of restoring some semblance of normalcy amid the violence and social chaos. Meanwhile, it's business as usual (by Indian standards, of course) in the rest of India.

The situation in the northeast sector of India has been perpetually more volatile than that of the rest of India. Because the region is a complex patchwork of several tribal and linguistic groups who are further divided by religion, there have been extensive demands for independence or statehood within India. Several violent insurgencies have accompanied these demands. These problems sometimes spill over into the neighboring states of Bangladesh and Myanmar, where similar insurgencies prevail among Chakmas, Shans, and Kachins. Insurgents in all of these countries are able to find sanctuaries for their operations across international boundaries. Three Indian ministates called Nagaland, Mizoram, and Meghalaya have already emerged out of the old state of Assam, and there are further demands for the creation of separate Bodoland and Gurkhaland states out of Assam. Separatist insurgencies have occurred in the other northeast Indian states of Tripura and Manipur, which border Bangladesh and Myanmar. The problems here are unlikely to lead to war between India and its two neighbors, but they call for cooperation in managing the separatist movements in all three countries. Demands for the creation of new "tribal" and "hill" states in northern India called Jharkhand and Uttarkhand further threaten to fragment the Indian political system.[13]

The most serious potential internal security problem India faces is Hindu-Muslim violence. This problem dates back to preindependence India and the movement for the creation of Pakistan. The partition of India in 1947 resolved little since many of the Muslims of central and northern India who had most vociferously demanded a separate state were left behind in India. While sporadic Hindu-Muslim violence continued with increasing frequency and growing numbers of lives were lost after independence, the problem took on a new dimension in the 1980s with the rise of militant Hindu nationalism. Hindu nationalism has been a response to increasing Muslim assertiveness throughout India. This is in contrast to three decades of relative Muslim submissiveness following the creation of Pakistan. The growing Hindu-Muslim confrontation and the decline in India's secular commitment was reflected in the Mosque-Temple ("Masjid-Mandir") dispute that took place in Ayodhya, Uttar Pradesh, between 1988 and 1993.

The campaign in the early 1990s by Hindu nationalists to construct a temple to the Hindu god Ram at the site of an existing mosque built by the first Moghul emperor, Babar, aroused passions among both Hindus and Muslims. Hindu zealots claim that Ram, a hero of the Hindu epic Ramayana, was born on the exact spot where the Emperor Babar had built the mosque around 1530. A Hindu temple built there centuries earlier had been torn down by the first Moghul for the construction of the mosque. The mosque itself, of no aesthetic value compared to later Moghul architectural wonders, had not been used by Muslims for decades. But the preservation of the mosque was depicted by some Muslims as symbolic of the security of Muslims and the future of Islam in India. The controversy provoked widespread Hindu-Muslim communal conflict in early 1993 when Hindu extremists managed to demolish the mosque. The Hindu-Muslim religious violence that followed threatened to drag in Pakistan, Bangladesh, and Afghanistan and create a wider Muslim-Hindu imbroglio in Southern Asia.

Caste divisions have also been a source of tension and conflict, but on a lesser scale than religion. The upper and lower castes of the Hindi-speaking Hindus of north-central India, who constitute nearly a third of the total population of India, are at present politically divided. In Bihar and Andhra Pradesh, this division has turned extremely violent, and occasional massacres and countermassacres took place between 1986 and 1992.[14] Since the mid-1990s, the lower castes, especially the Harijans, have become affiliated with violent Communist parties, such as the Maoist Communist Centre in Bihar and the Peoples War Group in Andhra Pradesh. The inspiration for these movements was the violent extremist Communist revolution in 1967 in Naxalbari, a district of West Bengal. The Naxalites, as they came to be known, had sought to establish a Communist state in India based on the Maoist slogan, "political power grows from the barrel of a gun." While the leaders of these movements have not been from the lower castes, their appeal has been largely directed toward the lower castes. The Indian government's reaction to these movements has been equally violent.

Caste and subcaste affiliations play an important part in Indian voting patterns and elections, and they form the basis for many of the economic demands made by the lower working classes. But territorial demands based on Hindu caste affiliations are difficult to generate since Hindu castes are not regional but form part of a social strata that is distributed over various regions.

Often, intercaste rivalry takes on the form of a power struggle at the state or national level. The struggle between the upper castes and the lower castes was evident in the violence that accompanied the efforts of V. P. Singh, the Janata Dal prime minister who himself came from an upper-caste princely background, to implement the Mandal Commission Report in 1989.[15] The Mandal Commission Report—published more than a decade before, but ignored by earlier Indian governments—pointed out that the "Backward Classes," comprising mainly the lower-caste Shudras, had failed to gain their fair share of resources and jobs. Prime Minister Singh's indication that up to 27 percent of government jobs would be reserved for these classes (in addition to the 22 percent already reserved for "Scheduled Castes and Tribes") triggered widespread demonstrations and several self-immolations by young upper-caste men and women during 1990-91. The plan was abandoned following the fall of the V. P. Singh government.

While Singh's Janata Dal party unsuccessfully sought to play the "lower caste" card, the Hindu nationalist Bharatiya Janata Party (BJP) managed to rally mainly the upper castes, both on the Mandal Commission Report that proposed quotas for the lower castes and on the anti-Muslim sentiment of Hindus that had been provoked by the "Masjid-Mandir" dispute in Ayodha, Uttar Pradesh.[16]

THE EFFECTS OF CIVIL-MILITARY RELATIONS ON THE POLICY PROCESS

The Indian political system may appear better equipped to deal with the problems of external security than to deal with the problems of internal security. But the increasing problems of internal violence and political instability complicate the formulation and conduct of defense policy. The problem largely arises from the interactive nature of many external and internal security issues and the integrated system of national security decision making that was set up in India by the late 1970s. One of the basic principles of democracy is civilian control over the military. Ultimately, it is the civilian authority that must make security policy. This has been the case in India, but when the internal and external security policy-making bodies are integrated, the areas of participation by the military in the decision-making process become ambiguous. Military leaders are supposed to participate in meetings dealing with external security policy-making, but when internal and external security are discussed together, the military gets excluded altogether. Civilian control over the military has had a tendency to become translated into civilian exclusion of the military from the security decision-making process.

Before the 1971 Indo-Pakistani war, security decision making was directed at threats from external powers, especially China and Pakistan. The Defense Committee of the Cabinet (DCC), the Defense Minister's Committee (DMC), and the Chiefs of Staff Committee (CSC) constituted a hierarchy of interacting committees that brought together political, bureaucratic, and military leaders to assess the security environment of India. By the mid-1970s, significant changes were made in the first and second tiers of the hierarchy of committees. The DCC became the Cabinet Committee on Political Affairs (CCPA), and the DMC became the Defense Planning Committee (DPC).[17]

Whereas the DCC had included only some cabinet minsters directly concerned with defense and the cost of defense (the ministers of defense, external affairs, finance, and industry), the CCPA included virtually all cabinet ministers since it was concerned with the entire spectrum of external and internal political and security issues.[18] The rationale for this change was twofold. First, Indian policymakers felt that the problems of external threats and weapons procurement could not be separated from the problems of internal strife and domestic political stability. Second, it was felt that resource allocations for defense should involve an assessment of the total resources available and the balanced distribution of such resources. Excessive defense allocations that might affect development or economic stability could prove disastrous for the defense effort in the long run and for maintaining domestic political stability. The security policy-making process therefore required inputs from a broad range of participants.

In October 1979, the Indian defense minister in the Janata government explained the reasons for the change as follows: "The concept of national defence must be much wider than the mere protection of the country's territorial integrity and sovereignty from perceptible military threats. What needs to be shielded equally is the whole spectrum of India's political, social, economic and technological progress from pressures arising out of the play of international forces."[19]

From the standpoint of defense planning, the most serious problem with the new committee was the reduced participation of the armed services in its deliberations. Lt. Gen. S. K. Sinha pointed out that although the service chiefs of the armed forces were technically expected to attend the meetings of the CCPA, "these occasions have inevitably got fewer because this committee is also involved with a host of other problems which are not connected with defence."[20] According to Sinha, the nature of the CCPA has led to a situation in which the service chiefs are often not invited even when defense issues are being discussed.

Instead, the services are often represented by the defense secretary, and direct military input into the highest policy-making forum is thus eliminated. Although Sinha made these observations in 1980, there is no evidence that matters have improved since then. No major wars have been fought in South Asia since the Indo-Pakistani war of 1971. India has been grappling with various problems of internal security so that the relevance of military input into the security policy-making process is not critical.

The DMC, which was at the middle level of the three-tier hierarchy, was replaced by the DPC in 1978. The DPC met under the chairmanship of the cabinet secretary and included the secretary to the prime minister, the secretaries of defense, defense production, external affairs, finance, and the planning commission, as well as the three chiefs-of-staff of the armed forces. Since the DPC consisted of seven high-ranking civil servants and three military chiefs-of-staff, military representation and inputs were overwhelmed by civilian representation and inputs. The DPC also did not provide any direct interaction between the military chiefs and the defense minister, which the DMC had provided. Indeed, even the defense minister's authority was reduced because the cabinet secretary who headed the DPC could report directly to the prime minister's office. Thus, while the service chiefs can discuss matters of inter-service concern in the CSC, their participation and direct input into the security policy-making process is low.

This situation may demonstrate that in India civilian control over the military is as complete as it should be in a democracy. But the frequent exclusion of the military from the security policy-making process produces grievances within the military. The military is expected to defend the country and has been used extensively in the maintenance of internal security without having much say in the security policy-making process. The Indian military has accepted this situation as unavoidable. As General Sharma noted: "What is the alternative? The police, despite its vast rising strength of armed battalions under the central Home Ministry or under the various states, with thousands of crores of expenditure, is unable to easily control the violent masses when the police itself is subservient to criminal political masters and their fawning bureaucrats."[21]

The military has also expressed grievances about the poor relationship between civil service officers in the defense ministry and the service chiefs. Lt. Gen. S. K. Sinha complained that a "thick layer of civil servants is interposed between the Defence Minister and the three Service headquarters, preventing direct interaction between the Minister and the Services."[22] Army chiefs have also complained that the existing CSC, which consists of three equal partners with no central command, prevents the military from assessing threats and presenting the military point of view from an integrated perspective. They have proposed a Chief of Defense Staff (CDS) system, along the lines of the system found in Britain and the Joint Chiefs of Staff (JCS) system of the United States, but it has been rejected by politicians because of their apprehensions about potential military takeovers and their view of it as a standing threat to democracy. Meanwhile, proposals from civilian military analysts and the military for instituting a National Security Council (NSC) to replace the CCPA continue to be made periodically but without success.

SECULARISM, HINDU NATIONALISM, AND DOMESTIC STABILITY

In India, the debate over whether India should move from a secular to a Hindu state (see chapter 2) is particularly important since one of the major external threats faced by the country is from the Islamic Republic of Pakistan. Threats emanating from other parts of the Islamic world tend to be transnational, including the spread of religious fundamentalism in India, which has been inspired by the revolution in Iran; and the infiltration into India's domestic Kashmir conflict of mujahideen warriors who once served in the Afghan war against Soviet forces. Moreover, many of the internal security problems of India are derived from religious differences; they include Hindu-Muslim communal violence and separatist movements among Punjabi Sikhs, Kashmiri Muslims, and Naga, Mizo, and Gharo tribal Christians in the northeast sector of India. India has experienced difficulties in coping with external and internal threats and conflicts that are manifestations of religious antagonisms and struggles while operating within the framework of its democratic constitution.

The choice between remaining a secular state or becoming a Hindu state affects India's external and internal security environments. However, a decision to declare India a Hindu state in either the near or distant future is not likely to increase the threat from Pakistan or raise the prospects of another Indo-Pakistani war. Pakistan has considered India to be a Hindu state ever since partition and independence in 1947. An official declaration from New Delhi that India is now a Hindu state would only imply (from the Pakistani standpoint) that India had finally decided to be honest about itself. Indeed, to see India as anything other than a Hindu state would be to question the raison d'etre for the creation of Pakistan. After all, Pakistan came into being on the basis of Mohammed Ali Jinnah's "two nation theory" that Hindus and Muslims constituted two separate nations on the subcontinent and that Muslims in a Hindu-majority India would always be an oppressed group of people. Thus, according to Pakistan, India's secularism was merely a facade for the purpose of retaining Muslim-majority Kashmir. Although an official declaration of India as a Hindu state is not likely to increase the prospect of war with Pakistan, Hindu-Muslim antagonism remains the underlying source of conflict between India and Pakistan. The prospects of war between India and Pakistan at any given time do not diminish either, irrespective of whether India is or is not formally a secular state.

A formal declaration that India is a Hindu state—or that it is not a Hindu state—could have great consequences within India, whatever the quality and effectiveness of its past secular policy. In a climate of rising religious nationalism and fundamentalism among Hindus, Muslims, Sikhs, and the northeast tribal Christians, an assertion or denial that India is a Hindu state could increase communal tensions and conflict. Either members of religious minorities will feel unhappy and less loyal to India if a Hindu state is declared, or members of the Hindu majority will feel unhappy and angry with India's religious minorities if a Hindu state is not declared. Either way, it may spell greater domestic communal conflict. At this stage, another Indo-Pakistani war over Kashmir could complicate the tensions and antagonisms between the major religious groups of India. A potential religious civil war, accompanied perhaps by another Indo-Pakistani war, could threaten the survival of India's democracy.

In the current situation, Hindu nationalists, represented by such parties and organizations as the Bharatiya Janata Party (BJP), the Rashtriya Swayamsevek Sangh (RSS), the Vishwa Hindu Parishad (VHP), and the Shiv Sena, argue that Hindus constitute 82 percent of the population of India, and therefore, India has every right to be a Hindu state. The arguments of the Hindu nationalists are reinforced by the fact that Pakistan is an Islamic state and that even Bangladesh, with a Hindu minority of 18 percent (which is proportionately larger than the Muslim minority of 12 percent in India), declared itself an Islamic state in 1988 under the military dictator General H. M. Ershad. And although Sri Lanka remains formally a secular democratic state, in practice it has been functioning as a Buddhist state. The state-owned radio and televisions routinely carry Buddhist prayers and programs, and Buddhist prayers are commonplace at official functions in which political leaders and public figures participate. Even in Britain and other states of Western Europe, prayers and religious ceremonies often precede official functions. Then why not in India?

Hindu nationalists now proudly endorse the long-standing Pakistani claim that India is a Hindu state, much to the satisfaction of Pakistani critics of India. Both Pakistani critics of India and Hindu nationalists now condemn India's "pseudosecularism." The following observations by Babu Suseelan, a pro-Hindu nationalist writer, reflect the attitudes of this rising group of

Indians: "The extraordinary preoccupation with tolerance and secularism encourages political leaders to peddle self-deception, self-delusions, and denial as realistic. . . . Minority Muslims and Christians are socialized to believe that they should occupy positions of power in India. The delusion of the majority Hindus is that they exist to serve the minorities."[23] Thus, Hindus have become the victims of the misguided policies of Hindu secularists whose concept of the Indian state was enunciated by first Indian prime minister, Jawaharlal Nehru. Indeed, Nehru's political stature and contribution to the Indian nation are being subjected to revisionism by present-day Hindu nationalists. And Sardar Vallabhai Patel, the powerful Hindu nationalist who challenged Nehru for the prime minister's post after independence, is now being elevated and glorified as the true representative of Indian national aspirations.

Such Hindu grievances have arisen in the face of nationalism and separatist movements among the Sikhs of Punjab, the Muslims of Kashmir, and the Christian tribals of Nagaland, Mizoram, and Meghalaya. The low-caste Adivasis of north-central India, who are now seeking a separate Jharkand state within India from the territories of Bihar, Uttar Pradesh, and Madhya Pradesh, are also perceived to have been influenced by Western Christian missionaries. However, there is not much basis for Hindu nationalist claims that religious minorities have gained at the expense of the Hindu majority. The converted tribal and lower-caste Christians of northeast and north-central India, who number less than 5 million, remain relatively backward compared to the rest of the Indian population. Although Christians in southwestern and southern India are found in much greater numbers than they are in the northeast tribal Christian states, they do not constitute a majority anywhere, not even in states such as Kerala and Goa where they form approximately 25 percent and 40 percent of the population, respectively. However, Christian organizations and missions own and run many schools and universities that cater to people of all religious communities. This makes Christians appear more prominent than their actual numbers. They also have much higher literacy rates than Hindus or Muslims and hence have entered various levels of white-collar employment where they are highly visible. However, they are by no means as wealthy as Hindu industrialists and businessmen. They form only 3 percent of the total population of India and numbered about 27 million in 1995; therefore they are not seen as a serious threat to the more than 750 million Hindus in India.

In general, Muslims have remained more economically and socially backward than Hindus, although like Hindu elites, certain Muslim elites have prospered. Muslim representation in central parliament and the state assemblies is proportionately less than the overall proportion of Muslims in the population. To a certain extent, this is to be expected. After the creation of Pakistan in 1947, all the Muslims from the part of Punjab allotted to India (some 5 million of them) fled to the Pakistani side of Punjab, just as a similar number of Sikhs and Hindus from the part of Punjab assigned to Pakistan fled to the Indian side of Punjab. Another 3 to 4 million Muslims from other parts of India, mainly elite bureaucrats and businessmen, moved to Sindh and East Bengal in Pakistan. The Muslims left behind in India were largely leaderless, except for a few Indian nationalist figures. They were also less economically advanced than Hindus, even before partition, which was a consequence of their failure to accept British education and other opportunities during the Raj, unlike the Hindus.

The creation of Pakistan made their condition worse. Especially during the first two decades after partition, most Indian Muslims, in their hearts and minds—whatever their public posture—were with Pakistan, the state that they, primarily, had pushed for and created. The creation of Pakistan meant that they had to cope with a more hostile and suspicious Hindu population in India that now constituted an even greater percentage of the total population than it had before partition. This identity crisis among Indian Muslims began to change after the breakup of Pakistan in 1971. The civil war between East and West Pakistan that resulted in the creation of Bangladesh, the expulsion of Bihari Muslims from the new state, and a violent struggle between Sindhi Muslims and Mohajirs brought about the realization among Indian Muslims that their destiny lay within India. Pakistan was not the promised land they had envisioned, and Pakistan could not and would not rescue them when they were in danger or distress. Since the 1970s, the relatively backward status of Indian Muslims has provoked their leaders to voice their grievances more openly and loudly and to demand political rights and a fairer share of development. This new Muslim assertiveness has produced a Hindu backlash, which has been made all the more acute because of the Muslim uprising in Kashmir.

The Sikhs of Punjab are clearly one of the most prosperous groups in India, but prosperity also has been achieved by Hindus in Punjab and Haryana. For that matter, the Muslims of Pakistani Punjab have achieved similar economic success. This suggests that the prosperity of all three groups may have something to do with the initiative and drive of Punjabi culture and character, irrespective of religion. As in the case of Kashmiri Muslims, who were perceived by Hindu nationalists to be the beneficiaries of heavy government subsidies but "ungrateful" toward the "tolerant" Hindu secularists, Sikhs are also now perceived to be ungrateful beneficiaries of Hindu largess. Again, such Hindu nationalist grievances are not entirely without basis. Beyond the initiative and hard work of the Sikhs, the economic prosperity of Punjab has had much to do with heavy central government investments in irrigation and agriculture in that state during the early Five Year Plans. The government of India decided to make

Punjab the showcase of the Green Revolution in India. Christians, Jains, and Parsees have also prospered, and Parsees and Jains are among the richest communities in India. (Jains number about 5 million and Parsees approximately 100,000.) Thus, despite Pakistan's constant derision of India's secularism, the Hindu secularists, beginning with the main protagonist of secularism, Jawaharlal Nehru, have made genuine efforts to assure all minorities that India welcomes all religions.

Whatever the objective facts concerning the status of religious minorities in India, a growing number of Hindus are becoming convinced that the minorities have prospered at their expense and that converting India from a secular state to a Hindu state will resolve this disparity and injustice. Just as the secularists believe that only their ideology will keep India united, the Hindu nationalists believe that it is the Hindu weltanschauung that will keep India united; that unless the Hindus assert their rights, the country will not last.

By mid-1993, to counter the rising tide of religious nationalism on all sides, the Rao government put forward two bills to reinforce the secular basis of national politics.[24] Those bills sought to amend the constitution and the electoral law. The proposed 80th Constitutional Amendment would have banned political parties and individual candidates that misused religion to gain votes. In particular, the 80th Amendment would have declared illegal the use of religious symbols in electoral campaigns or any other tactics that might promote hatred among people of different religions, languages, castes, or races. The second bill would have changed the People's Representation Act so that no association or body could be registered by the Election Commission as a political party if it bore a religious name or could in some way constitute an appeal to voters on the basis of religion and thus violate the secular principles of the Indian democracy.

These two bills were aimed particularly at two political parties, the BJP and the Muslim League. The BJP had acquired a national following—it had spread to areas in the south where it (and its predecessor, the Jana Sangh) previously had carried little appeal and had little support. After the creation of Pakistan in 1947, the Muslim League was disbanded all over India, except for a remnant section that was confined almost exclusively to Kerala. However, the appeal of this party was gaining strength, and new roots were being established outside Kerala. As was to be expected, the leaders of the BJP and the Muslim League, L. K. Advani and Ibrahim Suleiman Sait, both protested the new bills, arguing that they violated the basic principles of the constitution. Advani argued that low-ranked election commission officers would have discretionary powers to reject candidates seeking election. Sait claimed that the bills amounted to silencing the Muslim community and preventing it from gaining seats in the central and regional parliaments.

The proposed 80th Constitutional Amendment and changes in the People's Representation Act brought Hindu and Muslim parties together. A leading BJP member of parliament, Jaswant Singh, claimed in August 1993 that the party had entered into consultations with the Muslim League and another Muslim party, the Majlis Ittehad-ul-Muslimeen, to stop the bill because "they are as worried as us."[25] The BJP indicated that it was not against the new bills in principle, but was concerned with the Congress government's efforts to put down other political parties. The BJP, which had only two elected members in the Lok Sabha (the authoritative lower house of parliament) in 1984, had increased its membership to 119 in the 1991 elections.

Strangely, even some of the secular parties, such as the Communist Party of India, the Communist Party–Marxists, and the Janata Dal, objected to the bills. Somnath Chaterjee and Indrajit Gupta of the Communist parties welcomed the spirit of the bills, but had reservations about their proposed terms and implementation. George Fernandes of the Janata Dal claimed that the bills were yet another in a series of repressive acts passed by Congress governments to minimize democracy. These included the Maintenance of Internal Security Act in 1971 and the various national security ordinances and antiterrorist laws passed in the 1980s. At the end of 1993, neither bill had been put to a vote in the Indian parliament, and the proposed 80th Constitutional Amendment and the People's Representation Act remained in limbo and seemed unlikely to be revived in the near future.

THE USE OF FORCE AND HUMAN RIGHTS VIOLATIONS

When faced with armed separatist movements, the Indian authorities resort to an excessive and counterproductive use of force that leads to further violence by the secessionists and thereby increases the prospect of the disintegration of the state. In particular, the use of relatively undisciplined paramilitary forces has increased the level of violence between the state and the secessionists in Punjab and Kashmir. As noted in earlier chapters, the increasing use of armed force by the state has led to a corresponding erosion of democratic processes in India. As violence escalated in the 1980s, the constitution was amended and special legislation was introduced that gave the central government greater power to use force to suppress insurgency and terrorism by secessionists. The frequent use of military and paramilitary forces to suppress secessionists tends to politicize those forces and thereby increases the threat of a military takeover.

As India, Pakistan, and Sri Lanka have become more frustrated in their search for political solutions to problems of ethnic nationalism, the application of force has often been excessive. The use of force has sometimes served as a substitute for political negotiations and settlements. It frequently produces short-term solutions to problems without ensuring long-term peace and stability. After failing to crush Bengali separatism in East Pakistan in 1971, the Pakistan Army crushed Balochi separatism in 1974. In India, prolonged wars have been waged against Naga, Mizo, and Gharo tribes. The Sinhalese-dominated government of Sri Lanka initially sought to crush Tamil separatism; however, negotiations with the separatists produced tentative peace and a modicum of political stability in some Tamil regions. In mid-1995, the war between the Tamil Tigers and Sri Lankan government forces had erupted again. A similar situation exists in Assam, where the United Liberation Front of Assam (ULFA) was forced to sue for peace because of large-scale military actions. If the grievances of the Tamils and the Assamese are not alleviated, the potential for more violence in the future will remain. All such ethnic grievances and the desire for independence continue to lurk below the surface. In general, excessive force has proved to be counterproductive from the standpoint of the government. This is evident in the case of Kashmir.

Increasing problems of internal security arising from armed separatist movements have also increased the role of the military and paramilitary forces in domestic politics. In the case of Pakistan, which has been under military dictatorships much of the time since independence, this has been simply enhanced and consolidated the power of the military. In India, various forms of legislation have often been required to sanction the prolonged use of military force in response to domestic violence. As discussed in earlier chapters, this has led to an erosion of the democratic process in India. Occasional fears have also been expressed that the regular and frequent use of force to suppress secessionists may lead to a military takeover in India. Paramilitary forces, now taking the place of regular armed forces in India in dealing with internal security, are being increasingly politicized. Indeed, the paramilitary forces have become part of the problem because they are being perceived by many ethnic groups as the enemy of the people rather than their protector. Similar conditions exist in Pakistan and Sri Lanka.

The most disturbing aspect of the use of force for internal security in India has been the frequent allegations of human rights violations by international human rights organizations. Although India's external wars, conducted by its regular armed forces, have been played by the "rules of the book," internal security forces operate under ambiguous rules, or perhaps even no rules. The 1948 International Convention on Human Rights is the existing document closest to a list of suggested rules for regulating the use of force and determining acceptable standards for maintaining internal security. India and Sri Lanka have periodically been condemned by Amnesty International and Asia Watch for violations of human rights in their efforts to suppress Kashmiri, Sikh, and Tamil separatism. These organizations have also condemned similar violations by the separatists.

The pattern of human rights violations on all sides is becoming almost standard. In response to insurgency and terrorism by secessionists, state officials have often resorted to torture and indiscriminate killing of suspected insurgents and terrorists. And in order to further their chances of achieving independence, Kashmiri and Sikh secessionists hoping to alienate nearly all of their ethnic group from the state have through terrorist and insurgency tactics deliberately provoked human rights violations by the state. Human rights violations by the state's security forces then invite external political pressures from foreign governments and international human rights organizations. There have been various moves in the U.S. Congress to impose economic sanctions on India for human rights violations in Punjab and Kashmir. For example, one amendment, introduced by Representative Dan Burton in mid-1993, called for the suspension of $41 million in U.S. development aid to India unless India revoked its antiterrorist laws.[26] The amendment was narrowly defeated by a 203-201 vote, with 5 representatives abstaining. The Indian government, like the governments of other states with similar problems, such as Indonesia and China, considers international intrusions of this sort to be a violation of its sovereignty.

Developing countries faced with violent secessionist movements may consider some human rights violations to be unavoidable. All they may do is to minimize these violations while searching for a solution to the problem. Unlike the external enemy, the "internal enemy" is unknown, and the war against it is uneven. To expect government forces to play by the rules of international human rights organizations while the insurgents and terrorists do not may be considered not only to be unfair but also to amount to a losing battle. Thus, in Indian Kashmir and Punjab, thousands of suspects are rounded up and detained because the government has sweeping legislative powers. Sikhs have complained that Indian security forces have staged "faked armed encounters" with suspected Sikh terrorists in order to kill them without trial or proof of their involvement in terrorist activity. Some Indian legislation, such as the 42nd Amendment passed by Indira Gandhi during the 1975-77 Emergency, have constituted violations of the fundamental rights of citizens in a democracy. International human rights organizations have alleged that torture of detained suspects has taken place in India and Sri Lanka in their wars against Kashmiri, Sikh, and Tamil secessionists. Similar allegations were made against the Pakistani government when it was fighting Bengali and Balochi secessionists and are now being made because of its fight against Sindhi nationalists.

It is also important to note that there are deliberate attempts by secessionists to provoke widespread human rights violations by the state with the aim of gaining international attention and, hopefully, foreign political or military intervention. Western support is usually forthcoming if widespread human rights violations by government forces are perceived to have occurred. The experience of the Iraqi government of Saddam Hussein in dealing with Kurdish secessionists in the north and Shiite rebels in the south may be the objective of secessionists in South Asia, such as the Kashmiris and the Sikhs in India. Following the Gulf War, the Western powers had virtually partitioned Iraq, creating de facto Kurdish and Shiite states, and were about to create two independent states. It was only Turkish concerns about carving a Kurdish state out of Iraq because of its own Kurdish independence movement that may have prevented the United States from taking Iraq apart. The Western powers justified their actions in the Gulf on the grounds that Iraqi forces had committed human rights violations against the Kurds and the Shiites. For the time being, Iraq appears to have lost its sovereignty over these territories. Similar considerations prompted the West to swiftly recognize Slovenia, Croatia, and Bosnia as independent states from Yugoslavia. Such an erosion of sovereignty may occur in Kashmir and Punjab in India, the Tamil provinces of Sri Lanka, and Sindh in Pakistan if the problem of human rights violations by governments gets out of hand.

What Western governments sometimes consider intolerable human rights abuses are often deemed unavoidable by the governments of less-developed countries. The governments of these countries often see their internal security problems as part of a continuing process of state formation and consolidation. Secessionist-induced violence that results in human rights violations by all sides is the uncontrollable consequence of such state formation. Thus, whereas the Western industrialized states that are now secure and stable perceive human rights as absolute and universal, developing countries see them as relative and regional. After all, the Western states are not faced with widespread terrorism and insurgency. This divergence of perspectives was clearly displayed at the global conference on human rights held in Vienna in June 1993. In South Asia, maintaining the territorial integrity of the state is considered more important than preventing human rights violations, on the grounds that the potential disintegration of the state could lead to even greater human tragedies, as occurred in the partition of India in 1947, the breakup of Pakistan in 1971, and the disintegration of Yugoslavia in 1991.

4

The Constitutional

Dimension

THE CONSTITUTION AND STATE SECURITY

India's democratic constitution places the well-being of society and the security of the state above the fundamental rights of the individual. At least, this has been the interpretation of the constitution by the Indian Supreme Court since 1976. In India, fundamental rights are not always guaranteed when they conflict with the interests of society and the preservation of the state. Democracy and fundamental rights may be suspended if warranted by national security. The determination of whether the suspension of democracy is warranted or not is to be made by parliament. This essentially means that if the party holding the reins of government carries a two-thirds majority in parliament it may assume authoritarian powers through constitutional means.

This may suggest that the Indian constitution endorses the security first principle over democracy first arguments. However, the security versus democracy dichotomy has been a changing perspective in India, even in the judgments of the Indian Supreme Court. In various cases brought before it in the 1950s, the Indian Supreme Court favored the interests of the state over the individual; it then reversed itself in the 1960s and early 1970s by favoring the inviolability of individual fundamental rights. Following the declaration of the National Emergency in June 1975 and the passage of the 42nd Amendment in 1976, the

Supreme Court reversed its earlier judgments and favored the legislative powers of the state (provided proper procedures were followed) over the rights of the individual. Whatever the prevailing viewpoint of the time, a minority of Supreme Court judges always took up the opposing viewpoint.

Although the judicial view that supports the power of the state to override the fundamental rights of the citizen has prevailed since 1975, the Indian judiciary may reverse itself sometime in the future; however, the situation remains ambiguous and wavering. The unresolved question appears to be how far the state can go in compromising fundamental rights in order to protect its own survival. Underlying this question is the constant suspicion of whether governmental actions to restrict individual freedoms are really motivated by the need to protect the integrity of the state or are merely an excuse to protect and preserve the government in power. A fine line separates the motives of Indian governments that seek to suspend or restrict fundamental rights through legislative acts and executive orders from self-serving efforts to keep the ruling party in power. The political motives behind the suspension of fundamental rights during the Emergency declared between June 1975 and March 1977 by Prime Minister Indira Gandhi did not deceive many Indian and foreign observers. Even when the Indian Supreme Court has ruled that parliament's legislative powers are supreme (including the power to take away individual fundamental rights), the philosophy underlying this view appears to be that the intended purpose of emphasizing security over democracy is to secure democracy and individual rights in the long run. If the state fell into chaos and disintegrated then there would be no democracy and individual rights to protect.

Thus, the prevailing philosophy of Indian democracy is different from that of most Western democracies. It may reflect the fact that the needs of a less-developed country with enormous ethnic diversities are substantially different from those of the advanced, industrialized, and often more homogenous states of the Western democracies.

NATIONAL SECURITY EMERGENCY

One of the more controversial aspects of the Indian constitution pertains to the "emergency" powers granted to the central government to deal with problems of both external and internal security. Such powers are far more extensive than those found in Western democracies.

The constitution of India identifies three types of emergencies.[1] The first is "National Security Emergency" (Article 352), under which the president, acting on the advice of the prime minister, may proclaim a state of emergency if the "security of India, or any part of its territory is threatened by war, external aggression or armed rebellion." When Article 352 is invoked, Articles 353 and 354 then go into operation. They allow the central government to suspend the federal provisions of the constitution and thus give it direct control over the states and over all revenue. In effect, the central government may impose a unitary system of government. The second is "Constitutional Emergency in the States" (Article 356), under which the president, acting on the advice of the governor of a state and the prime minister, may proclaim a state of emergency in that state if he is satisfied that the normal process of government cannot be carried out in accordance with the constitution. The third type of emergency identified by the constitution is "Financial Emergency" (Article 360), which may be declared by the president, acting on the advice of the prime minister, if the financial or monetary stability or the credit of the country is threatened.

All of the above proclamations must be approved by parliament. Article 352, on external threats to national security, was invoked by the Congress government of Indira Gandhi during the year-long Bangladesh separatist movement in 1971, which culminated in the war with Pakistan in December of that year.[2] The same article was invoked, in the name of threats to internal security, by the Indira Gandhi government when it declared a state of National Emergency throughout the country between June 1975 and March 1977. Article 356, "Emergency in the States," has been invoked on different occasions in various Indian states, including Kerala, Assam, Punjab, and Kashmir. Article 360, "Financial Emergency," has never been used, although drastic economic measures, such as the banning of all industrial strikes, were adopted during the National Emergency between 1975 and 1977.

The government of India under various prime ministers, from Jawaharlal Nehru to P. V. Narasimha Rao, has resorted to Article 356, "Emergency in the States." This article has frequently been invoked when the ruling government of a state has been no longer able to muster the required parliamentary majority in the state legislature. This has led to "President's Rule," in which the state government is taken over directly by the central government until new elections can be held and a new state government put in place. More controversial, however, has been the resort to Article 356 in some Indian states where the central government is unable to cope with the crisis, irrespective of whether a parliamentary majority is retained by the state-based political party. This has been problematic in states such as Nagaland, Punjab, and Kashmir where separatist movements that resort to armed insurgencies or acts of terrorism have occurred. Similarly, widespread religious, linguistic, or ethnic rioting in a state has also led to the suspension of the state government, as has occurred in Assam. However, the suspension of the democratic process under conditions of internal security and instability has been ad hoc, regional, and temporary. After the crisis is over, the democratic process is restored.

The provisions of Articles 352 and 356 are supplemented by the provisions of two other articles—Articles 358 and 359—that enable the president, acting on the advice of the prime minister, to suspend the fundamental rights and protection clauses as guaranteed under Articles 13 to 32 of the Indian constitution. Such suspensions must be approved by parliament within six months. The suspension of the rights and protection clauses, especially Article 19, which embodies the "seven freedoms," is accompanied by the right of the central government to resort to preventive detention, that is, to arrest and detain persons to prevent them from indulging in acts, as yet uncommitted, that may be detrimental to national security and to the maintenance of law and order. Under the subtitle *Right to Freedom,* Article 19 of the Indian constitution states:

> Protection of certain rights regarding freedom of speech, etc. (1) All citizens shall have the right (a) to freedom of speech and expression; (b) to assemble peaceably and without arms; (c) to form associations or unions; (d) to move freely throughout the territory of India; (e) to reside and settle in any part of the territory of India; (f) to acquire, hold and dispose of territory; (g) to practice any profession, or to carry on any occupation, trade or business.[3]

Moreover, once the emergency is declared and approved by parliament, the constitution empowers the government to prevent citizens from appealing to the courts for the protection of their fundamental rights. Not even Article 32, which incorporates the "right to constitutional remedies" and the "writ of habeas corpus," can overcome central government powers made possible under Articles 352-360 that relate to national emergency.

In sum, when the security and stability of the country are threatened, one set of articles permits the central government in India to qualify and suspend the democratic freedoms provided under another set of articles that supposedly guarantees those freedoms. In effect, India's democratic constitution provides easy recourse for its own overthrow through constitutional means on the grounds of national security. No doubt, the suspension of the democratic constitution is only supposed to be temporary. But there is no guarantee that a prime minister who resorts to drastic constitutional methods will restore democracy. The liberal constitutional provisions in India are a would-be tyrant's dream. So far no prime minister has grossly misused the privilege although Mrs. Gandhi came close to doing so between 1975 and 1977. In the end, even she restored democracy after 22 months of Emergency rule that was declared in the interests of national security.

The imperial-type powers lodged in the Indian constitution are a legacy of British rule, which, ironically, also provided India with the basic structure of a democratic system. The Indian president's ability to proclaim a state of emergency when the country's security is threatened was a power held by the British viceroy under the Government of India Act of 1935.[4] The British had exercised these emergency powers between 1940 and 1945, when they were at war with Germany and Japan and simultaneously had to deal with the Indian struggle for independence and with Hindu-Muslim violence.[5] Such viceregal powers were reinforced by the British through the Defence of India Act of 1939, under the terms of which the British Indian government could resort to preventive detention of those not charged with committing criminal acts who threatened internal law and order for political reasons. The nature of these problems has not changed fundamentally since India obtained independence in 1947, nor have the far-reaching powers that were assumed by the newly independent Indian government.

THE DEBATE IN THE CONSTITUENT ASSEMBLY

The issue of whether to incorporate these emergency powers into the constitution produced serious differences of opinion among members of the post-independence Constituent Assembly of India, which was assigned the task of drafting a constitution for the country. Several members claimed that these provisions negated the central principles of freedom and democracy that were supposed to be the basis of the proposed Indian constitution. K. T. Shah, a member of the drafting body, claimed that the proposed provisions appeared to "arm the Centre [central government] with special power against the units [states], and to arm the government against the people."[6] Another member of the constitutional drafting body, H. V. Kamath, stated: "I fear that by this single chapter we are seeking to lay the foundation of a totalitarian State, a police State, a State completely opposed to all the ideals and principles that have held aloft during the last few decades, a State where the rights and liberties of millions of innocent men and women will be in continuous jeopardy."[7] A similar reservation was expressed by member Thakurdas Bhargava, who claimed that the proposed safeguards proposed in the chapter on fundamental rights did not do enough to protect the individual from the tyrannies of the police and the magistracy after arrest and detention.[8]

There were others who felt emergency powers were just that—to be used in an emergency, which would only occur occasionally or rarely, if at all. Indeed, one of the drafters of the constitution, Dr. B. R. Ambedkar, felt that emergency powers and President's Rule "will never be called into operation and that they would remain a dead letter."[9] However, that has not been the case. A national security emergency was declared between 1975 and 1977, and declarations of President's Rule in the Indian states has proved to be a routine method of maintaining law and order and the authority of the central government. Between 1950 and 1990, there were over 80 declarations of President's Rule in the Indian states and Union Territories of the central government. However, despite all the turmoil that occurred just before and after independence, most of the Indian constitution makers did not think that matters could get much worse. In fact, they believed that matters could only get better with the colonial yoke overthrown. As B. S. Raghavan, an Indian political analyst, put it: "Even if they had made more allowances than they did for human frailties, they could not have reckoned with the weight of the growing complexities inherent in the democratic government of a land of mind-boggling diversities entering an era when science and technology would scale unimagined heights, and population and related pressures and problems would multiply manifold."[10]

During the deliberations on drawing up the Indian constitution, the ability to suspend the right to appeal to the courts under Article 32 did come under attack from some opponents of the emergency provisions because it eliminated a citizen's ability to gain appropriate relief or remedy for what he might consider wrongful acts committed by the government. Others who argued against these provisions pointed out that no other similar constitution vested such extraordinary powers in the government. The Indian constitution, after all, was modeled on the constitutions of several Western democracies.[11] The basic political structure and process was modeled after the British parliamentary system of government; the fundamental rights were essentially derived from the American Bill of Rights; the federal system and the role of the central government with respect to the states were based on the Canadian system, but were more centralized in India; the idea of the preamble that incorporated the "Directive Principles of Social Policy" was obtained from the Irish constitution; and the concept of a finance commission that governed the grants-in-aid to be provided by the central government to the states was developed from the Australian constitution. However, none of these countries carried such far-reaching emergency provisions for national security purposes.

However, there were several other members of the Constituent Assembly who felt that the rights of society and the state should override that of the individual. B. N. Rau, a constitutional adviser to the assembly who helped draft the constitution, fluctuated between the two positions. After visiting the United States, Britain, Canada, and Ireland and consulting with justices, constitutionalists, and statesmen in these countries about the framing of the Indian constitution, he proposed a clause of liberty in October 1947 which would read: "No person shall be deprived of his life or personal liberty without due process of law, nor shall any person be denied equality before the law within the territories of the Federation."[12] But subsequently he proposed that "When a law made by the state in the discharge of one of the fundamental duties imposed upon it by the Constitution happens to conflict with one of the fundamental rights guaranteed to the individual, the former should prevail over the latter: in other words, the general welfare should prevail over the individual rights." Rau's proposed elimination of the "due process" clause and its substitution with "according to procedure established by law" was accepted by the assembly.[13]

The reasons for incorporating such extensive emergency powers, to be held by the central government, may be found in the political circumstances that prevailed between 1947 and 1950, when the proposed Indian constitution was being debated and drafted. The struggle for independence had also involved a concurrent struggle for an independent Pakistan for Indian Muslims, and this had led to widespread Hindu-Muslim rioting and killing. The eventual creation of the new state of Pakistan in 1947 produced a bloodbath among Muslims, Sikhs, and Hindus, and the struggle was especially fierce when the province of Punjab was divided along with the partition of the subcontinent. The new states of India and Pakistan immediately went to war over Kashmir in October 1947, and that war lasted until January 1949. Serious problems also arose because of attempts to incorporate the nearly 600 Indian princely states into the new Indian Union; these problems were especially severe in the Muslim-ruled states of Junagadh and Hyderabad. And on January 30, 1949, Mahatma Gandhi, the father of the nation, was assassinated by a Hindu extremist.

Because of such circumstances, the drafters of the Indian constitution felt that the central government needed extraordinary reserve powers if the fledgling Indian democracy was to survive in times of crisis. Moreover, because the circumstances of the polity and society of India were far more complex than those of the Western democracies, the Indian constitution makers felt that qualifications and restrictions ought to be placed on the Indian democracy even to the extent that temporary authoritarian measures might have to be applied.

NEW ACTS AND CONSTITUTIONAL AMENDMENTS

The resort to articles provided under the original constitution appears to have been less controversial than the passage of special acts and amendments to increase the powers of the government to deal with problems of internal and external security. Two early acts that dealt with problems of security were passed during times of war with external powers. The first was the Defence of India Rules (DIR), which was adopted in November 1962 following the breakout of war with China in October 1962 and was followed by the passage of the Defense of India Act in December 1962. Under the DIR, the right to move the Supreme Court for the enforcement of fundamental rights guaranteed under Articles 14, 21, and 22 was suspended by the president. The second was the passage of the Maintenance of Internal Security Act (MISA) during the height of the East Pakistani crisis that led eventually to war with Pakistan in December 1971.

More serious controversies in the security versus democracy struggle, as it were, occurred later, after the last major war with an external power was fought. They involved the passage of two constitutional amendments both relating to internal security: the 42nd Amendment, passed in 1976, during the Emergency under the government of Indira Gandhi, and the 59th Amendment, passed in 1988, under the government of Rajiv Gandhi.

The first of the legal resorts to deal with national security issues, namely, the Defense of India Rules of 1962, permitted the detention of any person "whom the authority suspects on grounds appearing to that authority to be reasonable, of being of hostile origin, of having acted, acting, being about to act or being likely to act in a manner prejudicial to the defence of India and civil defence, the security of the state, the public safety or interest, the maintenance of peaceful conditions in any part of India or the efficient conduct of military operations."[14]

The DIR remained in force until 1968, six years after the 1962 Sino-Indian war and three years after the 1965 Indo-Pakistani war had ended.[15] During the wars with China and Pakistan, Communists and Muslims whom the authorities felt may have been seeking to aid the enemy—there was no evidence that they had done so—were imprisoned without explanation or trial. After the termination of hostilities, the alleged suspects were released. However, since the DIR remained in force until 1968, these powers were occasionally used to justify the preventive detention of persons who were considered likely to commit crimes often unrelated to issues of national security. During the 1971 Bangladesh crisis and the Indo-Pakistani war, the DIR was reimposed; and after he Bangladesh crisis was over, it was again used to detain persons for acts unrelated to external threats. Thus, for instance, the DIR was invoked to arrest railway workers during the nationwide railway strike organized by the All-India Railwaymen's Federation in 1974. The large-scale detentions made during the 1975-77 National Emergency were also justified under the DIR.

The 1971 war with Pakistan over the Bangladesh issue not only brought back the DIR but also saw the introduction of new legislation known as the Maintenance of Internal Security Act (MISA). The provisions of this act were used to justify the detention of several opposition leaders in order to curb the violence in ethnic-strife-torn areas, especially in the border regions.[16] During the 1975-1977 Emergency, the powers of the central government were further strengthened by the passage in 1976 of the 42nd Amendment to Article 352. This was the infamous legislation that introduced the mechanics of an authoritarian state in India. The 42nd Amendment suspended the writ of habeas corpus and made the reasons for preventive detention state secrets.[17] Therefore, during the 1975-77 Emergency, a citizen could not appeal to the courts because he did not know the reason for his arrest and the government did not have to disclose it.

The provisions of the 42nd Amendment would appear to contradict two articles in Part III of the Indian constitution, which is entitled "Fundamental Rights":

21. *Protection of life and personal liberty.* No person shall be deprived of his life or personal liberty except according to procedure established by law.

22. (1) *Protection against arrest and detention in certain cases.* No person who is arrested shall be detained in custody without being informed, as soon as he may be, of the grounds for such arrest nor shall he be denied the right to consult, and to be defended by, a legal practitioner of his choice. (2) Every person who is arrested and detained in custody shall be produced before the nearest magistrate within a period of twenty-four hours of such arrest excluding the time necessary for the journey from the place of arrest to the court of the magistrate and no such person shall be detained in custody beyond the said period without the authority of a magistrate. (3) Nothing in clauses (1) and (2) shall apply (a) to any person who for the time being is an enemy alien; or (b) to any person who is arrested or detained under any law providing for preventive detention.[18]

The 42nd Amendment amounted to a miniconstitution in itself, and it even appeared to modify the preamble. "A new chapter on fundamental duties was incorporated and the supremacy of Parliament to amend the constitution was established."[19] It remained in force throughout the Emergency and was used extensively until the Emergency was lifted in February 1977. However, the 42nd Amendment, despite the draconian authoritarian rules that it embodied, did not appear to violate the Indian constitution. The subclauses under Article 22 provided several escapes for the government to bypass the above restrictions. Thus, according to Article 22 subsection (4):

> No law providing for preventive detention shall authorise the detention of a person for a longer period than three months unless (a) an Advisory Board consisting of persons who are, or have been, or are qualified to be appointed as, Judges of a High Court has reported before the expiration of the said period of three months that there is in its opinion sufficient cause for such detention: provided that nothing in this sub-clause shall authorise the detention of any person beyond the maximum period prescribed by any law made by Parliament under sub-clause (b) of clause (7); or (b) such person is detained in accordance with the provisions of any law made by Parliament under sub-clauses (a) and (b) of clause (7).[20]

The various provisions of Article 22 subsection (7) mentioned above read as follows:

> Parliament may by law prescribe (a) the circumstances under which, and the class or classes of cases in which, a person may be detained for a period longer than three months under any law providing for preventive detention without obtaining the opinion of an Advisory Board in accordance with the provisions of sub-clause (a) of clause (4); (b) the maximum period for which any person may in any class or classes of cases be detained under any law providing for preventive detention; and (c) the procedure to be followed by an Advisory Board in any inquiry under sub-clause (a) of clause (4).[21]

After the victory of the Janata Party in the March 1977 general elections, the DIR, MISA, and the 42nd Amendment were repealed through the passage of the 44th Amendment in 1978. The 44th Amendment declared that Article 21 could not be suspended even while an Emergency was in effect. In particular, the 44th Amendment rejected the 42nd Amendment's term "internal disturbance" in Article 352 and instead reintroduced the term "armed rebellion" as the justification for the declaration of an emergency.[22] Subsequently, however, some state governments enacted legislation that provided them with powers that were similar to the DIR and MISA. In mid-1979, the prime minister in the Janata government, Morarji Desai, declared that such measures were necessary to deal with internal problems of law and order. In effect, the motley group of opposition parties, which included the right-wing Jana Sangh and the left-wing Socialist Party, that had merged into the Janata Party in protest against the Indira Gandhi–led Congress government's undemocratic practices in the name of security found itself doing almost the same thing. The Janata government's recourse to such measures was not surprising for it should be remembered that the Indian constitution under Article 352 continued to provide any government in office with extensive emergency powers despite the repeal of the DIR, MISA, and the 42nd Amendment.[23]

The return of Indira Gandhi to power in January 1980 did, in fact, bring back a reworked combination of the DIR and MISA. This was initially incorporated in the National Security Ordinance promulgated by the president in September 1980 and the embodied in the National Security Act (NSA) passed in December 1980. NSA gave the central government the right to detain any person in order to prevent him from acting in any manner prejudicial to the defense of India or to the internal security of the nation.[24] NSA also enabled the central and state governments to detain anyone in the interest of maintaining public order and the flow of supplies and services to the community. This implied that industrial strikes and *bandhs* (efforts by political agitators to close all commercial and public activity in a city) that paralyzed the economic life of the country could be dealt with by widespread arrests and detentions.

Unlike the DIR, MISA, and the 42nd Amendment, the NSA contained safeguards against misuse, as well as provisions that attempted to ensure justice for the individual. Although members of the opposition in the Lok Sabha vigorously condemned the NSA, the new act provided individuals detained under its powers recourse to the courts if they believed their arrest was not justified. The new system also did not bar individuals from approaching the courts in cases involving the violation of fundamental rights.

Some of the safeguards did not last long. As a result of widespread terrorism by Sikh extremists from 1982 to 1984, the NSA was amended to deal with new and unprecedented conditions. In late June 1984, President Zail Singh, on the advice of Prime Minister Indira Gandhi, promulgated the National Security (Second Amendment) Ordinance.[25] According to this ordinance, a detention order was not to be "deemed to be invalid or inoperative merely because one or some of the grounds is or are: (i) vague, (ii) non-existent, (iii) not relevant, (iv) not connected or not proximately connected with such persons, or (v) invalid for any other reason whatsoever."[26] The ordinance also provided that the expiration or revocation of a detention order would not bar another detention order against the same person. However, the subsequent detention order would not extend beyond 12 months, as was stipulated in the original NSA, with the exception that it could be extended to 24 months in the "disturbed areas" of Punjab and the city of Chandigarh.

Legislation that eroded the democratic process continued under the Congress government of Rajiv Gandhi. In 1984, the Terrorist Affected Areas Special Courts Act was passed; it was followed in 1987 by the Terrorist and Disruptive Activities Preventive Act (TADA). Under TADA, suspected terrorists could be detained for up to one year without trial; and Court hearings and the testimony of witnesses could be conducted in secret.[27] The power to detain suspected terrorists without trial was subsequently further strengthened for the two regions where separatist violence was strongest, Punjab and Kashmir. This legislation was provided through the Armed Forces (Punjab and Chandigargh) Special Powers Act, the Jammu and Kashmir Public Safety Act, and the Armed Forces (Jammu and Kashmir) Special Powers Act. Again, this should not be surprising since terrorist activity by Sikh extremists and retaliation by government forces against suspected terrorists in the Punjab continued to escalate. The revolt and insurgency in Muslim-majority Kashmir from 1989 onward heightened the problems of internal security. The Muslim revolt in Kashmir was accompanied by an increase in the frequency and magnitude of Hindu-Muslim violence in northern India, especially in the states of Gujerat, Uttar Pradesh, Bihar, and Maharashtra.

The continuing deterioration of law and order in the 1980s led to the passing of the 59th Amendment in March 1988. This amendment nullified parts of the 44th Amendment by permitting the suspension of Article 21 in Punjab during an Emergency, and sought to further amend Article 352—the National Emergency Article—of the Indian constitution. As noted earlier, the 42nd Amendment had substituted the words "internal disturbance" for the words "armed rebellion," and then the 44th Amendment restored the original words so that the justification for an internal emergency would only take place in the case of an "armed rebellion." However, the more restrictive term "armed rebellion" did not seem to apply to the intensifying Sikh terrorist campaign in Punjab. Although it did not call for the return of the milder term "internal disturbance" in order to invoke the far-reaching Article 352, the Rajiv Gandhi government felt that something less than the term "armed rebellion" had to be adopted to be able to invoke the National Emergency clause of the constitution. Although the 59th Amendment sought to apply the national emergency provisions to only Punjab, several opposition members of both the Lok Sabha (House of the People) and the Rajya Sabha (Council of States) argued that the amendment would either tend to isolate Punjab "creating a constitutional

Khalistan," or be utilized eventually in other parts of India and thus amount to a "declaration of war on the people."[28]

Allegations have been perennial in India that TADA has been widely misused to address basic criminal and law and order cases all over the country that have had little to do with terrorism. The Act was considered to be a violation of the Rule of Law in a democracy. Kuldip Nayar noted:

> Of the 52,998 people arrested under the TADA between May 1985 [probable reference to the preliminary Terrorist Affected Areas Special Courts Act of 1984] and March 1993, 434 (0.8 percent) were convicted. And not a single conviction was under the Section relating to terrorist activity. The law was brought for two years in Delhi, one Union territory and one state. But today nearly the whole of India is reeling under it. The authorities like the TADA because it enables them to by-pass the normal process on inquiry and prosecution. Once arrested under TADA, the suspects do not have recourse to legal remedies which the other accused have. They are treated as a special category of prisoners, pursued in special courts and produced only before an executive, not a judicial magistrate. They are remanded normally for six months and then for another six months. In 88 percent cases, charge-sheets are never filed. . . . So long as TADA remains on the statute book, the government's tendency to use it to the exclusion of ordinary law will not be curbed.[29]

Periodic efforts were made by members of the ruling and opposition parties to revoke TADA since its passage in 1987. But Congress Party government's Home Minister S. B. Chavan declared in 1994 that TADA would not be repealed. He acknowledged that there had been widespread misuse of the act that was intended to deal with terrorists and stated that the chief ministers of the states had been warned not to misuse TADA. The government was endorsed by the Constitution Bench of the Supreme Court in September 1994 in the "Sanjay Dutt case" when it declared that "there is no reason, in law, to doubt its constitutionality or alter its proper construction."[30] In a 58-page judgment, the five members of the Constitution Bench headed by Justice A. M. Ahmedi affirmed the state's right to make special provisions for preventing and coping with terrorist activities.

The passage of the 42nd Amendment in 1976 and the 59th Amendment in 1988 occurred because the Congress government under both Indira Gandhi in 1976 and Rajiv Gandhi in 1988 held a two-thirds majority in the Lok Sabha, the majority that is required for passage of constitutional amendments. Indira Gandhi had obtained this overwhelming majority of seats in parliament in the

March 1971 general election. No national elections were held again until March 1977, one year beyond the constitutionally stipulated maximum five-year term. Rajiv Gandhi obtained the majority in the December 1984 general election. In a sense, such constitutional amendments were not unusual in India. Over 80 amendments were passed between 1950 and 1995. Congress governments under Prime Minister Jawaharlal Nehru had also carried a two-thirds majority in parliament and had passed several constitutional amendments. However, the amendments passed under Nehru were less controversial than those passed under his daughter and grandson. None of the amendments under the Nehru government affected the fundamental rights of the citizen to the same extent.

THE CONSTITUTION AND FUNDAMENTAL RIGHTS

The Indian constitution is easily amended. Following passage of the 42nd Amendment in 1976 during the Emergency, the Indian Supreme Court determined that nothing in the Indian constitution is beyond the amendment process, not even fundamental rights. Amendments are only subject to proper procedures provided by Article 368 of the constitution. If these procedures are followed, then the constitutional provision becomes amended. The amendment procedures may themselves be subject to amendment. The constraining factor on the destruction of India's democratic constitution through constitutional means would appear to be the unwritten tradition that no amendment may destroy the essence and spirit of democracy. The amendment process is subject to the implicit doctrines of "basic structure" and "implied limitation."[31]

Article 368 under Part XX, which in its original form is entitled "Amendment of the Constitution," delineates the procedures to be followed in amending the constitution."[32] One class of provisions in the constitution may be amended by a simple majority of the central parliament. It includes articles dealing with citizenship, salaries and allowances of ministers, the appointment of Supreme Court judges, and language policy. A second class of provisions requires a two-thirds majority of parliament and the concurrence of half the legislatures of the Indian states. This includes the mode and manner of the election of the president (Articles 54 and 55); the extent of executive power (Article 73); the powers of the states (Article 162); provisions relating to the union judiciary (Chapters 4 and 5, Articles 124-127); provisions relating to the distribution of legislative powers between the union and the states (Articles 245-255); provisions relating to the union, state, and concurrent lists delineating the respective jurisdictions of the central and state governments found in the Seventh Schedule indicated in Article 246.

The right of parliament to amend Part III of the constitution, which is entitled "Fundamental Rights" (Articles 12-35), was challenged almost immediately following the passage of the First Amendment Act in 1951. In the 1951 case of *Shankari Prasad Singh and Others versus The Union of India and Others,* the petitioners claimed that the First Amendment Act infringed on the Right to Property (Article 31), a fundamental right.[33] According to the plaintiffs, fundamental rights were subject to Article 13 (2), which reads as follows: "The State shall not make any law which takes away or abridges the rights conferred by this Part [Part III, Fundamental Rights] and any law made in contravention of this clause shall, to the extent of the contravention, be void."[34]

The Supreme Court ruled at the time that parliament did have the power to amend the constitution under Article 368 and that "the word 'law' in Article 13 (2) did not include 'amendment' of the constitution which was made by Parliament in exercise of its 'constituent' and 'legislative' powers."[35] In effect, the Supreme Court ruled that the right to property was a constitutional right and that parliament had the right to amend all aspects of the constitution. In the case of *Sajjan Singh versus State of Rajasthan* in 1965, the petitioners did not challenge the right of parliament to amend fundamental rights, but claimed that the 17th Amendment Act of 1964 did not fulfill the procedural provisions of Article 368. The Supreme Court again rejected the plaintiff's claims in favor of the right of parliament to amend all provisions of the constitution and ruled that the procedures had been followed appropriately.

However, between the judgment in the *Sajjan Singh* case in 1965 and the passage of the 42nd Amendment in 1976, the Supreme Court declared the inviolability of fundamental rights in two important cases. First, in *Golaknath versus State of Punjab* (1967), the petitioners claimed that Article 368, which indicated amendment procedures, could not override Article 13 (2), which declared that fundamental rights may not be abridged or taken away. This time the Supreme Court revoked the earlier judgments it had made in the *Shankari Prasad* and *Sajjan Singh* cases and ruled in favor of the plaintiff. A more definitive ruling came in 1972, in the case of *Kesavananda Bharati versus State of Kerala,* in which the petitioners challenged parliament's passage of the 24th, 25th, and 29th Amendments. The petitioners claimed an "implied limitation" on the power of parliament to amend fundamental rights through Article 368.[36] The plaintiffs also claimed that beyond fundamental rights, other provisions of the constitution, such as the right to vote and elect representatives to the central and state legislatures, the dual structure of the Indian Union, the separation of powers, the independence of the judiciary, and the basic secular nature of the

Indian state, could not be amended. These provisions represented the basic structure of Indian democracy, and therefore, parliament did not have the authority to amend provisions of the constitution that would change the nature of the democratic constitution itself.

In response to the plaintiff's complaint, the state claimed that parliament had unlimited power to amend any part of the constitution provided procedures under Article 368 were fulfilled. Indeed, individual fundamental rights were subordinate to Part IV, Articles 36-51, namely, the "Directive Principles of State Policy," that sought to bring justice to the whole nation. The attorney general of India, Niren De, representing the state, declared that "the only limitation upon the power vested in Parliament, if at all there was any, was that the whole of the Constitution" could neither be repealed nor re-enacted."[37] Any other interpretation would defeat the objective of parliament's amending powers.

The Indian Supreme Court, reversing its decisions in the *Shankari Prasad* and *Sajjan Singh* cases and reiterating its judgment in the *Golaknath* case, ruled in favor of the plaintiff. In the majority judgment, Chief Justice Subba Rao and Justice Mohammed Hidayatullah stated that parliament did not have the power to take away or abridge fundamental rights even through the amendment process.[38] In an assessment of the 25th Amendment and the amending power of parliament under the constitution, later Chief Justice S. M. Sikri declared that the "Directive Principles of State Policy" could not supersede "Fundamental Rights" as that would be a contradiction in terms.[39] To deny individual rights would be to deny society's rights. Other justices on the Supreme Court, concurring with the chief justice, declared that parliament had no right to abrogate the basic features of India's democratic constitution, and that amending powers under Article 368 were regulated by the doctrine of *implied limitation.* Thus, by 1972, the legal interpretation at the highest judicial level was that fundamental rights belonged to the basic structure of the Indian constitution, and that the amending power of parliament should be exercised "to preserve rather than destroy the essence of those rights."[40]

However, the passage, in 1976, of the far-reaching 42nd Amendment—virtually a new constitution unto itself—nullified the judgments made in the *Golaknath* and *Kesavananda* cases. Although many of the extreme provisions of the 42nd Amendment were reversed by the provisions of the 44th Amendment, which was passed after the Janata Party defeated Indira Gandhi's Congress Party in 1977, parliament's unlimited power to amend the constitution was retained. The principle established was that, in the national interest and in the name of national security, the rights of the state and society must come before the rights of the individual. Fundamental rights under the Indian constitution cannot frustrate the "Directive Principles of State Policy," and parliament's powers of amendment under Article 368 cannot be restricted by Article 13 (2), which declares that the basic character of fundamental rights is not amendable. Thus, Article 13 (2) would appear to be advisory or even ornamental. Fundamental rights in India are considered not to be *inherent* rights of the individual, but to be *derived* rights granted by the state to the individual.

In effect, the later Supreme Court interpretation appears to be that it is the state that grants the individual fundamental rights through the constitution and that the state may take away those rights in the interests of preserving the security and stability of the state, and thereby supposedly preserving democracy in the long run. This interpretation may not meet Western standards of freedom, but freedom (as seen in India, which faces myriad problems that are not faced by Western democracies) cannot be advanced at the cost of the state. Such an interpretation becomes crucial in understanding the manner in which India has dealt with problems of violent separatism in many parts of the country, especially in Kashmir and Punjab.

THE SUSPENSION OF DEMOCRACY IN THE STATES

Just as the fundamental rights of the individual may be suspended during times of emergency, the system of democracy and the powers of the Indian states may also be suspended if emergency conditions are considered to warrant such moves. Article 356 of the Indian constitution reads as follows:

> 356. *Provisions in case of failure of constitutional machinery in States.* (1) If the President, on receipt of a report from the Governor or Rajpramukh of a State or otherwise, is satisfied that a situation has arisen in which the government of the State cannot be carried on in accordance with the provisions of the Constitution, the President may by Proclamation: (a) assume to himself all or any of the functions of the Government of the State and all or any of the powers vested in or exercisable by the Governor or Rajpramukh, as the case may be, or any body or authority in the State other than the Legislature of the State; (b) declare that the powers of the Legislature of the State shall be exercisable by or under the authority of Parliament; (c) make such incidental and consequential provisions as appear to the President to be necessary or desirable for giving effect to the objects of the Proclamation, including provisions for suspending in whole or in part the operation of any provisions of this Constitution relating to any body or authority in the State.[41]

Needless to say, all of such presidential actions are to be undertaken on the advice of the prime minister who, in effect, holds executive power in the Indian parliamentary system. Sections (2) to (4) of Article 356 set conditions and limitations on the exercise of "President's Rule." The central parliament must approve of such a proclamation within two months, and approval for the continuation of President's Rule must be sought every six months thereafter, but not to continue for longer than three years from the date of the first proclamation.

Defining what constitutes a condition of emergency in the states has often been ambiguous and arbitrary. When no party is able to gain a majority in a state, and when no coalition or minority government appears possible, the central government has invariably declared President's Rule until new elections are held. Although such interventions have been frequent, they have not been controversial, especially if new elections are held within six months or a year. But in the case of Andhra Pradesh, the Telugu Desam government of N. T. Rama Rao was dismissed by Prime Minister Indira Gandhi in 1984 despite the fact that it held a majority of seats in the state legislature. Following a protest, the Rama Rao government was reinstated.

Declarations of President's Rule in a state because of a breakdown in law and order and the inability of the state government to handle the problem have proved to be controversial since there is usually a government with a majority of seats in the state legislature and central government intervention implies the dismissal of that legitimately elected state government.[42] How much breakdown in law and order is unacceptable is not easily determined, and states such as Punjab, Kashmir, Kerala, and West Bengal have complained that the central government's interventions have not been justified. Invariably, such interventions have occurred when parties opposed to the ruling Congress Party held power in the states—the National Conference in Kashmir, the Akali Dal in Punjab, and the Communist Party–Marxists (CPM) in Kerala and West Bengal.

A disturbing trend has been the increasing frequency of declarations of emergency in the states, as may be seen in the following figures, which cover the first four decades following the adoption of the Indian constitution in 1950:[43] There were 8 declarations of President's Rule during the 15-year period 1950-64; 9 during the 5-year period 1965-69 (including 7 during 1967-69 alone); 19 during the 5-year period 1970-74; 21 during the 5-year period 1975-79 (including 9 during 1977 alone); and 18 during the 10-year period 1980-89 (including 9 in 1980 alone).

In addition to these 75 cases of emergency being imposed in the states, President's Rule has been imposed another 10 times in the Union Territories of Arunachal Pradesh, Goa Daman and Diu, Mizoram, and Pondicherry. (The first three are now full-fledged states of the Indian Union.) The most frequent resorts to President's Rule have occurred in Kerala (9 times), Punjab (8 times), Uttar Pradesh (6 times), Orissa (6 times), Bihar (5 times), Manipur (5 times), West Bengal (4 times), and Gujerat (4 times).[44] Interestingly, there have been only two declarations of President's Rule in the state of Jammu and Kashmir, and these occurred only after 1986. But the state has been under a state of emergency and under "Governor's Rule" since 1990. There was also a six-month period of Governor's Rule in Kashmir between March and September 1977.

Apart from the 22-month National Security Emergency declared between June 1975 and March 1977, the suspension of the parliamentary process has been confined to the regional level. With the exception of the severe cases of Punjab and Kashmir since the mid-1980s, elections have been invariably held within six months to a year, in accordance with the limits placed on President's Rule by the constitution. In Assam, where there was a major interethnic struggle between Assamese and non-Assamese, along with a violent Assamese secessionist movement against Indian forces, elections were held in February 1983, following a period of President's Rule. This election was held despite warnings that there might be extreme violence by various Assamese political groups if such elections were held. The elections led to the massacre of over 5,000 Bengali Muslims. On the other hand, the prolonged crisis and instability in Punjab produced a constitutional amendment in parliament to extend President's Rule there to October 1985, an extra year beyond the mandatory time limit imposed by the constitution. In doing this, parliament was no doubt influenced by memories of the disaster in Assam the previous year. But again, despite the threat of extreme violence by Sikh extremists, the central government held elections in Punjab in February 1992. The turnout was less than 35 percent, and participation was mainly by Hindus in the cities. Most Sikhs and Sikh parties boycotted the elections either out of opposition to the Indian government's policies or because of fear of retaliation by Sikh extremists.

By 1995, insurgency and terrorist violence in Punjab had subsided and the crisis appeared to be dissipating in spite of the assassination of Congress Party Chief Minister Beant Singh in 1995. The government of India, under Prime Minister Narasimha Rao, had begun to address the basic grievances of the Sikhs in the hope that this would restore peace in Punjab. These grievances include demands that families of the victims of the 1984 massacre of Sikhs in the aftermath of Indira Gandhi's assassination be compensated and that the killers be apprehended and punished. They also include demands for the transfer of land from Haryana to Punjab; the sharing of irrigation waters between the two states; and the transfer of the city of Chandigarh to Punjab, to serve as the state's exclusive capital instead of the capital of both Punjab and

Haryana. The Rao government is attempting to reach settlements on these demands. The likelihood of a settlement based on India's policy of repression and rewards was reflected in the *panchayat* (village council) elections in Punjab in early 1993, in which Sikhs came out to vote in overwhelming numbers, rejecting extremist demands not to participate in any elections. Their return to the ballot box suggests that Sikh secessionists are losing their stranglehold over Punjab. However, hard-line Sikh extremists within India, together with their overseas supporters, are unwilling to give up their struggle for an independent Khalistan. India is determined not to give Punjab independence either.

The frequent resort to and prolonged imposition of President's Rule in the states is a barometer of growing troubles in India arising from internal security problems. The frequent suspension of democracy in the states also indicates an underlying problem with the Indian body politic that may call for drastic changes in the nature of the Indian political system.

THE ADEQUACY OF THE INDIAN POLITICAL SYSTEM

Since the amending power of the Indian parliament is unlimited subject only to proper procedures, presumably the basic structure of the Indian political system may also be changed. However, the doctrine of "implied limitation," which does not appear to have been rejected by the Indian Supreme Court at any time, would indicate that any change in the basic structure must still conform to a democratic system. Thus, the Westminster system of parliamentary democracy may be discarded in favor of an American or French presidential democratic system or some other form of democracy. A constitutional amendment that incorporates an alternative democratic model is all that would be needed. But it is also important to keep in mind that the theory of implied limitation has never been fully tested in India. If anything and everything could be amended by Article 368, then a not-so-democratic model, or a non-Western democratic model that is not based on adult franchise and majority rule, may also be adopted.

In Pakistan, for instance, President Ayub Khan introduced a system of "Basic Democracies" in which national representatives were indirectly elected through a pyramid consisting of layers of elected representatives at lower levels. During martial rule, there has also been talk in Pakistan of distinguishing between Western concepts of democracy and Islamic concepts of democracy. In India, there is no talk of a "Hindu democracy," a "Communist democracy," or any other democracy that does not follow the basic Western norms of democracy. But there has been a great deal of soul-searching about whether the existing Westminster form of government meets India's needs as it approaches the end of the twentieth century.

By the 1990s, security pressures and stress on the Indian democracy had increased as a result of two new conditions. Internal security problems were paramount. Indeed, problems of external security were the spillover effects of domestic security issues in the border states and the growth of violent communalism in general. First, there were outbreaks of two more violent separatist movements—in Assam beginning in 1986, and in Kashmir beginning in 1989. The separatist movement in Kashmir threatens to trigger another Indo-Pakistani war. Second, weak, "minority" state governments began to assume office, making it more difficult for the central government to deal with the increasing problems of internal security.

Following the general elections of November 1989, a shaky coalition government led by the minority Janata Dal–National Front group of parties and backed by the right-wing Bharatiya Janata Party and the left-wing Communist parties assumed office. The National Front government's staying power was dependent on its ability to placate and receive continuing parliamentary support from the incompatible outside parties that backed it but were not members of the ruling "coalitional" government. (Both the earlier Janata government and the later Janata Dal governments were not coalition governments because various parties had formally merged to create a new party.) Unable to maintain loyalty within the party and the support of the outside parties, the Janata Dal government fell in early 1991 and a new national election was called. Just prior to the election, Rajiv Gandhi was assassinated while campaigning in Madras, and leadership passed on to P. V. Narasimha Rao. In the elections held in June 1991, the Congress Party was elected with a plurality of votes but not a clear majority. This government, too, became dependent on outside support from the BJP on the right and the CPM on the left to remain in power. By 1995, through by-elections, the Congress Party had obtained a slim majority.

In July 1993, Subodh Kant Sahai, who had been minister of state for home affairs under the Janata Dal government, expressed the general apprehension in India of perpetually weak, ineffective, and short-lived governments.[45] Speaking in New York, Sahai claimed that since Rajiv Gandhi's election in December 1984, successive Indian leaders have had to make a choice between concentrating on national affairs or party affairs. A prime minister cannot do both very well, especially when there exists the constant threat of an early dismissal of the government if the ruling party cannot muster enough votes in parliament. A presidential system, which need not be identical to either the

American or French systems, would provide the remedy. According to Sahai, under a presidential system, prime ministers "will have to deal with party affairs before the elections, not after it. The last four prime ministers have been too busy looking after their seat to look after the country. Second, the parties will necessarily have to throw up leaders who are acceptable to all sections of the population, which means the system will help curb militant tendencies among certain parties."[46]

The broader problem of domestic stability arose from periodic doubts about the adequacy of the existing British-Canadian democratic federal system in India. The root cause of internal security problems was perceived to lie with the failure of the Westminster parliamentary system and the federal structure. Minority governments in the parliamentary system were very weak and ineffectual, and the center-state system was not federal enough, causing the rise of religious, linguistic, caste, and tribal minority dissatisfaction and ethnic conflict. At an even broader level, doubts have been raised about whether the prevailing parliamentary system of government, which does not guarantee a fixed term for the executive branch of government, is adequate to deal with the kinds of severe domestic security problems that India faces today.

The debate on whether to adopt an alternative system of government to replace the parliamentary system became louder during and after the declaration of Emergency by Prime Minister Indira Gandhi. Although those who drafted the constitution between 1947 and 1950 reached a majority decision that a parliamentary system was preferable to a presidential system in India, since the 1970s there were politicians and political pundits who began to suggest that a presidential system of the American or French variety might be more suitable for the maintenance of external and, especially, internal security.[47] The question of adopting an alternative system of government arose again in 1993 with the emergence of three successive minority governments after the defeat of Rajiv Gandhi's Congress government in 1989. The Janata Dal government of V. P. Singh, elected in 1989, the even smaller Janata faction government of Chandrashekhar, which took office briefly in 1991, and the Congress government of Narasimha Rao elected in 1991, have all functioned with uncertain support from parties outside the ruling party. In mid-1993, as the Rao government was put to an unsuccessful vote of no confidence, doubts began to arise as to whether any party in the near future would be able to muster a clear majority of seats in parliament. The era of the Nehru family–led Congress Party dominance appeared to be over.

The problem of unstable governments had been perennial in the states, especially after 1967, when the Congress Party was no longer able to gain the majority of the seats in many of the Vidhan Sabhas (state legislative assemblies).

A basic problem that had plagued state governments in the past and increased their instability was the practice of "floor crossings," in which members of state legislative assemblies crossed over to the opposition or to ruling government benches. State governments were easily toppled in the 1960s, and the political instability of the Indian states was considerably increased. This problem was resolved by Prime Minister Rajiv Gandhi in 1985 when an antidefection law—the 52nd Amendment—was passed. It deprived legislators of their membership in the legislature if they quit the parties under which they were elected after a period of six months, or if they were expelled by the party in accordance with parliamentary procedures.[48] The main exception to this rule was when parties split or merged. However, this has not prevented some ambiguous switches from one party to another.

A controversial case of alleged floor crossing arose in July 1993, when a faction of the Janata Dal Party led by Ajit Singh joined forces with the Congress government of P. V. Narasimha Rao to defeat a no-confidence vote against the Congress government in parliament.[49] The measure was defeated by a vote of 265 to 251, a margin of 14 votes, which meant that without the 7-vote switch by the Ajit Singh faction, the vote would have been tied at 258 and would have produced the fall of Rao's Congress government. (In July 1993, the ruling Congress Party had 257 votes in parliament, which has a total of 532 seats.) The Ajit Singh faction appeared to have formed a coalition with the Congress Party or even perhaps joined it. Opposition parties argued that the seven MPs who switched had violated the antidefection law, which prohibits any group from crossing the floor unless the defectors constitute one-third of the members of that party in parliament. The weakening of the antidefection law may imply the greater instability of central governments in India in the future.

The debate on whether to adopt a political system other than that based on the Westminster model dates back to the deliberations by the Constituent Assembly between 1947 and 1950 to devise a constitution for the newly independent India. Four alternatives have been proposed periodically since 1947: the American presidential system, the post-1958 Gaullist French presidential system, a combined presidential and parliamentary system, and structural revisions to the existing British parliamentary system.

At the outset, the 1947-49 Constituent Assembly rejected the American presidential system in favor of retaining the British system. One of the foremost architects of the Indian constitution, Dr. B. R. Ambedkar, declared that while the American presidential system may give the chief executive, the president, greater stability through his election on a national basis and through guaranteeing him a fixed term of office, it also gives the executive less responsibility. According to Ambedkar, "the British system on the other hand gives you more responsibility but less stability."[50] In rejecting the American system, the majority of those who drafted the Indian constitution felt that the independence of the legislative and executive bodies would result in frequent deadlocks, particularly in situations in which the legislature was dominated by one party and the executive by another. As English jurist Walter Bagehot noted, under the American constitution, "the executive becomes unfit for its name since it cannot execute what it decides on; the legislature is demoralized by liberty by making decisions of which others (and not itself) will suffer the effects."[51]

The Gaullist presidential system, in which a nationally elected president appoints a prime minister but the executive and the legislature are separate, has also been proposed. Although the Gaullist system in France ended the almost biannual fall of governments and brought about greater stability, there were still structural problems that brought about frequent confrontations between the president and the prime minister. In 1978, Sri Lanka, under Julius Jayawardene of the United National Party, adopted the Gaullist system, except that the nationally elected president was still responsible to parliament; the system was, in essence, a combination of the presidential and parliamentary systems.[52] But the president would remain in power for six years unless he were impeached. However, as in the American system, the majority of the elected members of the Sri Lankan legislature could be from opposition parties, making the powers of the executive less effective.

Three main reasons for the adoption of a presidential system in India are usually advocated. First, because the president would be nationally elected, he or she would be acceptable to the majority of the people from all over the country. This would give the executive leader greater authority to conduct national security affairs. Because the prime minister in a parliamentary system is elected from a single constituency of a particular state, there is no guarantee that he or she has a national following. While there may have been national support for Prime Minister Jawaharlal Nehru, for Prime Minister Indira Gandhi during various periods of her rule, and for Prime Minister Rajiv Gandhi, such support for Prime Ministers Morarji Desai, V. P. Singh, Chandrashekhar, and P. V. Narasimha Rao has been much less certain. Second, because a president would have a fixed term, there would be sufficient time for him or her to adopt and implement policies. Under the weak minority governments of V. P. Singh and Narasimha Rao, strong actions to deal with the problems of rising communal violence and armed separatist movements could not be adopted since all such policies would require the support of loosely allied outside parties in parliament. Both the Singh and Rao governments were dependent on votes in parliament from members of the Communist parties on the left, the Bharatiya Janata Party on the right, or the regional parties from states such as Tamil Nadu and Andhra Pradesh. Third, a nationally elected president with a fixed term of office would be able to appoint cabinet ministers or secretaries, none of whom would have to worry about election during their appointments. The president and his appointed cabinet would be able to adopt policies that might be unpopular but effective in dealing with external and internal security problems.

No serious effort has been made thus far to move away from the parliamentary system toward a presidential system. In April 1995 Speaker of the Lok Sabha Shivraj Patil circulated a 10-page "confidential" document titled, "A short note on what can be done to provide reasonable stability to the government at the Centre."[53] The document proposed re-examining the American and French presidential systems. Alternatively, it proposed introducing substantial amendments to the existing framework of the constitution to avoid hung parliaments after 1996. These changes would include requiring a vote of more than a two-thirds majority for the removal of the central government, giving greater powers to the Lok Sabha, allowing MPs to vote according to their inclination instead of the party line and no-confidence votes to be directed against individual ministers instead of the ruling party as a whole.

The most substantive changes that might occur before the end of the twentieth century, if any changes do occur, would be some structural revisions to the existing system, perhaps some method of granting a fixed term to a newly elected government.[54] The prevailing sentiment to "Reform not Reject" the existing constitution may be seen in the observations of P. G. Mavalankar, a former member of India's parliament:

> The parliamentary form and system of government must be retained and, indeed, be strengthened. The presidential model, as is practised in the United States, need not be transplanted in the Indian soil. What is good and workable in one large democracy is not necessarily so in another. The British pattern, which we have adapted, not adopted, suits us admirably; it guarantees a more meaningful principle and a purposeful practice of responsible government in a democratic polity. We have been, by an historical accident, fairly familiar with the 'Westminster Model' since pre-independence days; this too prompted the constitution-makers to opt for it. Our experiment and experience with it has spanned over the last 45 years, and it is by no means an adequate or a sufficient period of time to arrive at a judgement against it. Moreover, why make a gamble in deserting the known constitutional mould and embracing the unknown outfit?[55]

5

The Military Dimension

THE MILITARY AND POLITICS

The military has played an important and forceful role in the domestic politics, economy, and society of many developing countries. Indeed, the essential security function of the military in many Latin American and African countries has not been in the international arena, deterring or defending against armed attacks against the state. Instead, the military has been occupied in the domestic arena, dealing with armed insurgencies and acts of terrorism committed by dissident ethnic or tribal groups. The internal security role of the military has often led to military coups and the perpetuation of praetorian states.[1] Before 1990, the military was the dominant political actor in Pakistan and Bangladesh. On the other hand, despite its size and power, the military has played a much lesser role in the domestic political arena in India. In general, the principle of civilian control of the military has prevailed in India, and the military's incursions into domestic politics has been only on the invitation, and under the control, of the civilian authorities.

Although the military has remained in the background in India, its large size, its disciplined organization, its demand for budgetary allocations, its control over considerable resources, and its potential ability to intrude into the domestic political arena make it a significant force in national life. In a diverse and multiethnic society such as India, the recruitment policy of the military and the location of its defense production programs are cause for competition between and concern in the different regions. The military may be perceived also either as a threat to various ethnic groups that are seeking greater autonomy or as the protector and unifier of the nation.

With some qualifications, the military in India may be viewed as an integrating force in its role as the defender of the nation against external threats. It may also appear as an integrating force when it serves as a showcase for the secular, noncaste, and nonreligious values that Indian leaders have sought to impose on it since independence. But it may be viewed as a disintegrating force when it is deployed to deal with problems of internal security, especially when it appears to function in the role of a British colonial–type native constabulary force. When it serves as an integrating force, the democratic aspirations of the country are enhanced; when it is viewed as a disintegrating force, the democratic ethos of the country becomes diminished.

Stressing the effects of the outward and inward deployment of the Indian military may seem like stating the obvious, but it would be reasonable to ask whether some Third World states would have survived as relatively stable political entities if the military had not played a role or been deployed in counterinsurgency and antiterrorist campaigns. Although controversial, the overthrow of civilian regimes and the seizure of political power and authority may have sometimes prevented such newly emerged countries from falling into a state of anarchy. Could civilian democrats in many developing countries have provided the political and economic stability for prolonged periods of time that military dictators or military-backed civilian dictators have provided? Military or military-backed dictatorships in Pakistan and Bangladesh, as well as in Chile, Argentina, Brazil, Nigeria, South Korea, Taiwan, and Thailand, have all claimed that their intervention into the political sphere prevented the disintegration of the state and provided prolonged spells of sustained economic development.

Compared to most developing countries, India has been unique because of its continued civilian political control of the military within a Western parliamentary-type democratic system. One of the reasons for this happy situation has been that the military, and especially the army, has always had a broad-based, socially prestigious identity in India. At the same time, the military's acceptance of civilian overlordship, combined with a generally honest give-and-take approach to military growth and development between civilians and the military, has done much to dissipate the tensions that might otherwise have arisen from the relationship. This has resulted in over 40 years of amicable civil-military relations. On balance, therefore, the military in India may be seen as an integrating force and as the defender of democracy—not as its enemy.

On the other hand, the size, growth, and potential political power of the military and its frequent use for internal security purposes could undermine the prevailing democratic norms. When the military is used to deal with insurgency, terrorism, and the general breakdown of law and order in the states, often this is done through various ordinances and amendments to the constitution that are passed by the ruling government. The basis for such actions usually bypasses normal democratic and judicial procedures. Moreover, the use of the military for internal security through such authoritarian measures has usually aggravated the fissiparous tendencies among the various ethnic groups in India. Rather than being seen as a symbol of unity, the military may be seen as an obstacle to rectifying political injustices or achieving political freedom. Under these circumstances, the military in India may be viewed as a disintegrating force and a potential threat to democracy.

Two other issues need to be considered in dealing with the impact of the military on India's democracy. First, what powers does the Indian military wield in the security decision-making process? Second, is the Indian military capable of and willing to overthrow the civilian democratic system on grounds of ineffective government, corruption, or allegations of civilian anarchy? These have been the grounds for the overthrow of civilian governments by the military in other developing countries, including Pakistan and Bangladesh.

THE MILITARY AND NATIONAL INTEGRATION

Until the Indian Army's assault on the Sikh's Golden Temple in Punjab in 1984, the military was viewed by much of the Indian population as a symbol of national unity. The military was, and still is, to most Indians, the trusted friend of the people. Indeed, the Indian military sees itself as the defender of the nation and as an important symbol of national unity, and it would like to keep things that way. The military as an *integrating force* may be found in the following policies and roles: (a) its national recruitment efforts; (b) its role as the defender of the nation against external aggression; and (c) its role in providing disaster relief and other assistance to the civilian authorities during natural calamities. The recruitment policy and composition of the Indian military have much to do with the stability of India's democracy. Conditions in India may provide clues to why democracy in Pakistan failed even though Pakistan inherited one-third of the British Indian military services.

However, the Indian military has, at times, contributed to national disintegration. Especially since "Operation Blue Star," the Indian Army's assault on the Sikh's Golden Temple in Amritsar in June 1984, perceptions of the regular armed forces as symbols of national unity and integrity began to decline.

The military as a *disintegrating force* arises mainly from its reluctant role in the maintenance of internal security. Controversy over the internal use of force to quell armed insurgencies, of course, surrounds both the paramilitary forces and the armed forces. In the case of the paramilitary forces, the issue is not whether they have a role to play in the maintenance of internal security; they were, after all, raised for that purpose. The issue is whether such special internal security forces are likely to be misused by the government in power. Perhaps the argument could be made that the greater the size of paramilitary forces, the greater the probability that democratic processes and the freedom of the citizens are likely to be undermined. On the other hand, in the case of the regular armed forces, the question is whether such forces should be used at all in the maintenance of internal security.

THE ETHNIC FACTOR IN RECRUITMENT POLICY

It should be apparent that military recruitment and the socialization and integration of diverse ethnic groups in the Indian armed forces has a stabilizing effect on the nation. Although recruitment by the Indian Army has tended to follow the pattern of recruitment by the British in the pre-independence era, which was based on the concept of the "martial races" of northern and western India, the continuation of this policy after independence has been partly due to historical accident rather than deliberate design, and partly due to an unstated "evolutionary" policy followed by the Indian military establishment that is aimed at minimizing dislocations and breaks with British Indian military traditions.[2]

Indian politicians, however, have sought to end this undemocratic British mentality and legacy. The concept of martial races, for instance, is considered to be a British-generated myth. In any case, in the age of modern technology, the size and physique of a soldier is irrelevant. Politicians have advocated, therefore, a policy of proportional recruitment and representation from different regions and ethnic groups, and the mixing of these groups in common regiments to foster national integration.

The earlier British rationale for communally separated regiments was that the various ethnic groups in India had different customs, traditions, and eating habits that could not be easily integrated. The British also argued that communal regiments produced better esprit de corps, and therefore better fighting units. But these arguments may be misleading since no efforts were made to separate Indian ethnic groups in the Royal Indian Air Force (RIAF) and Royal

Indian Navy (RIN). No doubt, these two services were much smaller than the British Indian Army. The reasons for communal representation may have had more to do with the policy of divide and rule than with concern for the special interests of the various ethnic groups. An integrated British Indian Army could have posed a threat to the empire itself. On the other hand, when separated and commanded almost exclusively by British officers before and during both world wars, the British Indian Army not only did not constitute a threat to the empire, but also was effectively wielded to defend the empire against rebellious forces within India and was used in Britain's overseas campaigns in Asia, the Middle East, Europe, and North Africa.

While the army was conducive to such communal divisions and representation in the formation of regiments, the air force and navy were not conducive to communal separation. It would have appeared absurd to create a destroyer full of Sikhs only, or a submarine full of Gurkhas, or a combat air squadron full of Marathas. The policy of divide and rule would have been too obvious if applied to the air force and navy. The RIAF before the Second World War was only in a nascent stage, and the extensive use of air power was an interwar development. Given the small size of the RIAF, the British could perhaps have argued that communal separation was unnecessary. Likewise, because Britain's Royal Navy commanded the Indian Ocean, it could have been argued that a large Royal Indian Navy organized into communal units was unnecessary. In comparison, the threat from a potentially large and communally integrated British Indian Army was ominous, and this may have been an important reason for communal separatism in the regiments. The historical experience of the Great Indian Mutiny of 1857-58, when Hindu and Muslim soldiers of the British East India Company revolted against their British masters, was not lost on the British. In this context, it may be interesting to note that the small but integrated Royal Indian Navy mutinied against the British in 1946, thereby accelerating the move toward independence a year later.

Not unexpectedly, the British legacy was difficult to reverse in the short run. Quite apart from the understandable resistance to change by privileged ethnic groups within the army, the military's overarching concern is to maintain combat effectiveness. It is, therefore, unwilling to sacrifice the qualities of cohesion and esprit de corps of the fighting men, especially in the infantry and armored divisions. The military high command in India still believes in the need to generate such qualities based on caste and community in the frontline regiments. Even as recently as 1980, Lieutenant General S. K. Sinha argued that some British military traditions need to be maintained so long as they are not incompatible with Indian traditions.[3] Regiments based on ethnic communities and castes may be perceived to fit Indian traditions and need not be seen as undemocratic. At the same time, the continuation of such military traditions might serve a similar purpose for India as it did for the British. It would keep the post-independence Indian Army divided by community and caste so that it would, therefore, pose little threat to civilian democratic rule. It would also keep the Indian Army pleased and content.

Thus, the main Indian infantry divisions remain largely Sikh, Jat, Gurkha, Rajput, Dogra, Maratha, Mahar, Kumaoni, Garwahli, and Madrasi (Tamil).[4] And many old armored units such as Skinner's Horse, 17th Horse, Deccan Horse, and Central Indian Horse, to mention a few, still have Sikh, Jat, Dogra, Maratha, and Rajput Tank squadrons. In fact, army headquarters has been so determined to conserve tradition and keep the "sword sharp" that mechanized outfits raised after independence, such as the 63rd, 64th, 65th, 70th, and 71st cavalry, all feature both "mixed" squadrons and separate Jat, Sikh, Dogra, and Rajput tank squadrons along the lines of the older and more renowned units.

However, as a demonstration of its intent to move gradually towards a more communally integrated military, the Indian Army has acquiesced to the induction of "outsiders" into many previously "pure" regiments. Thus, Gujeratis, who were labeled by the British as nonmartial, were permitted to join the Rajputs, many Rajputs themselves being Gujerati-speaking. Several Mahar regiments now include non-Mahars. But the most conspicuous move in this direction was the raising of the only new infantry regiment in the last four decades—the raising of the elite Brigade of Guards in the early 1950s. In order to make it a showpiece regiment, the Brigade of Guards was cobbled together by transferring the best battalions from each of the established regiments and forcing these disparate fighting groups to merge their identities.

Recruitment to the Indian armed forces is, therefore, a compromise between the tradition set by British rule and the political needs of post-independence India. Politicians over the years have been content with this arrangement because of their respect for the military's sensitivity and their unwillingness to trespass into the army's professional concern for maintaining superior fighting formations. In turn, the Indian Army has been sensitive to the politicians' concern for fighting units that are communally integrated. And since the 1980s, it has increasingly made concessions in this direction.

Unfortunately, efforts to recruit proportionately on the basis of regional populations and to integrate the various groups have been one of the grievances of the Sikhs. Members of the main Sikh party, the Akali Dal, as well as other Sikh politicians, have demanded on various occasions that fitness and merit be the primary criteria for recruitment to the armed forces.[5] This demand was part of the Akali Dal's Anandpur Sahib Resolution, passed in 1973, and the issue had been raised with the central government by former chief minister of Punjab, Giani Zail Singh, who was to be become president of India later.

Other Sikh complaints included the failure to appoint a single Sikh general as chief of army staff despite the large number of Sikh officers in the Indian Army. On at least three occasions, a Sikh general in line for the position of army chief had been superseded. On two occasions, this was done was done by extending the term of the existing army chief, although on the last occasion, it also had to do with not offending Sikh susceptibilities by appointing a shorn and clean-shaven Sikh general. Note, however, that two Sikhs have held the position of chief of staff of the air force, a service in which approximately 20 percent of the officers are Sikhs.[6] Despite such Sikh complaints, it should be noted that Sikhs constitute up to 8 percent of the Indian armed forces and at least 12 percent of the Indian Army combat divisions. No doubt, these figures are down from the 20 percent Sikh composition of the British Indian Army, but the percentage of Sikhs in the military remains a high proportional representation, as Sikhs constitute only 2 percent of the Indian population.

Whatever these military grievances, there was confidence in the loyalty and discipline of the Sikh forces in the Indian military until the Indian Army's assault on the Sikhs' Golden Temple in June 1984. The launching of Operation Blue Star by Prime Minister Indira Gandhi triggered mutinies and desertions among Sikh soldiers from Sikh regiments and military encampments in Ramgarh (Bihar), Sri Ganganagar (Rajasthan), Poona (Maharashtra), and the state of Tripura. At Ramgarh, 600 Sikh soldiers deserted their unit and wounded about 600 people, including 25 army officers, in a fierce battle.[7]

Although the Sikhs were greatly alienated by the government's assault on the Golden Temple—the Sikh equivalent of St. Peter's Basilica in Rome or the Grand Mosque in Mecca—there is no evidence that the recruitment of Sikhs into the Indian armed forces has declined. This may be because of the gap that remains between Sikh demands for more recruitment into the armed forces and the government's efforts to seek greater proportional national representation in the military. Therefore, there are still plenty of Sikh volunteers to fill the vacancies in Sikh and other mixed regiments in the Indian military. Even after Operation Blue Star, Sikhs remained prominent in the operations of the Indian Peace-Keeping Forces (IPKF) in Sri Lanka, which was commanded by a Sikh general.

Efforts to create proportional representation in the military may cause resentment among those groups that were once favored under the British Raj, but the new Indian policy should gain favor with the rest of the population, which fell outside the historical and traditional sources of military recruitment during British rule. Thus, Sikh alienation in the recruitment process may be more than offset by a favorable Hindu reaction elsewhere in the country, especially given the new level of Hindu revivalism and nationalism. After all, Hindus constitute 82 percent of the population of India. In a democratic system, pampering such an overwhelming majority could not hurt any party seeking to gain or maintain power, whether Congress, Janata, Janata Dal, BJP, or some other party aspiring to win the next general or local election.

Once a sensitive issue, but now a receding factor, has been the recruitment of Muslims into the Indian armed services. After the partition of India in 1947, virtually all Muslim soldiers, both officers and *jawans* (enlisted men), numbering about one-third of the total British Indian Army, were transferred to the new state of Pakistan. The transfer of Muslims to Pakistan applied to the Royal Indian Air Force and the Royal Indian Navy, although a few Muslim airmen and seamen chose to remain within the newly constituted Indian units since these services were more communally integrated than the army.

After the 1947-48 Indo-Pakistani war, there was little development and growth of Indian military manpower. During this time, there were considerable purchases of military equipment for the army and the air force to counter the weapons acquisition in Pakistan through its participation in the American-sponsored Southeast Asian Treaty Organization (SEATO) and the Central Treaty Organization (CENTO). However, even the annual recruitment to replace retiring military personnel did not attract many Muslims, either because the recruitment process eliminated Muslims as security risks or, as is just as likely, because Muslims were deterred from joining the Indian armed services that were most likely to be deployed against Pakistan, a country to which many Indian Muslims were sentimentally attached.

All the same, the Indian Army, with the concurrence and approval of the government, has endeavored to act very professionally on this issue.[8] When the 1965 Indo-Pakistani war began, a Muslim-majority battalion of the Rajput regiment stationed in the crucial Poonch sector of Jammu and Kashmir state, far from being hastily withdrawn, was allowed to play its part in the execution of the army's forward actions. According to several high-ranking Indian Army officers, the fact that the battalion did not flinch and carried out its assigned role creditably demonstrated the loyalty of Indian Muslim soldiers.[9] However, this may have been an exceptional case and may indicate hopeful thinking within the Indian military.[10] Muslim representation in the Indian armed forces remains very low in proportion to the Indian Muslim population and their deployment in combat against Pakistan is rare.

On personnel matters, the Indian Army has attempted to act objectively, appointing and promoting Muslim officers on the basis of seniority and merit. Thus, the longest serving commandant of the National Defense Academy at

Khadakvasla—India's equivalent of a joint West Point, Air Force Academy, and Naval Academy—was Major General Enayat E. Habibullah, who was in charge for over six years, starting in the late 1950s. It was General Habibullah who began "Indianizing" the ethos of the officer corps from its old British military mentality. Similarly, Major General Shami Khan, a member of the Indian Muslim nobility of Rampur (and hence a cousin of retired Pakistani General Sahabzada Yaqub Khan, who was military governor of East Pakistan and later the Foreign Minister of Pakistan), was given several postings on the West Pakistani front during his career. Eventually, he attained the rank of deputy adjutant general.

THE ROLE OF THE MILITARY IN EXTERNAL DEFENSE

The wars against Pakistan and China generally produced a sense of national unity and purpose. This observation was probably more true of the war with China in 1962 than the wars with Pakistan in 1947-48, 1965, and 1971. Indo-Pakistani tensions have generated political sensitivity and emotion and have confused and strained the loyalty of Indian Muslims. Hindu nationalists may claim that such loyalty among most Indian Muslims, who in 1995 numbered about 120 million, or about 12 percent of the population, never existed and therefore the wars with Pakistan have heightened Hindu-Muslim tensions in India. On the other hand, external wars have produced a high sense of nationalism among Hindus, Sikhs, Christians, and Parsees, and perhaps also among many Muslim elites who had never supported the concept of Pakistan and who felt that their future lay with India.

Especially during the 1965 and 1971 Indo-Pakistani wars, the government of India went to considerable pains to highlight the fact that war between India and Pakistan was war between two different political systems and ideologies: a democratic and secular state versus an authoritarian and theocratic state. The courage, bravery, and sacrifice of the few Muslims who served in the Indian Army, Air Force, and Navy to defend India's secularism and democracy have been given a great deal of publicity to the point of exaggeration. For instance, during the 1965 Indo-Pakistani war, the bravery and death in the line of duty of a Muslim soldier, Abdul Hamid, was given much fanfare by the Indian press; much of the story had been orchestrated by the Indian government, which constituted virtually the only source of information on such matters.

The 1962 war with China produced a feeling of nationalism and unity in India. The war was portrayed as one between a free and democratic state versus a Communist and expansionist state. Unlike the wars with Pakistan, which one American author described as a domestic Hindu-Muslim "communal riot with armor," the war with China could readily unite India's many religious and linguistic communities.[11] There was no Chinese community in India. To be sure, there were some tensions and misgivings among some Indian Communists who had always looked to the Communist experience in the Soviet Union and China for inspiration. More particularly, Mao Zedong's political philosophy and the Chinese Communist revolution carried greater relevance for the Indian Communist movement than did that of the Soviet Union since economic conditions were similar in India and China.

However, at the time of the October-December 1962 Sino-Indian war, the Sino-Soviet split was already intensifying and Communist movements all over the world were being split into pro-Chinese and pro-Soviet factions. This was to occur in India as well toward the end of 1963, following the open rift between Moscow and Beijing in July 1963. During the Sino-Indian war, several suspected pro-Chinese Indian Communists, especially in the states of Kerala, West Bengal, and Andhra Pradesh, were arrested under the newly instituted Defense of India Rules. But they were few in number, and they were released following the termination of hostilities.

In short, political confrontation and war against China would appear to be good for the consolidation of democracy and national integration in India. War against Pakistan tends to produce solidarity among the myriad linguistic and caste groups that form the Hindu majority, but may polarize relations between Hindus and Muslims. Some opposition members of parliament have even alleged that Prime Minister Indira Gandhi promoted conditions of imminent war in order to gain political support and perpetuate Congress government rule in India. Similarly, Prime Minister Rajiv Gandhi periodically alluded to the "foreign hand," implying Pakistan, inciting violence in Punjab and referred to "war preparations" across the border. Such statements, in response to Pakistani reactions to India's massive "Brasstacks" war exercises in early 1987 in the Rajasthan desert, were made on the eve of state elections in three states. However, Rajiv Gandhi's Congress Party lost to the Communist parties in two states, West Bengal and Tripura, and managed a "victory" only as a junior partner of the National Conference in the infamous elections in Kashmir. Again, the Congress Party—now in opposition, but still led by Rajiv Gandhi—tried to use the threat of war with Pakistan, over its support of separatists in Kashmir and Punjab, to undermine the minority government of the Janata Dal/National Front under Prime Minister V. P. Singh.

Although Indian politicians may see opportunities to drum up support by sounding the alarms of war with an external enemy, the military has usually tried to ignore these claims or maintained a moderate posture. In general, it should be apparent that the greater visibility and role that the military achieves with regard to a foreign enemy, the greater the solidarity and confidence within the military, and the greater the sense of national unity among the public at large. But it should also be noted that India's external wars have been of short duration. Prolonged war could well undermine the stability and unity of the country.

THE MILITARY AND INTERNAL SECURITY

Almost to a man, the leaders of the armed forces are convinced that the regular military should not be used to maintain internal security. The military argues that to use the armed services "against their own people" would not only produce a breakdown in the military-civilian trust that has been built up over several decades, but also—if the army were deployed on domestic security missions in the border provinces such as Punjab, Kashmir, and Assam—undermine its own ability to fight a war properly, because of the alienation of the people living in those regions.[12] The military would be seen eventually as the enemy of the people, a situation that may be found in Pakistan and several other developing countries in Asia, Africa, and Latin America.

In Pakistan, the military had a record of violent suppressions in Balochistan and in East Pakistan before the latter broke away to become the independent state of Bangladesh. The military regime of Zia-ul Haq was engaged in political battles against various opposition groups in Pakistan, especially the faction of the "Movement for the Restoration Democracy" led by Benazir Bhutto. After Benazir came to power through the electoral process, the military continued to be a threat to her government. Eventually, she was deposed by the civilian president of Pakistan, Ghulam Ishaq Khan, but there were suspicions that the military was behind the dismissal of her government. This is the kind of situation that the military in India would like to avoid.

Second, the armed services are not equipped or trained to deal with problems of internal law and order. As Lieutenant General M. L. Thapan noted: "A fundamental principle of war is concentration of men and materiel at the right place and at the right time."[13] Internal security duties, on the other hand, "require dispersion and the use of minimum force since our own countrymen are involved." Similarly, Lieutenant General A. M. Vohra observed that because the army does not mingle with the crowds as the police are required to do, the army's ability to sense and deal with internal riots is severely limited.

Third, the use of the armed services for internal security may produce a breakdown in military training and in readiness for dealing with external security. It may also encourage politicization and corruption. Frequent use of the military for internal purposes would invariably create friction and arouse the emotions of both civilians and soldiers and could eventually result in struggles between the two, leading to military coups and takeovers.

Ironically, the deployment of the military in India as an internal constabulary force to maintain law and order is more reminiscent of the British Raj than of an independent democratic state. The British colonial strategy was to use "alien" Indian troops to suppress political demonstrations and to wage counterinsurgency warfare both in India and in its overseas empire. For example, the British used Gurkha troops to fire on peaceful demonstrators at Jalianwallah Bagh in Punjab, causing the massacre of hundreds of civilians. Similarly, in independent India, the Sikh Light Infantry and other lightly armed and mobile north Indian units (except for Gurkha regiments or paramilitary units like the Assam Rifles, who may have felt some ethnic or racial empathy) were fielded at various times against the Chinese-backed guerrillas in the northeastern tribal states of Nagaland and Mizoram.[14] When this option, for social or political reasons, is considered too risky, the preferred solution is to deploy the integrated Brigade of Guards to ensure that no stigma attaches to any one communal regiment as the executor of British colonial–style "police action."

The British strategy of maintaining law and order also went as far as deploying troops in their own regions and against their own communities. Presumably, this fostered a sense of discipline and obedience to line of command in the security forces. Local police forces and other armed constabulary were used routinely to suppress both peaceful and violent demonstrations during the Indian independence struggle. This strategy may be seen in one of the major actions taken in the Punjab toward the end of British rule. In the 1930s, in what was known as the Khaskar Rebellion, under instructions from the Muslim chief minister of pre-partition Punjab, Sir Sikander Hayyat Khan, a Muslim deputy commissioner led mostly Muslim troops against armed Muslim fundamentalist dissenters in a mosque in the Jhelum district of Punjab (now West Punjab in Pakistan). Thus, the rebellion was crushed while the British remained at a distance. Elsewhere in the world, parallels may be seen in the use of Black security policemen by the earlier White-controlled state of South Africa to suppress Black demonstrators.

Similarly, Operation Blue Star, the assault by the Indian Army to dislodge well-armed Sikh secessionists entrenched in the Golden Temple in Amritsar, was under the command of a Sikh general, Lieutenant General Rajeshwar Singh

Dayal, and the Brigade of the Guards elite strike force was led by a Muslim colonel and included Sikh soldiers.[15] The selection of a Sikh commander and the inclusion of Sikh soldiers was probably not a coincidence. It appeared consistent with the colonial practice of "neutralizing" a rebellious community by carrying out military action under the leadership and support of persons from that community. In the Punjab case, it did not work. Apart from triggering Sikh mutinies and desertions from Sikh regiments elsewhere, it alienated most moderate Sikhs, who until then were with the government, even if they had some grievances. However, government officials have claimed, and quite rightly, that most Sikh soldiers remained loyal to their units. This was also demonstrated by the fact that the Sikh commander and the Sikh soldiers that formed part of the assault team did not flinch from carrying out civilian orders for military action against the Golden Temple. A somewhat similar situation may be seen in Kashmir, where the head of the Indian Army sent to deal with the Kashmir uprising that broke out in 1989 was a Muslim, Lieutenant General Mohammed Abdullah Zaki.

When dealing with problems of internal security, the Indian military has sometimes continued yet another of the policies of the British in India. The government, by accident or design, has sent military regiments comprised of neutral ethnic groups to deal with various problems of internal violence: it has sent Gurkha, Rajput, or Maratha regiments to Kashmir or Punjab; Sikh or Madras regiments to Assam; and so on.[16] In comparison, what makes the Sri Lankan situation difficult is that there is no significant neutral third ethnic group to deal with the problem between the Tamils and the Sinhalese. Even if substantial forces can be raised from the mainly Tamil-speaking Muslim Moors, the policy may aggravate Hindu-Muslim tensions between Tamils and Moors. The Sri Lankan military is almost exclusively Sinhalese, and the civil war is between armed Tamils and Sinhalese government forces. Until recently, the Colombo government was not able to recruit Tamils to fight the rebellious Liberation Tigers of Tamil Ealam. But with the alienation of many Tamils from the Tigers, Tamil militia are fighting alongside Sri Lankan forces against the Tigers.

In Pakistan, the problem is similar. The military is 80 percent Punjabi, with much of the rest being Pashtuns from the North-West Frontier Province. Even the "Balochi" regiments are now becoming increasingly Punjabi and Pashtun. The Sindhis are barely represented in the armed forces, and the Pakistan Army operation in Sindh is being conducted almost entirely by non-Sindhi forces. In the past, mainly Punjabi soldiers were used to suppress insurgencies among Bengalis, Sindhis, and Balochis, thereby aggravating ethnic perceptions of Punjabi domination and persecution.

The deployment of 55,000 Indian Peace-Keeping Forces (IPKF) "overseas" in Sri Lanka from 1987 to 1990 has been an unusual experience for the Indian armed forces. The Indian military, having argued that its job should not include the control and suppression of internal ethnic insurgencies, was then sent to do just that in another country, on a very large scale. The Indian Army, which was initially dispatched to disarm the Tamil insurgents and protect Tamil civilians, found itself engaged in a bloody war with a faction of the ethnic group it was sent to protect. The IPKF was ambushed and mauled by female Tamil fighters.[17] That the enemy was usually unknown, that it could appear from anywhere, and that it could include women, contributed to the general demoralization of the IPKF in the field. The result of the three-year IPKF operation in Sri Lanka was a lowering of military professionalism and effectiveness, something that the Indian Army would like to avoid in India. If the Indian Army learned a lesson from its military involvement in Sri Lanka, it was that civil wars among ethnic groups cannot be easily policed by "neutral," external, third-party armed forces. The intervening military gets sucked into the quagmire.

CIVILIAN RULE, THE MILITARY, AND INTERNAL SECURITY

Despite military opposition, civilian leaders feel that domestic situations may sometimes exist in which limited military participation becomes inevitable, even if undesirable. In an interview in 1981, Jagjivan Ram, former defense minister in the Congress government and deputy prime minister in the Janata government, stated that in cases of extreme breakdown of law and order, the mere introduction of army units in troubled areas tends to produce a pacifying atmosphere without those units having to resort to any actual force.[18] Indeed, the army rarely uses force when deployed in riot-torn areas and this results in a lower number of deaths than might be caused if police were deployed and compelled to open fire on violent mobs. With some exaggeration, former chief of army staff General V. N. Sharma noted:

> The main reason for military success in law and order duties is the complete trust of the citizen in the reasonably fair conduct of the soldier and that the military would never take political sides nor ever become a slave of any "political party weighted" orders of the central government. Army leadership at all levels has a good idea of causes of political upheavals and largely get excellent support from officials of the civil administration

and police officers. When such support from local officials and police does not exist, the military may not be too successful though it does use its own intelligence to try and get at the truth. . . . It appears that the use of the army [for internal security duties] is only going to increase until criminalized politics and corruption are corrected.[19]

However, military leaders interviewed in 1981 pointed out that the army had succeeded in maintaining law and order only because the armed forces had thus far been used sparingly. Because frequent use of armed forces could destroy their pacifying effect, military leaders felt that the goal of the central government should be the total avoidance of the use of the armed services for internal security. In strife-torn Punjab and Kashmir, the Indian Army was deployed, but failed to bring peace and was largely withdrawn to be replaced by paramilitary forces.

However, military leaders agree that the use of the armed forces may prove unavoidable in two domestic areas. The first concerns the problem of dealing with insurgencies, such as those in the northeast of India and Kashmir. But even in the case of insurgencies, the military leaders caution against frequent use of the armed forces. Persistent insurgencies like those that prevailed in Nagaland and Mizoram, as Generals Vohra and Thapan pointed out in the early 1980s, suggest the need for political settlements rather than military solutions. Their advice was taken to heart by the government of India, which has negotiated deals with the Nagas and Mizos whereby the rebel leaders have accepted Indian nationality, foresworn violence, entered the political mainstream, won elections, and are now holding power in their own states. Similar conditions are being brought about in Punjab and Assam. That political gestures of accommodation are not succeeding in Kashmir would imply that government concessions to the dissidents have not gone far enough, or that the process of alienation of the ethnic community has gone too far.

The second area in which the military agrees it has a contribution to make is the provision of aid to civilian authorities, especially during times of natural disasters. There is general consensus within the military that this constitutes one of its essential tasks. However, a somewhat ambiguous line separates military relief operations and reconstruction in the aftermath of a natural calamity from prolonged participation in civilian reconstruction efforts. No doubt, the military's mechanical, civil, and electrical engineers and military labor could contribute much toward civilian reconstruction beyond the immediate natural disaster. But if such support moves toward becoming a more permanent operation, it turns into a major military role in civilian development programs, something the Indian military has rejected.

The Indian Army has carried out aid to civilian authorities almost routinely, especially when providing rescue operations and assistance to victims of floods during heavy monsoon rains. The Indian Air Force has provided aircraft and helicopter transport during such rescue missions. The domestic nonsecurity role of the armed services is good public relations and projects the military as a friend of all Indians of every class, creed, and community. Since the personnel from the armed services that are utilized in this role are drawn from all over the country, a sense of national unity and support in the "hour of need" of those less fortunate is provided.

While the military's role in providing disaster relief is generally taken for granted, there have been periodic suggestions that during prolonged periods of peace, the armed services should be utilized on a more regular basis in India's development programs. An extension of this argument is that a much larger "People's Liberation Army" should be formed, along the Communist Chinese model, whose functions would be defense against external aggression during times of war, as well as participation in various economic development projects during times of peace. In this way, a large standing military would not prove to be an economic liability to the nation, and the interaction of the military with the people would keep the military in touch with the mainstream of civilian life.

The military has no objections to the role of providing disaster relief, but has strongly resisted any attempt to engage it in regular development projects.[20] From the standpoint of the military, such a policy would politicize the armed forces, draw it into the underground economic system of bribery and black marketeering, and increase the probability of its direct or indirect involvement in national politics. The temptation to engineer a military coup against the civilian government might not then be far behind. Even the proposal to use the vast army-held cantonment lands for the "Grow More Food" campaign of the early 1950s, which was endorsed by the first Indian commander-in-chief, General K. M. Cariappa, was resisted by other high-ranking Indian military commanders. All such "civilian" tasks are perceived to reduce the professionalism and combat effectiveness of the armed forces, which are necessary to maintain in case of the sudden eruption of hostilities. Military training and military alert need to be maintained at all times. Otherwise, slackness and ineptitude may creep into the military system and lead to a breakdown of military command and control, with disastrous effects for defense against external attacks.

In any case, the idea of a large-standing People's Liberation Army of about 10 million soldiers is unacceptable to most Indian politicians, who fear threats to democratic civilian rule. It would lead to the fusion of the civilian and military domains and to the potential loss of civilian control over the military.

INTERNAL SECURITY AND
THE RISE OF PARAMILITARY FORCES

The government's response to the demands of the Indian armed services not to use the military for internal security has been to increase the size of existing paramilitary forces, or to raise new ones.[21] The paramilitary forces, which are under the control of the Home Ministry and/or the Cabinet, are now being used in place of the Indian Army in areas of insurgency and terrorism. They include the Provincial Armed Constabulary (PAC), the Central Reserve Police Force (CRPF), the Border Security Force (BSF), and the Assam Rifles, which have been utilized extensively in Uttar Pradesh, Kashmir, Punjab, and Assam. Additionally, after the debacle in 1984 of Operation Blue Star, the Indian government raised a new elite force called the National Security Guards (NSG) who were recruited mainly from the Indian Army. The NSG was used in 1988 in the second operation against the Golden Temple (code named "Operation Black Thunder") to root out the terrorists ensconced within. This time there were few casualties and the operation provoked relatively little alienation among the Sikhs. In 1993, a new paramilitary force known as the Rashtriya Rifles (National Rifles) was formed under the command of the Indian Army and jurisdiction of the Ministry of Defense to deal exclusively with problems of internal security.

The security forces operating in Kashmir and Punjab are now mainly paramilitary forces. Intervention by the regular armed forces usually occurs when an external military factor may be involved. This includes interception of arms and of armed guerrillas moving across the frontiers with Pakistan, China, Bangladesh, and Myanmar. The exception was in Assam, where four Indian Army divisions joined several paramilitary companies in operations against the United Liberation Front of Assam in the 1980s and early 1990s.

While this has satisfied the Indian military, other problems associated with the policy of deploying paramilitary forces have arisen. First, the paramilitary forces, especially the PAC, have often proved to be undisciplined, reckless, and destructive. Instead of solving the problem of Hindu-Muslim killings and ethnic insurgencies, they have added to the problem or become part of the problem itself. The PAC has taken sides with the Hindus and has massacred Muslims indiscriminately in Moradabad and Meerut in Uttar Pradesh. Similarly, allegations of human rights violations, including torture and rape, have been leveled at other paramilitary forces by both Indian and foreign groups. There have been some allegations against units of the Indian Army as well in Kashmir, but not as many as against the BSF and the CRPF operating there.

Table 5.1 Armed Forces in South Asia								
(In thousands)								
1986	1987	1988	1989	1990	1991	1992	1993	1994
India 1492	1502	1362	1260	1262	1265	1265	1265	1265
Pakistan 573	560	560	560	597	565	580	577	587
Bangladesh 91	101	101	103	103	106	107	107	115
Sri Lanka 37	48	47	47	65	88	105	110	126

Source of information: *The Military Balance,* an annual publication of the International Institute for Strategic Studies, London.

The Indian Army claims that atrocities committed by their forces, wherever proven, have been quietly dealt with through court-martials and punishment.

As noted earlier, former defense minister Jagjivan Ram's observation that the use of paramilitary forces aggravates internal security issues while the introduction of the regular military produces a calming effect in troubled areas carries limited validity. Frequent or excessive use of the military clearly does not produce a calming effect. This is evident in Kashmir, Punjab, and Assam. Moreover, a large standing paramilitary force involved in the maintenance of internal security can threaten democratic values and practices as much as the regular military. While the size of the regular armed forces has not increased much since the 1965 Indo-Pakistani war, the size of the paramilitary forces has been increasing steadily since the mid-1970s. The regular armed forces reached a peak of 1.3 million uniformed personnel in the mid-1960s and remained approximately at that figure thereafter; but since the total Indian population has doubled in the 30 years since 1965, the proportionate size of the military to the population has actually halved. This clearly has implications for hundreds of thousands of able-bodied men who see the Indian military as a source of stable and well-paid employment with only a remote prospect of actually seeing life-threatening combat during their 7- to 15-year commissions. The comparative figures of South Asian armed forces shown in table 5.1 are illustrative.

In comparison, there are about 960,000 paramilitary forces, plus another 460,000 Home Guard forces. If one includes the Home Guard, which mainly does disaster relief work and social development work, but which may also be called on to maintain law and order, the total number of paramilitary forces would add up to almost 1.5 million, exceeding the 1.3 million members of the

			(In thousands)		
Table 5.2 Paramilitary Forces in India					
	1990	1991	1992	1993	1994
National Security Guards (Cabinet)	5.0	5.0	7.5	7.5	7.5
Central Reserve Police Force (Home)	90.0	100.0	125.0	125.0	120.0
Border Security Force (Home)	90.0	140.0	171.0	171.0	120.0
Ladakh Scouts (Home)	5.0	5.0	5.0	N.A.	N.A.
Indo-Tibetan Border Police (Home)	14.0	22.0	29.0	29.0	29.0
Special Frontier Force (Cabinet)	8.0	10.0	10.0	10.0	10.0
Central Industrial Security Force (Home)	70.0	55.0	74.0	74.0	50.0
Defense Security Corps (Defense)	30.0	30.0	31.0	31.0	31.0
Railway Protection Force (Railways)	70.0	60.0	70.0	70.0	70.0
Provincial Armed Constabulary (Home)	250.0	250.0	400.0	400.0	N.A
Rashtriya Rifles (Defense)	—	—	—	10.0	30.0
Home Guards (Home)	N.A.	N.A.	N.A.	464.0	462.0

Source: Pervaiz Iqbal Cheema, "Arms Procurement Policy of Pakistan," Paper presented at the Stockholm International Peace Research Institute, September 22-24, 1995.

regular armed forces. The growth of paramilitary forces in India are shown in table 5.2.

This rise in paramilitary forces may appear even more disturbing when set against a parallel increase in various legislative acts and constitutional amendments.[22] Since the declaration of the National Security Emergency between 1975 and 1977, President's Rule or special ordinances have been invoked in many states, including Kashmir, Punjab, and Assam. Other acts and amendments passed since 1975 for security purposes include the 42nd Amendment in 1976, the National Security Act of 1980, the Terrorist Affected Areas Special Courts Act of 1984, the Terrorist and Disruptive Activities Preventive Act of 1987, the 59th Amendment to Article 352 in 1988, and the Defamation Bill, restricting press freedom, in 1988. All of these acts and amendments imply an increase in demand for, and use of, paramilitary forces. Thus, as more legislative acts restricting individual freedoms are introduced in parliament, the internal military capabilities to enforce such legislation are also being increased.

Could paramilitary forces constitute a threat to democracy in India? No doubt, it would be difficult for paramilitary forces in India to organize a coup against civilian rule because the regular armed forces could almost certainly be relied on to intervene and crush such a move. Like the regular military, which is divided according to service and commands, the paramilitary forces are also divided and separated according to functions and regions. Just as the regular military has no central command (such as a chief of defense staff) except civilian control under the Ministry of Defense, the paramilitary forces have no central command except civilian control under the Home Ministry. Nevertheless, if the size of the paramilitary forces were to continue to increase, it would indicate that the internal security problems of India are not being resolved satisfactorily, and it would conjure up visions of a growing police state in India.

THE CONSEQUENCES OF MILITARY
INVOLVEMENT IN INTERNAL SECURITY

The dilemma remains that the use of the regular armed forces for internal security is unacceptable in a democracy. The perennial use of the regular armed forces to combat insurgency and terrorism within the state can lead to the politicization and corruption of the military. In a democracy, the principle of military subordination to civilian authorities will be compromised, and this may eventually lead to military coups and the overthrow of civilian regimes. If external threats exist, defense preparations may be undermined. The chief of staff of the Indian Army, General S. F. Rodrigues, stated in June 1992 that "large scale and frequent deployment of troops to combat insurgency certainly affects the training of troops in their primary role of combatting external aggression and safeguarding the security of national borders."[23] During the 1971 Bengali revolt in East Pakistan, the Pakistani military was not merely engaged in combatting the insurgents, but was also responsible for the massacre of thousands of civilians. These conditions produced a general deterioration in

Pakistani war preparations and the demoralization of the Pakistan Army. The army became ineffective as a fighting force and provided little resistance to the Indian military invasion, surrendering within two weeks of the war.

The continued use of the armed forces for the maintenance of internal security will also alienate the military from the people, who increasingly will see the military as the enemy rather as than their protector. These observations provide an increasing dilemma for the states of South Asia, all of which are now civilian democracies. To what extent should the regular military be used for the maintenance of internal security? The answer becomes more difficult when a proxy war is being waged through the training and arming of insurgents across international frontiers, and the lines between internal and external wars become blurred.

On balance, the Indian Army's misgivings over its use in the maintenance of internal security appear to have been justified. Although there have been minor mutinies and desertions in the police and paramilitary forces in the past, the army's assault on the Golden Temple in Amritsar in June 1984 set off the first, though brief and limited, military mutiny in independent India. Only two other mutinies had occurred in the history of the Indian armed forces in the nineteenth and twentieth centuries, and both had occurred under the British. The first was the Great Indian Mutiny of 1857-58, in which Indian sepoys (foot soldiers) revolted against the commanding British officers. The second was the mutiny by Indian seamen of the Royal Indian Navy against British naval commanders in 1946. In retrospect, both mutinies were seen as milestones in the road toward Indian independence. In a similar manner, Sikh separatists claimed that the mutiny by Sikh soldiers in the immediate aftermath of the attack on the Golden Temple in 1984 would be a milestone toward an independent Khalistan. An independent Khalistan may then herald the beginning of the disintegration of India.

The Sikh mutiny of 1984, though minor and confined, raises fundamental questions about the domestic role of the armed forces. In the short term, following the army's assault on the temple, the Indian government sought to restore the holy shrine to Sikh civilian control and to pacify the anger felt by most Sikhs throughout India and abroad. At the same time, the military establishment sought to restore the confidence and commitment of the army's Sikh soldiers, who have historically distinguished themselves in the defense of India.

In the long term, the solution to avoiding a breakdown in civilian-military trust lies in separating (or shielding) the military from the role of maintaining internal security. In the aftermath of Operation Blue Star, representations to this effect were made by the military to Prime Minister Indira Gandhi and resulted in the creation of the National Security Guards, a special elite paramilitary force separate from the regular armed forces but raised partly from retired enlisted men and officers from the armed forces.[24] The distinction between the regular armed forces and the elite paramilitary forces has often appeared to be thin or not properly recognized by the civilian population. Where paramilitary forces have been sent into operation, as they have been in the Punjab and Kashmir, this may also cause the reputation of the regular armed forces to become tainted. Part of the problem arises from overlapping roles. Some paramilitary forces, such as the Border Security Force, the Indo-Tibetan Border Police, and the Assam Rifles, play a role in the maintenance of external and internal security, while the Indian Army has been frequently deployed to deal with large-scale domestic violence.

The decision in 1993 to create the 30,000-strong Rashtriya Rifles (RR) poses special problems.[25] Since it is to be commanded by the Indian Army and controlled by the Ministry of Defense, its deployment for internal security will not help the Indian Army to remain aloof or impartial in internal struggles. The RR will be identified with the army by the public. If the RR replaces many units of the paramilitary forces, this will only generate unhealthy political competition among forces under the Ministries of Home and Defense. The policy of raising paramilitary forces in order to keep the regular armed forces out of domestic struggles, with all its pros and cons, will have been reversed.

6

The Economic
Dimension

DEMOCRACY AND THE DEVELOPMENT FIRST THESIS

In addition to the question raised in earlier chapters of promoting security at the expense of democracy, a corollary issue is one of emphasizing economic development over democracy in order to achieve both faster rates of economic growth and greater defense capability and overall national security. Rapid economic development may be seen as a prerequisite for a strong defense program and for the ability to maintain internal stability through the advancement of general prosperity. Faster rates of economic growth, the generation of more foreign exchange, and higher levels of GNP imply not only the ability to procure more weapons from home and abroad, but also greater economic well-being and satisfaction at home. Both external and internal security are thereby enhanced.

Based on the experiences of East Asian and Southeast Asian countries, a development first approach may suggest that authoritarian regimes are more likely to deliver economic growth. South Korea, Taiwan, Singapore, Indonesia, and Thailand have achieved high rates of economic growth and strong defense programs under authoritarian systems. Political dissent and economic and political disruptions within the state have been kept largely under control. In Japan, despite the prevalence of democratic structures and procedures, the economy and the labor force have functioned in a disciplined manner that is typical of the authoritarian systems of the other East Asian countries. The tradition and custom of authoritarian values appear to have been maintained in Japan under a democratic system and may have contributed to Japan's economic success. In Latin America, the experience of Chile is equally revealing. After the overthrow of the democratically elected Marxist government of Salvador Allende in 1971, Chile was ruled by a military dictatorship led by General Augusto Pinochet for more than 20 years. Despite the lack of political freedom, and amidst accusations of widespread human rights violations, Chile experienced rapid economic growth and prosperity.

According to this line of reasoning, exemplified, for instance, by the writings of Barrington Moore, a Leninist state like China was likely to modernize faster than a democracy such as India.[1] Democracies are unable to provide the political and economic discipline needed for national security and economic prosperity. Conversely, authoritarian systems are better able to ensure stable political order and thus promote faster rates of economic growth and higher levels of defense capabilities.

Order and disorder during the process of economic development are starkly visible in China and India. Although the visitor can "see" the economic boom in the bustling cities of Beijing and Shanghai in China, and New Delhi and Bombay in India, the Indian cities appear to be buckling under the pressure of large-scale migrations of people from the rural to the urban areas. Under authoritarianism, China has been better able to manage development in the city and the countryside.[2]

However, there is disagreement on this issue. The Soviet or Chinese type of totalitarian political systems and command economies did not succeed. Comparing China and India's performance, Edward Friedman observed the following:

> At the end of the Mao era, China was no more industrialized than India; standards of living were similar. In fact, China had, in many ways, experienced far less material progress than India. It lacked India's international level corps of scientists and technicians that permitted India to become the leader in Third World computer software exports. In China's capital, Beijing, at Mao's death, only 2 percent of government offices had telephones. Leninist states, after exhausting the productivity of dragooned corvee labor left in place wasteful, militarized, heavy steel companies incapable of efficiency, competition, innovation or moving up the value added labor.[3]

Nevertheless, China operating under a Leninist political system and a free-market capitalist economy appears to have outclassed India in economic growth. Economic growth rates since 1980 have annually averaged between 8 and 10 percent in China compared to India's average of about 3 to 5 percent. But this may be considered misleading because China introduced its reforms in the mid-1970s while India embarked on its economic reforms in 1991. The optimistic expectation of those who back India's democratic free-market economy as more likely to succeed in the long run than that of China's Leninist free-market economy is reflected in the following views of Karen E. House in the *Wall Street Journal:*

> India is a nation breaking loose from the self-imposed shackles of socialism but doing so without rejecting the richness of its deep and diverse culture. Having rejected both Confucianism and Maoism, China today venerates only the god of rampant materialism. India is a nation in only its fourth year of a determined program of economic liberalization, but more importantly it is approaching its 50th year as a genuine democracy and its third century of commitment to a British-based rule of law. By contrast, China, in its second decade of economic liberalization, remains an authoritarian society ruled not by law but by the whims and anxieties of old men. . . . Finally, India offers what in a competitive world may be the most valuable software of all—minds that have been permitted to be open, inquisitive and creative, and men and women who are fluent in the global language of business, English. . . . "On the surface, China looks stable, but underneath it's not," says a Japanese diplomat. "On the surface, India looks chaotic, but underneath it is stable." . . . The issue for investors, of course, doesn't have to be China or India. Opportunity exists in both. But for the foreseeable future—five to ten years—the tortoise of India is a safer and better bet than the galloping hare to its north.[4]

There was another reason for the spectacular success of the non-Communist East countries, including democratic Japan: state intervention and support to promote export-oriented economies. The postwar Japanese economy has been directed by institutionalized and centralized decision-making structures commanded by a powerful state bureaucracy. As Shalendra Sharma observed:

> Specifically, the pervasive belief that the secret of the East Asian miracle was (and is) their free-market oriented development strategy is fundamentally flawed because it fails to take into account the role of East Asia's interventionist states in guiding economic development. . . . The East Asian states went far beyond the norms of prescribed neutral policy. The

market-oriented policies were accompanied by discretionary state intervention that complemented and directed rather than negated market forces.... In their path-breaking works, Barrington Moore and Alexander Gerschenkron have lucidly shown that capitalist industrial development required some sort of an "alliance" between the state and the emerging bourgeois classes.[5]

The economic miracles in Japan, South Korea, Taiwan, and Thailand also carry another common thread. These states were all part of the American security network to contain the Communist threat. In all of them, security pressures, and especially American security interests, resulted in a high level of American military involvement and presence. These security ties with the United States resulted in extensive economic ties that have been mainly advantageous to the East Asian countries themselves and less so for the United States. The economic explosion of Japan, South Korea, Taiwan, and Thailand has had much to do with American investments in these countries and the generous markets the United States allowed them, which served as springboards for an extended economic boom during the Cold War. Similarly, the United States preferred a military dictatorship rather than a Marxist regime in Chile. The more politically stable and open economy under the Chilean generals led to a generous infusion of American investment. As in the case of East Asia, this may explain why Chile prospered, but it does not explain why other Latin American countries under military or civilian dictatorships did not. Perhaps the explanation is that economic performance is largely a function of economic policy and economic capacity, irrespective of whether a country is a democracy or a dictatorship.

INDO-U.S. SECURITY AND ECONOMIC COOPERATION

Since the mid-1980s, India has been seeking closer security ties with the United States, a policy that took on greater momentum with the collapse of the Soviet Union in 1991. However, this search for collaborative security arrangements has occurred without mutual perceptions of common external enemies, the standard prerequisite for forging a military alliance relationship. As a consequence, Indo-U.S. military collaborative effort has not gotten very far. However, Indian economic liberalization and reform is producing an explosion of American investment in India. This growing economic interdependence between India and the United States may provide the grounds for security collaboration. K. Subrahmanyam, the Indian strategist who has lobbied for the development of nuclear weapons by India, and who was at one time a severe critic of the United States and an advocate of strong ties with the U.S.S.R., observed the following in 1995:

> The U.S., as has been seen in its relations with China, is prepared to subordinate its other foreign policy aims in favor of expanding commercial relations. The U.S. policies on Kashmir, and on Indian nuclear and missile options, will undergo appropriate changes if Indo-U.S. commercial relations intensify and Indo-U.S. trade reaches the levels of U.S.-China trade. Every U.S. investor, U.S. exporter to India and importer from India will listen to the Indian point of view from his business partners and will exhibit more empathy towards Indian problems and policies.[6]

Thus, while common security interests have generated greater economic ties between the United States and the East Asian countries, greater economic ties between India and the United States may generate more common security interests between the two countries in the future.[7] Such an unusual trend would imply that the priority of development in India's relationship with the United States would advance both security and democracy.

In the United States, political conservatives and Southern Christian fundamentalists argued for strong defense against the Soviet Union during the Cold War. Periodic attempts by liberals and moderates to cut back defense programs were considered dangerous to national security and unpatriotic. Although a strong American economy was considered essential for a strong American defense, American right-wing conservatives assumed that their demands for a stronger defense were not going to be at the expense of a strong economy or the erosion of democratic principles in the United States. In contrast, liberals and racial minorities in the United States were concerned with the opportunity costs high defense spending would have on domestic economic and social programs. Defense programs and military actions abroad were perceived to be disadvantageous to minorities and the poorer sections of the United States.

So, too, in India, political conservatives and Hindu nationalists have been more inclined to advocate the primacy of security needs and strong defense programs (including a nuclear weapons program) even if this implies that economic and social programs would be adversely affected and that some democratic rights would need to be curtailed. On the other hand, liberals and religious minorities in India would prefer to push economic development programs and the advancement of individual and democratic rights over the pursuit of expensive national security programs. In both democracies and authoritarian systems, the territorial integrity of the state against outside aggression and the maintenance of law and order at home are the familiar goals of conservative agendas. Conservatives have usually considered the economic consequences of such external and internal security programs to be greatly exaggerated or to be unavoidable burdens.

A long-standing question, which was the subject of considerable controversy in the past, is whether defense programs and the maintenance of a large military force adversely affect development programs. In India, the issue assumed an element of urgency following the wars with China in 1962 and with Pakistan in 1965. While the debate has not gone away, the issue has been given less attention since economic reforms were initiated in India. As former defense secretary G. C. Katoch observed: "Gone are the days when phrases like 'hostile security environment' and 'the imperative needs of modernisation of the Armed Forces' were dinned into one's ear so that a large section of public opinion had become conditioned to look upon a high level of defence spending as not only inevitable, but perhaps even desirable."[8] In the post–Cold War era, the debate revolved around the issue of moving from a mainly socialist economic system to a private-sector capitalist system and the extent and speed of economic reforms necessary to make this transition. The question here was whether such a transition from socialism to private-sector capitalism would contribute to domestic and regional political stability and overall national security.

DEFENSE AND DEVELOPMENT

The end of the Cold War and the new Indian commitment to economic liberalization, privatization, and marketization have affected the traditional defense-development debate in India. Whereas in the past this debate took place in a socialist context, it must now take place in a private-sector capitalist context. A change in the economic system may not make a difference to the debate, except perhaps in the actual or perceived efficiency of socialist and capitalist economic systems. In other words, if a private-sector capitalist economic system is considered more efficient than a socialist one, then "the economic burden of defense" is less because of a more healthy economy and higher rates of economic growth. The economic burden of defense may be defined broadly as the impact of defense programs on the national economy. The ability of the economic system to absorb defense expenditures and diversions to weapons production without unsettling effects on the economy may be considered a low burden of defense. Conversely, adverse effects on the economy because of large defense programs may be considered a high burden of defense. Such a consequential definition provides a more realistic measure of the defense burden. Annual defense expenditures as a percentage of GNP provide a standard fixed indicator of the burden of defense and may be more useful for cross-national comparisons.

However, as discussed below, countries with high defense/GNP percentages have not necessarily fared worse economically than those countries that spend a lower percentage of their GNP on defense. The ability of a country to shoulder a high defense burden depends greatly on the prevailing health of the economy. Some national economies are able to sustain more defense programs than others without sowing the seeds of their own destruction. Hence the argument many development economists advance is that Third World countries cannot afford the costs of defense programs even if their defense/GNP percentages are not substantially different from those of advanced industrialized states.

Such observations and definitions may be considered debatable. Whatever the failures of the Soviet Communist economic system, it was able to deliver weapons systems that were competitive technologically with those of the United States and Western Europe. But the economic burden of defense programs in the Soviet Union (where they cost approximately 15 percent of GNP) was much higher than that of defense programs in the United States (where they cost approximately 6 percent of GNP). This may have contributed to the collapse of the Soviet economy and to the eventual disintegration of the Soviet Union itself in 1991. On the other hand, the privatization of defense production through government contracting, or defense production undertaken by state-owned enterprises that involves a great deal of subcontracting to private corporations, may have proved to be a more workable and effective economic arrangement in the United States and Western Europe than in the Soviet Union and China, where defense production was in the public sector. Thus, it was not so much the defense/GNP burden that proved the downfall of the Soviet Union as much as the inefficient economic system, although some conservative U.S. Republican Cold War strategists are inclined to believe that the pace set by the United States in the arms race drove the weaker Soviet Communist system into bankruptcy.

Compared to other developing and developed countries, India's defense expenditures expressed as a percentage of GNP or GDP have not been excessive. Ever since the period before the 1962 Sino-Indian war when defense/GNP percentages were around or below 2 percent, they have ranged between 3 and 4 percent, with some exceptions when they may have marginally exceeded 4 percent. However, even these figures must be treated with caution. Japan, which

Table 6.1 India's Defense Burden

	Percent of Total Government Expenditure	Percent of Gross Domestic Produce
1982-83	16.9	3.16
1983-84	16.4	3.14
1984-85	16.2	3.40
1985-86	15.2	3.41
1986-87	16.7	4.02
1987-88	17.5	4.07
1988-89	16.9	3.82
1989-90	15.5	3.67
1990-91 (Estimates)	14.8	3.55
1991-92 (Estimates)	14.4	3.55

Source: G. C. Katoch, "Defence Expenditure: Some Issues," *Indian Defence Review,* January 1992, 36.

spends only 1 percent of its GNP on defense, actually spends almost four times as much as India does on defense in absolute terms. The figures provided in table 6.1 are indicative of Indian defense expenditures relative to GDP and total government expenditure:

Since the sudden outbreak of the Sino-Indian war of 1962, which was followed three years later by the Indo-Pakistani war of 1965, the question of whether defense programs retard economic development has been subject to opposing interpretations.[9] The standard interpretation that is favored by most development economists is that there is an inverse relationship between defense expenditures and economic growth. Defense allocations represent opportunity costs for development. Thus, the greater the level of defense expenditures the lower the rate of economic growth, and vice versa. An opposing viewpoint claims that, within prudent limits, allocations to defense may boost development and economic efficiency through the sharing of technology and production facilities, through the generation of demand in civilian sectors of the economy, and through providing economies of scale in civilian and military production in areas such as aeronautics, automotive vehicles, shipbuilding, communications equipment, computers, and the like.

The first viewpoint—that defense programs represent opportunity costs for development—prevailed in India before the 1962 Sino-Indian war. This view did not change except that some came to believe that from a political and security standpoint, development without adequate defense might be futile. However, from the early 1970s onward, some Indian defense experts began to question the standard proposition that defense programs retarded development. Instead, defense may in fact boost the development program. This belief emerged following the findings of an empirical study of 44 developing countries undertaken by Emile Benoit, whose findings were published in 1973.[10]

In his empirical study, Benoit discovered that in 1963 and 1964, the years immediately after the Sino-Indian war, when Indian defense expenditures reached heights of 4.5 and 3.8 percent of GNP, India's GNP increased at an annual rate of 6.3 percent. This compared to a 4.5 percent annual average rate of economic growth between 1950 and 1961, when defense received annual allotments of about 2 percent of GNP. Moreover, this happened despite the fact that agricultural output rose at only 2.7 percent per annum in 1963 and 1964, thus eliminating the possibility that the spurt in economic growth may have been due to favorable monsoon rains. Additionally, Benoit's study indicated that the sudden increase in Indian defense expenditures after 1962 did not take place at the expense of investment. The average annual investment ratio (that is, investment relative to GNP) was about 16.5 percent during the three years from 1962 to 1964. This compared to an average annual rate of only 12.3 percent for the period 1951-64. Benoit, therefore, concluded that "while this historical experience could be coincidental—it does tend to support the possibility that rising defense expenditures may have been, on balance, favorable to growth in India."[11] Similar findings were evident in almost all of the 44 countries studied by Benoit, and the basic correlation seemed strong enough "so that there was less than one chance in a thousand that it could have occurred by accident."[12]

Benoit also found that in developing countries, only a small part of income not spent on defense was put into highly productive investments, although in theory direct channeling of defense funds into civilian production might have produced much better results. In reality, most income went into consumption and the rest into social investments, such as housing and social welfare benefits, rather than into investments that produce net capital formation and an increase in future civilian production. On the other side, defense programs indirectly or inadvertently contributed to the civilian economy through investments in roads in border areas, electronic communications, and spinoffs from shipbuilding, aircraft, and automotive vehicle production.

Similar findings, with qualifications, were made by Robert E. Looney and David Winterford after a detailed statistical study of countries in South Asia and the Middle East. They observed:

> Many analysts have argued that the expansion in military expenditures undertaken in the Middle East and South Asia over the last two decades has preempted resources capable of contributing to physical capital formation. As a result, they believe that military expenditures may have tended to frustrate national development programs, especially those of non–oil exporting countries such as India and Pakistan. While this view makes intuitive sense, we have argued it is conceivable that military expenditures do not necessarily reduce economic growth in developing countries. Defense expenditures may act as an economic stimulus in such ways as financing heavy industry and the acquisition of advanced technologies, providing employment, and attracting investment.[13]

However, with the reference to the Indian case, Looney and Winterford concluded that "defense expenditures in India cease to have a positive impact when they grow at rates greater than 3.0 percent per annum for a decade or more."[14] Between 1977 and 1987, the annual increase in defense spending averaged 6.8 percent, but since then average annual defense spending increases have not exceeded annual rates of growth of India's GNP.

When Indian defense analysts, such as K. Subrahmanyam of the Institute for Defence Studies and Analyses in India and David Whynes of Britain, began to project the Benoit thesis in the mid- to late-1970s, other American and Indian economists such as Nicole Ball, P. Terhal, and Ved Gandhi attempted to contradict Benoit's assessments.[15] Ball concluded that Benoit's study had a "number of serious analytic shortcomings, which are related to the availability of statistics, the methodology employed, and the kinds of information Benoit chose to include or exclude from his regression analysis."[16] A later empirical study undertaken by D. D. Khanna and P. N. Mehrotra concluded that the positive spin-off effects of defense expenditures on the economy could not be confirmed.[17] According to Khanna and Mehrotra, some of the empirical findings of high growth rates in countries with high defense expenditure (such as OPEC and East Asian countries) differed from those of other developing countries such as India because there were major differences in resource endowments and political, economic, and social structures.

Whatever the relative merits of arguments regarding the impact of defense expenditures on economic growth rates, comparative levels of military and social expenditures in India may indicate misguided priorities. Air Marshal Vir Narain

(Retired) of the Indian Air Force noted appropriately: "I have elsewhere (*Times of India*, 31 July 1991) ventured to suggest that the military expenditure of a nation cannot be considered affordable unless certain *minimum* standards of health, education and welfare of the people have first been met. . . . After Pakistan, Egypt and India represent countries with significant levels of military expenditures and low levels of health, education and welfare."[18]

One argument advanced in India in the 1960s soon after Indian rearmament began was based on the level of investible savings available in developing countries. Unlike the Western industrialized nations and Japan, which have highly developed and extensive financial institutions capable of tapping substantial savings for investment, poor countries are characterized by high consumption pattern economies and a general lack of banking and financial institutions. Thus, although Indian defense spending may have been less than 4 percent of GNP, this constituted a substantial part of the savings that could be generated for investment, about 15 percent of GNP in the 1960s and 25 percent of GNP in the 1980s.[19] The diversion of more than one-fourth of the national savings to the defense sector could considerably affect India's GNP growth rate, a conclusion reached by Khanna and Mehrotra in their study.[20] Ultimately, a lower growth rate, or even a negative growth rate, would mean that the absolute amount available for defense at the rate of 4 percent of GNP would be less than what might have been available with a lower rate of defense spending but a higher growth rate. While such observations may be true in theory, in reality defense allocations in India appear to have had no effects on savings generated, which have steadily increased since the early 1950s. Moreover, the official record of investible savings does not display the entire Indian economic picture. A substantial part of the Indian economy operates in the thriving black market, which suggests that India's GDP and level of investible savings may be higher than what official figures indicate.

Two areas in which the impact of defense expenditures on the economy may be less controversial suggest that a diversion of resources to defense is likely to be harmful to developing economies. The first is the development opportunity cost of foreign exchange expended on defense programs. The second is the inflationary effects of defense spending on the economy.

Due to India's chronic foreign exchange crisis, the expenditure of billions of dollars on the import of sophisticated combat aircraft, such as the Mirage-2000, and ships has cut deeply into the available foreign exchange needed to import machinery and other advanced technology. In the late 1980s, it was suggested that India give up its self-imposed restriction on exporting weapons and thereby alleviate the foreign exchange burden of importing weapons. But the foreign exchange value of such Indian arms exports that were earned turned out to be marginal compared to the annual foreign exchange cost of the Indian arms import bill. As regards inflation, military expenditures imply large-scale payments for goods and services that are not consumed, but "wasted" through obsolescence or utilization during war. Even government-produced industrial and agricultural goods are sold to private and public corporations and individuals for a price that covers at least the costs of production. But weapons and the payment for military services, whether produced in the private or the public sector, are paid for by the state from tax revenues. Particularly in the case of India, the location of defense in the public sector implies unnecessarily large bureaucracies and massive wage bills that may further aggravate inflation.

Sweeping economic liberalization, privatization, and market reforms may not substantially influence the debate on whether defense allocations affect economic development in negative or positive ways. However, with the advent of such reforms, the question of whether defense industries should be located in the public or private sector will need to be addressed once again. Allegations of managerial and financial inefficiency and lower product quality would apply to both civilian and defense production in the public sector. In that case, moving defense production from the public to the private sector would suggest greater efficiency and quality. The American model of defense procurements may appear more appropriate in the context of Indian economic reforms.

The extension of economic liberalization and privatization to the defense sector may prove difficult to implement. The Congress government's decision under its Industrial Policy Resolution of 1956 to locate all defense industries in the public sector was based largely on political and moral considerations. This was unlike the decision to locate other heavy industries in the public sector, which was based on the belief that socialist planning and government ownership would produce better economic results. In the case of defense, the Congress government judged profiteering based on the pressures of national security as immoral and harmful to the state. In any case, the American system of defense procurement is not based on market forces of supply and demand but on security assessments and competitive bids submitted to the U.S. government by corporations for the production of weapons. Political manipulation and cost overruns have been perennial in the American defense procurement system, and there is no reason to believe that such a system implanted in India would prove any different. What is likely to happen in India is that as public-sector undertakings are reduced in number and size or are privatized entirely, there may be an increase in subcontracting to the private sector by the Indian public-sector defense undertakings such as Hindustan Aeronautics, Bharat Electronics, and Mazagon Docks. This process had already begun in the early 1980s and is being continued in the 1990s.

DOMESTIC CRITICISM OF
ECONOMIC LIBERALIZATION

The transition from an emphasis on public-sector capitalism to an emphasis on private-sector capitalism was begun rather slowly in the mid-1970s under Prime Minister Indira Gandhi. The tempo of economic change was increased under Prime Minister Rajiv Gandhi after the election of 1984, in which he won 79 percent of the seats in the lower house of the Indian parliament. However, it was only after the minority Congress government of P. V. Narasimha Rao took office in June 1991 that sweeping economic liberalization and reform was introduced into the Indian economy.

There is relatively little dispute among the mainstream members of the three major political parties—Congress, Bharatiya Janata Party (BJP), and Janata Dal—that India must move away from socialism. But there are differences of opinion among these parties on how much reform there should be, and how fast reform should take place. There is also opposition to economic liberalization or the type of reform that should take place among factions within the three major parties. Members of the Communist Party–Marxist (CPM) and a minority of left-wing members within the Congress Party and the Janata Dal remain opposed to abandoning India's primarily socialist system. However, misgivings among the small group of Communist members of parliament in the Lok Sabha about the radical change of economic direction by the Congress government was not shared by the Communist government of West Bengal under its chief minister, Jyoti Basu. Acting under the Communist label and mantle, Jyoti Basu's government has gone further than many other non-Communist states in India in attempting to privatize industry and attract indigenous and foreign private-sector capital.

Within the ranks of the Hindu religious right-wing BJP, which had always included (or been viewed sympathetically by) prominent members of the business community, there are differences of opinion on the nature of economic reform that should be adopted. Hindu nationalist leaders such as L. K. Advani, B. R. Malkani, and A. B. Vajpayee are enthusiastic advocates of an open free-market system that would provide incentives to both Indian capitalists and foreign investors. However, other BJP leaders, such as Murli Manohar Joshi, who are more Hindu "fundamentalist" in their ideology, advocate a reform movement that would emphasize *swadeshi* (indigenous capitalism).[21] Underlying this pro-Hindu belief in promoting "Made in Bharat" capitalism is the fear that the influx of Western or Westernized multinational enterprises would corrupt Hindu values and the Indian way of life.

In 1995, the BJP, allied with the more extreme Hindu party, the Shiv Sena, was voted to power in elections held in the highly industrialized state of Maharashtra. The party's platform of economic nationalism was immediately implemented by the cancellation of the $2.8 billion contract signed by the previous Congress Party state government with the American company, Enron, to construct a power plant at Dhabol in Maharashtra.[22] The power project was not only the largest of its kind in the world, but also the largest contract signed by India with a foreign company and was expected to demonstrate India's commitment to economic freedom and hospitality toward foreign investors. To the BJP–Shiv Sena state government, the contract showed that foreign investors were getting too many concessions at unreasonably high prices. Endorsing the BJP–Shiv Sena decision, Rashmi Mayur declared that the cancellation of the deal by the state government was a great victory for India: "We are given the justification that the larger plant, the cheaper the cost of producing energy. But paradoxically, the cost of constructing the plant was more than double that of a similar plant constructed by Enron at Teeside in Britain."[23] The power plant allegedly would have displaced local villagers and caused environmental damage. Interestingly, after considerable criticism of the cancellation accompanied by threats to sue the state, Enron offered to cut its tariff and offered to take on an Indian partner for the construction of the project.

Criticism of economic liberalization was enunciated in 1995 by 13 prominent Indian economists. They included Ashok Mitra and Deepak Nayar, former chief economic advisers to the Indian government; Arun Ghosh, former member of the Indian Planning Commission; S. P. Shukla, former secretary of commerce and finance; highly respected academics such as K. N. Raj, P. C. Joshi, L. S. Gulati, and C. T. Kurien; and Krishna Raj, editor of the *Economic and Political Weekly* published in Bombay.[24] Some of their criticisms and fears included the following: the globalization of Indian prices without the globalization of Indian incomes; the potential inflation of the prices of food and other necessities; the lack of transparency in the privatization of government-owned enterprises; "the spate of agreements" with large international companies in the power, petroleum, and telecommunication industries; extraordinarily generous tariff and trade concessions to advanced industrialized countries without reciprocal benefits; the dispensation of the Indian patents act without parliamentary debate; the pruning of outlays in social sectors such as public health and education; and the almost blind faith in the principle that "markets know best."

Opposition to liberalization has been voiced occasionally and quietly by Indian industrialists and businessmen who are concerned that foreign competition may be unfair or difficult to cope with. Large Indian conglomerates such as Birlas and Tatas would like to control the entry of foreign competition. Small firms are fearful of being driven out of the marketplace.

THE NATURE AND PROSPECT OF ECONOMIC REFORM

In India, unlike some of the former Communist countries of Europe that are attempting to convert to a capitalist system, private business initiatives, entrepreneurial skills, and market-oriented capitalism have always been deeply ingrained in certain sections of society. These traits and skills are mainly found among traditional merchant and business communities within one level of the Hindu caste hierarchy, namely, the Vaishyas. Indian capitalists were kept on a tight leash during 40 years of Indian socialism, but continued to operate private business enterprises successfully under the most difficult political and economic handicaps. They were hampered by severely restrictive government regulations that were accompanied by demands for bribery from government officials and a hostile trade union system that resorted to frequent labor strikes and city *bandhs*. (The Hindi word *bandh* means to close down.) For a variety of reasons, not always related to economic grievances but provoked by ethnic political disputes, trade unions would attempt to close an entire city down so that there would be no public transport in operation, or offices, factories, and shops open for work or business. Failure to support city closure could lead to severe violence against the life and property of the private businessman or industrialist. The losses suffered by the private sector in such *bandhs* were always enormous.

In July 1992, the *Financial Times* of London described the Indian business community as being composed of some of the most "buccaneer capitalists" found anywhere in the world. Again, in India, unlike the former Communist countries of Europe, all of the institutions and processes of capitalism were already in place and functioning so that what was required was merely the unshackling of an existing system. On the other hand, it must be remembered that there are various sections of Indian society, and especially in the Hindu caste hierarchy, that regard the business community and private greed as distasteful and immoral. The civil service, the military, the medical sciences, and engineering were occupations that honest Indians were expected to strive for. Indeed, it was Jawaharlal Nehru, the British-educated high-caste Brahmin, who insisted on implementing Stalinist-type socialist economic plans in India, albeit within a democracy that conformed to his high moral and political ideals. These two conflicting intellectual, social, and political forces in India will continue to outmaneuver each other as they have in the past. However, for the time being, the capitalist experiment has been given a chance, and the success of this experiment could irretrievably change the direction of Indian economic policy in the decades ahead.

Prime Minister Rajiv Gandhi's reforms earlier had emphasized international technology transfers and domestic technology development as the key to modernization. Since cutting down the Indian bureaucracy seemed like such a hopeless task, Rajiv Gandhi attempted instead to circumvent the bureaucracy in order to speed up the licensing of new industries or the promoting of joint industrial ventures with overseas firms. There were other liberalization measures adopted by Rajiv Gandhi that were intended to attract foreign investment and, especially, to develop those projects that carried a foreign exchange–generating potential.[25] These piecemeal reforms and liberalization schemes under both Indira Gandhi and Rajiv Gandhi resulted in an average annual economic growth rate of about 5 percent beginning in the mid-1970s. This was a considerable improvement from the average 3 percent, often derisively referred to as the fatal "Hindu rate of growth," that prevailed in the 1960s and early 1970s.

The "new" reforms under P. V. Narasimha Rao were essentially a continuation of the liberalization process introduced by Rajiv Gandhi in 1985. The difference was the scale and speed of the reforms following the collapse of the Soviet Union and the end of the Cold War in 1991. The Rao government abolished the industrial licensing system that used to be the scourge and despair of private-sector industrialists.[26] Indeed, post-independence India had been nicknamed the "Licensing (or Permit) Raj" by its domestic critics. (Licenses, however, are still required in those industries that may carry strategic value or generate hazardous effects or environmental damage.) Likewise, the monopoly regulation act was considerably loosened by the Rao government. Firms no longer needed to obtain prior approval for new production, mergers, or expansion of production. Most significantly, foreign corporations were entitled to own 51 percent equity in their Indian subsidiaries—and even more in the case of special industries that generate exports or contribute to essential economic development goals. The Indian government also designated 34 industrial sectors in which foreign investors would be given automatic clearance.[27]

The reforms were welcomed by the West and by world bodies such as the IMF and the World Bank. Within the first six months of Rao's reform initiatives, seven major foreign collaborations worth a total of Rs. 1,100 crores ($440 million) were approved by the government of India.[28] Clearly, the actual investment value of these initial, high-profile joint ventures was not as significant as the reputations and visibility of the collaborators themselves. The foreign firms included General Motors, Ford Motors, General Electric, Du

Pont, Motorola, Kellogg, McDonalds, and Coca Cola of the United States, Gerb and BMW of Germany, and Buhler of Switzerland. Almost every major U.S. computer firm—IBM, Compaq, Dell, Apple, Hewlett-Packard, and Digital—joined the competition for India's $1 billion hardware/software information technology industry. Earlier, an agreement had been reached with Suzuki of Japan for expanding the production of the Suzuki-Maruti car in India. Donor nations also increased their aid commitments from $6.7 billion in 1991-92 to $7.2 billion for 1992-93, perhaps as a reward and incentive to promote further reform.[29]

U.S. companies have led the entry of new international investment in India. Former U.S. Ambassador to India Thomas Pickering stated in February 1993: "We estimate that India enjoyed a $1.2 billion surplus in trade with the U.S. last year, as over 18 percent of India's total exports landed in America."[30] Approximately one-fourth of the 10,000 foreign collaborations in India in 1992 were with American firms. In 1991-92, U.S. investment grew tenfold over the previous year's level. According to Pickering, "Roughly 150 new Indo-U.S. collaborations were signed last year [1992] alone."[31] He predicted that about $2.5 billion in U.S. investment would flow into India over the next three years. American investors' preference for India over China has much to do with India's democratic political system compared to China's continued authoritarian, if not totalitarian, system. As Indian-born economist Jagdish Bhagwati pointed out: "The combination of democracy with market reforms gives India a prospect that will outweigh the temporary advantage that economic reforms have given to totalitarian China. The Indian giant is awakening later than the Chinese giant. But it will step on to firmer ground."[32]

However, progress toward privatization in India has been slow compared, for instance, to neighboring Pakistan. Unlike Pakistan, which had put all of its more than 100 public sector undertakings on the auction block at the start of its economic reform campaign, India under Prime Minister Rao was hesitant to move too fast in the direction of privatization. In the early 1990s, there were fears in India that such a move would lead to extensive corruption charges and political recriminations, as proved to be the case in Pakistan, and that it could produce a sudden political backlash from left-wing politicians and from the millions of workers in the public-sector enterprises.[33] Consequently, few of the 260 public-sector undertakings corporations, which employed 2.3 million people, were privatized during the first year of Rao's tenure. Instead, emphasis was placed on restructuring the undertakings, and restructuring was to be followed by a gradual transition to privatization through government disinvestment. Initially, 900 million shares of 30 public-sector undertakings were sold to public-sector banks and financial institutions.[34] In 1992, however, 400 million shares of 8 major public-sector undertakings were auctioned off to prospective investors in the private sector.

Restructuring also meant eliminating inefficient production methods by cutting back on costly over-employment. In 1991, with the prospect of large-scale layoffs looming in the next few years, the Indian government allocated about $100 million to finance an employee retraining program called the National Renewal Fund.[35] By the end of 1991, at least 60 public-sector units employing more than 400,000 people had been identified as chronically loss-making enterprises that would need to be immediately restructured or eliminated. The total cost of restructuring these public-sector undertakings was estimated at about $2.4 billion. Such trends were expected to continue and perhaps accelerate during the second half of the 1990s.

The Congress government's economic reform movement had become cautious and hesitant for what appeared to be political rather than economic reasons. Even those who advocated the shift from socialism to private-sector capitalism believed that reforms in India had to be implemented slowly rather than suddenly. This was contrary to the recommendations of Professor Jeffrey Sachs of Harvard University, an adviser to Russia and Poland, who suggested that former Communist governments were better off taking the "shock therapy" approach: that is, suffering some extreme hardships in the short term for the sake of lucrative long-term gain. According to proponents of the "shock therapy" argument, a half-hearted approach was more likely to prolong the disadvantages of state socialism without achieving the benefits of private-sector capitalism. Moreover, a cautious approach was more likely to give time to opponents so that they could marshall political support to thwart the reform movement.

The increasingly cautious policy of the Rao government was reflected in the prime minister's speech to the forty-fourth meeting of the National Development Council in New Delhi in May 1992. Rao declared that the market mechanism could not be the "sole vehicle" of development and that it should be dovetailed with planning so that they could be complementary.[36] The market, according to Rao, had limitations, and these would have to be supplemented by direct state intervention. In particular, he argued that state planning was necessary to take care of the poor and the downtrodden "who are for the most part outside the market system and have little asset endowment to benefit from the natural growth of the economy."[37]

In sum, the overall nature of India's reforms appears to be threefold. First, there will be no more new public-sector undertakings or expansion of existing ones, but they will continue temporarily as restructured units. Second, privatization will occur through a slow process of government disinvestment whereby the shares of public-sector undertakings will be auctioned periodically, thereby diluting government ownership. Third, India will remove all obstacles to foreign and domestic private-sector investment and industrial expansion through the elimination of licenses and permits.

INITIAL RESULTS AND CONSEQUENCES OF REFORM

The results of the reforms thus far have been mixed.[38] The failure to produce spectacular results has been largely due to the worldwide recession, which has begun to hit the Indian economy. National expectations for the reforms have also been much too high, and a year was hardly sufficient time to produce results. In mid-1992, doubts were raised about the effects of the reforms.

On the negative side, the growth of India's GDP declined to 1.5 percent in 1991-92, the year the new reforms were enacted.[39] This compared to GDP growth rates of 9.4 percent in 1988-89, 6 percent in 1989-90, and 5.6 percent in 1990-91. Inflation, which was supposed to have been brought down from 12 percent to single digit figures, continued to hover at around 10-12 percent. On the positive side, the annual fiscal deficit had been brought down from 8.4 percent of GDP in 1990-91 to 6.5 percent in 1991-92, and to 5 percent in the 1992-93 budget.[40] Although exports had declined from $18.1 billion in 1990-91 to $17.8 billion in 1991-92, the trade deficit had been reduced to $1.6 billion through a cutback in imports. The foreign exchange reserves had increased from $1.3 billion in 1990 to $5.4 billion in 1991. As is evident, most of these positive changes had taken place before the new reforms were implemented. However, by late 1992, the Indian economy began to show signs of modest recovery.[41] The inflation-adjusted predicted growth for 1992-93 had risen to 4 percent on the basis of current monthly growth rates, and inflation had been brought down to 8 percent in August 1992. In 1994-95, the economic growth rate was 5.3 percent; export growth rate was averaging 19 percent in U.S. dollar terms; the balance of payments deficit had come down from $10 billion in 1990-91 to $1 billion; foreign currency reserves had climbed from $1 billion in June 1991 to $4.5 billion in 1994-95; foreign investment flows had risen from $200 million in 1991-92 to over $4.5 billion in 1994-95; and food grain production had reached an all-time high of 186 million tons.[42]

The major reaction to economic reform has been the predictable opposition from trade unions representing public-sector corporation employees. National one-day strikes were called in November 1991 and again in June 1992. Both strikes were only partially successful.[43] Opposition groups, especially socialists in the Janata Dal and the two Communist parties, alleged that the Rao government had sold out to the World Bank and the IMF under pressure instead of pursuing an independent economic policy. The BJP, while supporting the government's economic reforms in principle, disagreed with the scope and thrust of the liberalization program. According to Jay Dubashi, the main economic adviser to the BJP, "where we fundamentally disagree with the government is that unlike the external liberalization that is being done now, we are more in favor of internal liberalization."[44]

A serious problem that sprang up in 1992 was a stock market scandal involving brokers and bankers who colluded to use large amounts of money from bank deposits to speculate on the country's stock markets.[45] Several major banks and financial institutions in India, including three foreign banks, the Australian ANZ Grindlays, the British Standard Chartered Bank, and the American Citibank, faced huge losses. The financial scam was made possible by faults within the Indian banking and stock market systems and was probably exposed only because of the new economic openness introduced by the reforms. But the economic liberalization of the Rao government has been blamed by opposition politicians and critics for encouraging private greed and corruption.

The stock market scandal and the economic liberalization program led to the introduction of a no-confidence motion in parliament in July 1993. Parts of the motion introduced by Ajoy Mukhopadhyay of the Communist Party–Marxist criticized the Rao government for indulging in "anti-people economic policies based on total surrender to the IMF-World Bank," for the government's "compromising attitude to communal forces," and for its "all-pervading corruption."[46] The motion was defeated by a vote of 265 to 251 only because seven members of the Janata Dal's faction led by Ajit Singh switched loyalties in favor of the Congress Party. If this faction had supported the opposition, the vote would have been a tie and the motion sustained, thus bringing down the Rao government. Indeed, one of the reasons advanced by Ajit Singh for the switch by his faction was that "nobody wants elections because our feeling is that they would only help the BJP."[47]

The Rao government seemed determined to proceed with reforms. According to Finance Minister Manmohan Singh, it will take about three to five years for the reforms to show significant results. Even then, it is unlikely that the growth rate will considerably exceed the average 5 to 6 percent annual growth rates of the 1980s. However, as Manmohan Singh pointed out, "India cannot solve its problems of poverty and underdevelopment by going the command economy type of route where you find so much corruption, so much mismanagement, and there will be neither growth nor social justice. The economy cannot be run in the way we used to run it in the '50s and '60s and early '80s."[48]

THE EFFECTS OF SECURITY
PROBLEMS ON THE ECONOMY

Frequent interstate wars and problems of internal security tend to erode investor confidence, especially the confidence of foreign investors. The economic reform movements in India, Pakistan, and Sri Lanka have been affected by periodic threats of war and by armed separatist movements in Kashmir, Punjab, Assam, Sindh, and the Tamil area of Sri Lanka. The last major war in the subcontinent was fought in 1971 between India and Pakistan over the Bangladesh issue, and a potential war has continued to simmer in the 1990s over the Kashmir issue. To a considerable extent, domestic insurgencies have been confined to specific regions often along the periphery of the state. Therefore, the problem has not proved to be debilitating thus far.

The exception is Hindu-Muslim strife in India, which could occur throughout northern and western India where large numbers of Muslims reside. Hindu-Muslim conflict threatens to be more serious since it occurs in industrialized metropolitan areas such as Calcutta, Kanpur, Meerut, Delhi, Ahmedabad, and Bombay, causing dislocations or disruptions in production. In 1993, the destruction by radical Hindu nationalists of the mosque in Ayodhya built by the first Mogul emperor, Babar, in 1528 led to widespread Muslim demonstrations and rioting throughout India and threatened to trigger a war between India and its Muslim neighbors, Pakistan, Bangladesh, and Afghanistan. Those riots, in turn, produced mainly Hindu attacks on Muslims. Most significantly, in 1994, Hindu-Muslim rioting and killing spread to the heart of Bombay, India's most industrialized city.[49] The chain of bombings in Bombay in March of that year, including the bombing of the Bombay Stock Exchange by Muslim extremists, added a new dimension to sectarian violence in India.

Such fears were aggravated in early 1995 when the right-wing Hindu nationalist parties—the BJP and Shiv Sena—were elected to power in two of the most industrialized states of India, Gujerat and Maharashtra. Both states were traditionally strongholds of the secular-oriented Congress Party. However, Hindu-Muslim strife in India has arisen before and then faded away. By 1995, there were signs that Bombay, the capital of Indian private enterprise, would likely remain vibrant and resilient in the future. On achieving their electoral victories in Gujerat and Maharashtra in 1995, the coalition of the Hindu nationalist parties—the BJP and Shiv Sena—was quick to assure the security of Muslims in these two states and the continuation of the economic liberalization policies of the central Congress governments.

Violent regional secessionist movements in Kashmir, Punjab, and Assam have not adversely affected the overall Indian economy in a significant way, but they do carry long-term implications about the future of the Indian state. The armed insurgency in Kashmir by Muslim separatists demanding an independent Kashmir or accession to Pakistan has brought the economy of Kashmir to a virtual standstill. Kashmir's main industries were tourism, timber, horticulture, and handicrafts. While some efforts are being made by the government of India to promote the sale of Kashmiri handicrafts in other parts of India, the end of foreign tourism in Kashmir has deprived both the state and the national economy of valuable foreign exchange.

The violent Sikh separatist movement for an independent Khalistan would be expected to have a more substantive impact on the Indian economy. Strangely, terrorism and insurgency in Punjab has produced no measurable adverse consequences for the Punjab economy, which has continued to thrive through more than a decade of violence. Punjab, the granary of India and the showcase of India's green revolution, has continued to increase its foodgrain output annually, while several small-scale industries have continued to emerge and flourish in the state. With Sikh separatism on the wane from 1993 onward, Indian and foreign industrial investments in Punjab have been increasing rapidly. Separatist demands and insurgency in Assam since the early 1980s have been similar in outcome to those in Punjab. Assam's main economic enterprises are oil, tea, and timber, none of which have been badly affected by internal war between the United Liberation Front of Assam and the Indian military and paramilitary forces.

Although the impact of violent separatist movements in Punjab and Assam has not severely affected the overall Indian economy, fears that such violence may spread throughout India could have a long-term bearing on investor confidence. Underlying most religious, linguistic, and ethnic grievances are economic grievances, as is the case in both Punjab and Assam. In the case of Punjab, the very success of the green revolution created a class of wealthy farmers and well-paid farm labor, on the one hand, and large numbers of unemployed youth, on the other. It produced dislocations of the traditional social structure. In Assam, dissatisfaction among the Assamese had to do less with the state's economy than with the feeling that Bengalis from West Bengal, Muslim Bengalis from Bangladesh, and others from various parts of India have usurped much of the oil, tea, and timber industries and trade. The influx of outsiders to Assam has reduced the Assamese to a minority in their own state. That the economy of Assam has suffered has less to do with insurgency and sectarian strife than with declining oil reserves, decreasing timber forests, and the slack in the export of tea to international markets arising from competition from East Africa and elsewhere.

The optimism in Indian and international circles regarding the future of India's security, political stability, and economy, especially as compared to China, may now go too far compared to the pessimism of the past. Periodic Indian claims that the country has a large middle class of approximately 300 million people (one-third of its population) may be misleading. In reality, compared to the middle class in North America and Western Europe where the average household may maintain a residential space of about 800 square feet, a fridge, a television, a telephone, possibly a car and the like, the middle class in India with similar living standards and purchasing power may not exceed 20 percent, 60 million, of the alleged 300-million middle class. As Emma Duncan wrote in the *Economist* of London:

> India has an economy slightly smaller than Belgium. Its GDP per head is $310. Fewer than half of its 950 million people can read. [The literacy rate is actually about 60 percent.] Between them, they have only just over 6 million telephones and 35 million television sets. Some 14 percent of the population has access to clean sanitation—a lower proportion than anywhere else except for a handful of Sudans and Burkina Fasos. According to the World Bank, 63 percent of India's under-five-year-olds are malnourished. Perhaps 40 percent of the world's desperately poor live in India. Apart from a tiny elite in Delhi and Bombay, India's rich are poor by anybody else's standards; according to the National Council for Applied Economic Research, only 2.3 percent of the population has a household income of more than 78,000 rupees ($2,484).[50]

The similar claim that India possesses one of the largest pools of scientific and technical manpower in the world surpassed only by the United States, Japan, and Russia, can be quite misleading since this is a quantitative rather than a qualitative statement. India's manpower resources have not produced defense self-reliance or technological self-sufficiency in India. Apart from the elite institutes of technology and science, most Indian universities churn out massive numbers of graduates whose training and capabilities do not compare to that of the West. Moreover, some of the best and the brightest scientific and technical Indian personnel are lost to the West in a steady brain drain. With far better resources and training facilities, the emigré Indian scientific technical personnel in the United States, for instance, could well produce combat aircraft, tanks, and submarines that have thus far eluded their counterparts in India. The residue pool of scientists and engineers in India does not possess the same advanced research and resource facilities and intellectual climate and incentive enjoyed by the counterpart Indian emigré community abroad. The Indian technological community may have gained sufficiently high standards at home to develop and generate comparatively substandard civilian goods and services within a hitherto highly protected public and private-sector economy; but for the greater part it has not absorbed the technology even in this area nor been competitive with those of the advanced industrialized countries.

India's ability to acquire and absorb advanced technology capable of generating innovative and competitive weapons will depend on its success in the wider arena of science and technical advances and accomplishments. Until a broader and internationally competitive industrial technical base is first established, India's objective of defense and civilian technological self-sufficiency will remain unfulfilled. Since much of weapons systems today is derived from dual-use technologies, civilian and military technological capabilities cannot be separated. Much will therefore depend on the success of economic reforms in India and the country's ability to compete with the rest of the world in the development and production of sophisticated products in general.

7

Optimizing Democracy, Security, and Development

THE FUTURE OF INDIA'S DEMOCRACY

In developing countries, democratic processes and values have especially great problems surviving amid external and internal security pressures. It is not a coincidence that few democracies have emerged in the Third World, although several have emerged in the 1990s. Introducing democratic institutions in developing countries is difficult, and when such institutions are established, it is difficult to sustain them. Undoubtedly, security pressure is not the only force that prevents democracy from taking root. Poverty, illiteracy, the lack of political maturity and experience, or decades of authoritarian rule contribute to the difficulties of establishing and sustaining democracies. On the other hand, there are many industrialized or oil-rich countries, such as South Korea, Taiwan, Saudi Arabia, and the Persian Gulf kingdoms, in which democracy has yet to find a home. In other countries, as industrialization continues and literacy rates increase, democracy has taken root, as in Brazil, Argentina, and Chile, or there are new pressures to introduce democracy as in South Korea, Taiwan, Singapore, and Thailand. But in countries such as South Korea, Taiwan, and Pakistan, where external and internal security pressures are high, democracy movements have had a hard time. After a few fits and starts, Pakistan has experienced sustained democracy since 1989 although the future still looks uncertain. Meanwhile, in India, the democratic process has had trouble keeping on track amid growing security pressures.

No doubt, the roots of the Indian democracy are deeper than those of the more recent democracies. Therefore, India's longer democratic political experience may endow the state with greater resilience in dealing with security pressures. But since the mid-1970s, a growing malaise has set in on the Indian body politic. Reflecting on the question of whether the Indian state would degenerate into a coercive one, veteran Indian socialist parliamentarian Madhu Limaye, a long-standing observer of the Indian political scene, made the following gloomy assessment in 1989:

> The menacing cloud of terrorism and mindless violence, the aggravation of the troubles in Jammu and Kashmir, the continuing insurgency in the North-East, the growing discontent in the west tribal belt which encompasses parts of Madhya Pradesh, Bihar, Orissa and West Bengal, the increasing fury of caste conflicts in the countryside and the rising wave of communal tension and rioting in the urban areas, and, above all, the general breakdown of law and order, have put the very existence of our nation in jeopardy. Scarcely have we completed 40 years of independence than the edifice of the constitutional structure and network of institutions built up by Nehru, Patel and their colleagues has begun to crumble.
>
> India, with its background of centuries of anarchy and fragmentation, must put the task of preserving the rational and ordered state at the top of our list of priorities. It is the existence of this rational state and the rule of law that is now threatened. Freedom cannot be realized by the common people in conditions of anarchy. It can thrive only in an ordered state. In a democratic country, with a written constitution and fundamental rights and a hierarchy of courts to enforce them, the law enforcement agencies should be the chief upholders of the ordered state. But in India, these agencies have, over large parts of the country become thoroughly demoralized, brutalized and corrupt. Not only Punjab, but Bihar too is far gone towards the destruction of the ordered state.[1]

Some of Madhu Limaye's suggestions to resolve the crisis of India's democracy are as follows:

1. Greater discipline should be enforced in the ruling and opposition parties.
2. Select committees should scrutinize all major legislation.

3. The central and state governments should embark on a major civil service retrenchment program to reduce the tyranny of the bureaucracies.
4. Central, state, and local police forces should be retrained and disciplined to enforce law and order more equitably.
5. In order to speed up the administration of justice, written arguments should be substituted for long oral arguments in the higher courts.
6. An ad hoc committee should formulate a more rationale and functional allocation of resources among the central, state, and local governments.
7. The political power base should be broadened by giving fair shares to neglected sections of society.
8. The government should downgrade religious programs and programs that appeal to people's superstitions through the formulation of guidelines for television, radio, and other media.

Limaye's recommendations appear to be in the vein of fixing or patching up the *process* of Indian democracy, which is faced with increasing security pressures from within and without. However, use of temporary measures to keep the Indian political system alive may be insufficient in the long run. What the Indian state may need is a radical reorganization of the *structure* of its political, economic, and military systems if it is to adequately meet its security and development objectives and maintain its democratic traditions.

•• The erosion of the Indian democratic process also arises from the threat of war with external powers. Thus far, this has implied meeting the security threats from Pakistan and China. However, strains on the Indian democratic system could also arise indirectly through the economic burden of defense. This burden is increased whenever military aid begins to flow to India's two traditional adversaries and whenever there are arms buildups in the Middle East, Southeast Asia, and the Indian Ocean region. In general, the greater the internal and external threats to the country, the greater the probability that individual and group democratic rights may be curtailed by the government. And more security programs may imply less resources available for development programs.

Perhaps the above problems may be addressed by decentralizing the political, economic, and military structures within the Indian political system and establishing a loose confederation of states in South Asia as a whole. The decentralized Indian state may be expected to mitigate, if not resolve, the problems of violent separatist movements and internal security issues. A confederation of South Asian states may be expected to promote larger markets and free trade, thereby ending the threat of wars in the region. These two possible hypothetical measures for reorganization are discussed below.

FEDERALISM AND INTERNAL SECURITY

When there is an acute security crisis in India, the instinctive reaction of the government is to invoke the centralizing powers provided by the emergency clauses of the Indian constitution. If these laws are not sufficient, then new legislation is passed to increase the authority of the central government. Thus, the Indian government, especially under Indira Gandhi, injected incremental doses of political centralism to address the problems of external threats and to resolve the problems of violent ethnic separatism and the nationwide breakdown of law and order.

Until the introduction of sweeping reforms in 1991, the tendency toward political centralization during times of acute security crisis was paralleled by policies of economic centralization, albeit these were mainly for ideological reasons. While the Indian constitution lays the framework for a federal system, its "Directive Principles of Social Policy" tends to foster a mixed socialist-capitalist economy. A socialistic Indian economy in which all heavy industry and defense production were to be in the public sector was reinforced through two Industrial Policy resolutions passed by the Congress Party in 1948 and 1956. Both the push of political policy and the pull of economic ideology have tended to aggravate the pressures on the Indian democratic system by reducing the individual freedoms and economic incentives of diverse ethnic groups.

A major cause for the breakdown of Indian democracy may be traced to the government's inability to cope with unconventional modes of conflict. Resolving problems of internal security calls for counterinsurgency and antiterrorist tactics, both of which have defied the state's military policy-making apparatus. Meeting external threats is also becoming complex as India may have to cope simultaneously with internal insurgency and terrorism aided and abetted by external enemies during times of war. Both counterinsurgency and antiterrorist tactics by the government have a tendency to devolve into undemocratic methods and practices. Indeed, the advocates of security first may even argue that democracy may have to be dispensed with in order to deal with such problems. President's Rule in Indian Punjab and Kashmir, the dismissal of the Zulfikar Ali Bhutto government by General Zia-ul Haq in 1977, and, perhaps, the dismissal of the Benazir Bhutto government by President Ghulam Ishaq Khan in 1990 may be seen as examples of the collapse of democratic systems in South Asia arising from the breakdown of internal law and order.

The needed political decentralization in India would involve the devolution of power from the central government to the various levels of state governments, the village *panchayats*, and town councils. The central government would hold the portfolios of only defense (but excluding the defense industries), foreign affairs, communications (including railways, air transport, and telecommunications), and currency (but excluding banking). The rest of the portfolios would be held by state governments.

This would be a radical departure from the present constitutional division of power between the center and the states, which provides substantial power to the former and only limited residual power to the latter. At the time the Indian constitution was being formulated, between 1947 and 1949, there were serious differences on the distribution of power between the center and the states.[2] Critics at the time alleged that the final resolution made the Indian political system only "quasi-federal." According to Indian constitutional specialist M. V. Pylee, "it [the Indian constitution] establishes a unitary State with subsidiary federal features rather than a federal State with subsidiary unitary features."[3] Indeed, there were allegations at the time of the formulation of the Indian constitution that the unitary system was deliberately made so strong that the federal aspects were a mere facade to placate the states.

At present, the constitution provides for a Union (federal) List, a State List, and a Concurrent List.[4] The Union List consists of 98 items and includes defense and defense production, the armed forces, atomic energy, shipping and navigation, air transportation, railways, radio and television, mines and oil resources, atomic energy, income tax and customs, and nearly all heavy industries. The State List consists of 61 items and includes law and order, prisons, public health and sanitation, irrigation and agriculture, education, and intrastate communication, trade, and commerce. The Concurrent List consists of 52 items and includes detention for reasons connected with the security of the Indian state. Other items on the list are contracts, bankruptcy and insolvency, economic and social planning, commercial and industrial monopolies, trade unions, trade and commerce in a number of areas, utilities, newspapers, and the legal, medical, and other professions.

While this distribution may appear equitable and substantially federal in appearance, in key areas of governance, the states have little control. Thus, for example, although law and order is under the prerogative of the states, in practice central government intervention is not only permitted, but is frequently used if the center determines that the states cannot cope with the breakdown of law and order. More importantly, most heavy industries are owned and controlled by the central government, and the states' access to income to conduct government is limited.

Consequently, along with political decentralization, there is also a need for economic decentralization. One of the major complaints of the Sikhs in Punjab, for instance, has been that the economic control held by the central

government over the states through standardized agricultural price-fixing policies leaves the Punjabi Sikh farmer little room for profit. Similarly, the Assamese
have claimed that they are not the beneficiaries of the oil wealth of that state
but that the rest of India is. States such as Punjab, Assam, Maharashtra, Gujerat,
and Karnataka may also argue that through a federal system of progressive
taxation and redistributive grants, the less efficient states benefit at the expense
of the more prosperous and efficient states, which are being denied their due
economic share. The central government's position reportedly is that its policies
are applied uniformly in all the states. If India is to remain one country, then
progressive taxation and redistributive grants are inevitable in order to produce
an equitable and egalitarian national society.[5]

Before sweeping economic reforms were introduced in 1991, there was
greater centralism in the economic sphere than in the political sphere in India.
Indeed, the facade of federalism, which was alleged by the critics within the
Indian constitution-making body during its deliberations between 1947 and
1950, turned out to be greater than envisaged at the time. Centralized economic
planning was done through the creation of the Planning Commission, which
was empowered to formulate, organize, and execute India's Five-Year Plans.
The creation of this permanent commission in 1950, was in itself subject to
controversy between Prime Minister Jawaharlal Nehru, who supported it, and
then Finance Minister John Mathai, who opposed it. Claiming that such a body
would undermine the functions of the Finance Ministry and the Indian states,
Mathai resigned in protest in 1952.

Because nearly all the major industries were under the public sector, the
Planning Commission wielded enormous power in determining the location of
those industries. In turn, the central government was able to wield undue
influence on state policy through a system of economic rewards and punish-
ments. States that did not fall in line with central government policy, or that
were ruled by opposition parties, were likely to be denied new industries. For
example, few public-sector industries were located in the states of Kerala and
West Bengal, where Communist parties periodically gained or maintained
power, or in the states of Punjab and Kashmir, where Sikhs and Muslims are
in the majority and are threatening to secede from the Indian Union.

The Indian states have much less control over their own economic destiny
than do the states in the United States. The essential difference may be found
in private entrepreneurship and ownership of industries in the United States
and centralized planning and public ownership in India. Lack of economic
control in the Indian states implies lack of political control. These conditions
are also found in Pakistan, where the provinces are held together by a highly
centralized Punjabi-dominated government in Islamabad. Underlying factors

in the secessionist movements in Indian Punjab and Pakistan's Sindh province and in the secession of Bangladesh from Pakistan in 1971 were the relative economic domination of the central government and discrimination by the central government against the states and provinces.

Thus, decentralization or privatization of the federal economic system needs to accompany decentralization of the federal political system. The latter will not work unless the former is also implemented. The Indian states need to compete with each other to attract private industries and entrepreneurs whose decisions are more likely to be based on the economic advantages of locating industries in a particular state than on politically motivated considerations, such as party politics or ethnic and caste preferences and prejudices.

This may suggest the need to privatize defense industries as well. The central government of India needs to subcontract to private industries, through a system of public bidding, the production of defense goods, as is done in the United States. In issuing such contracts to private entrepreneurs, the Indian government may still require that these defense industries be spread throughout the country to reduce security risks and generate a more equitable distribution of defense-sector benefits among the states. Unlike civilian industrial production, which needs to be based mainly on economic criteria, defense industry production may be based on political criteria.

However, decentralization cannot be extended to the military sector, especially in the case of the regular armed forces intended to maintain external security. Coordination and control in the command structure and high levels of integration among the forces are needed for the maintenance of discipline, efficient decision making, and speedy force deployment. Meeting external threats appears to call for a policy of centralization and consolidation. On the other hand, military decentralization may be more desirable in the case of paramilitary and other police forces intended to maintain internal security. Meeting internal threats appears to call for a policy of localization and distribution of military power. Local and state authorities may know best in such cases, although local prejudices and the inability to see the national picture may prove to be handicaps in promoting internal security.

Neither centralization of the military forces nor decentralization of paramilitary and police forces are all that clear-cut because the roles of the two types of military forces may be interchanged at times. The regular armed forces have been used to quell internal disturbances in the states, giving them a domestic security role as well. Such deployment may be necessary in cases in which the state and local paramilitary forces may be unobjective and ineffective in dealing with armed violence in their own provinces. And, conversely, paramilitary forces, especially those deployed along the border areas such as

Punjab, Kashmir, Rajasthan, Uttar Pradesh, and Arunachal Pradesh, may be used for external defense. Such forces include the Border Security Force, the Indo-Tibetan Border Police, and the Assam Rifles. If the civil authorities in India have concerns about creating a chief of defense staff organization to provide a unified command for the army, air force, and navy, they may also have concerns about creating a highly centralized military organization for internal security purposes. Such a unified internal military security organization may politicize the internal security forces and provide them with opportunities to overthrow the civilian government through armed coups.

Decentralization may be extended to the point where the states achieve complete autonomy short of independence. In essence, this would imply the creation of a new confederation out of the existing federation. Such a solution was in fact proposed in 1946 by the British Cabinet Mission in order to avoid partition and salvage a united India. Under the Cabinet Mission proposal, British India would have been divided into a three-part confederation. The western and eastern parts would have constituted what essentially became West and East Pakistan. While Mohammed Ali Jinnah and Mohandas Gandhi accepted the proposal, however reluctantly, Jawaharlal Nehru rejected it.

Although the underlying reason for Nehru's rejection of the Cabinet Mission proposal was not made clear, it may have been that the plan was merely a first step toward eventual separation by the western and eastern parts into the new state of Pakistan. Indeed, Jinnah accepted the plan merely because it would have provided a period of gradual transition. If the plan had been adopted, then the confederation first would have legitimized the new semi-internal boundaries that it had created and then made them the boundaries of the new state of Pakistan. That would have given Pakistan all of Punjab and Bengal, together with the rest of the eastern sector, including Assam. In 1990, a similar confederal arrangement was proposed by Slovenia and Croatia as a means of keeping the former Yugoslavia together. Serbia rejected this arrangement because accepting it may have implied legitimizing the internal boundaries of the new confederation, which would become external boundaries if Slovenia and Croatia were eventually to secede. That would have merely legitimized the existing boundaries disputed by Serbia. It would not have solved the problem of boundaries and minorities and would have left large Serb populations outside Serbia. Likewise, the British Cabinet Mission plan would have left large numbers of Hindus and Sikhs in Pakistan if it were to secede from the confederation. Moves from federation to confederation have rarely held together. The Commonwealth of Independent States forged out of members of the former Soviet Union has been weak and largely inoperative. However, existing independent states seeking to establish a confederation appear to have a greater chance of success.

CONFEDERALISM AND EXTERNAL SECURITY

If releasing central government powers is the solution to the problems of internal security, then encompassing the independent states of South Asia into a larger confederal union may be the solution to the problems of external security in the region. Centuries of violence and wars that have plagued the different linguistic and religious groups of Europe are now being resolved through European integration. No doubt, this integration has gone through some rough times, especially since the end of the Cold War. But the chance of wars between the states of the European Union are now remote. South Asia may benefit by emulating the European experience. Whole or partial restoration of the economic and political ties that once linked the peoples of South Asia under British rule may end the secessionist movements for independent states: of Kashmir, Khalistan, Assam, and Nagaland from India; Sindhudesh, Balochistan, and Pashtunistan from Pakistan; and Tamil Ealam from Sri Lanka. It may also end the wars of the subcontinent and thus reduce the pressures of both internal and external violence that make the democratic process difficult or impossible.

The Western European experiment of regional economic and political integration initiated in the 1950s was intended both to deal with the loss of European economic and military power in a new world of superpowers and to meet external threats emanating from the Soviet-bloc Communist countries. With the end of the Cold War, the latter has dissipated, but regional conflict issues that lay dormant under Communist dictatorships have resurfaced in Eastern Europe and in the former Soviet republics. These conflict issues may be resolved through an expansion of European regional integration that may include the Eastern European states. An early promise to allow the former Yugoslavia into the European Community would have made the subsequent struggle over boundaries and minorities following the disintegration of the state quite irrelevant. East and West Germany have already been integrated into a single state. Together, they are part of the European Community, despite their divergent political and economic experiences for over 45 years. In spite of all the linguistic, religious, and ethnic nationalism that has prevailed for centuries, a common European historical experience and identity is becoming increasingly recognized.

There are similarities between conditions in Europe and South Asia. Logically, the Indian subcontinent may be perceived as one state or at least 30 to 50 based on religious and linguistic differences. One could argue that Tamils, Sinhalese, Kashmiris, Bengalis, and Punjabis, for example—whether Hindu,

Muslim, Sikh, or Christian—have little in common. Yet despite all the differences and antagonisms between the various linguistic and religious groups of South Asia, a common geography, history, and culture unite them all. In retrospect, it should be apparent that not Islam but a common "Indian" heritage is the primary bond between East and West Pakistan. Rejection of that common heritage was one of the underlying causes for the breakup of Pakistan in 1971.

Although it is now too late to make amends, in retrospect the partition of British India in 1947 would appear to have been a mistake. The Muslims of north-central India who spearheaded the movement for Pakistan benefited the least. Fearing domination by a Hindu majority when the British were about to leave India, they demanded a separate homeland for Indian Muslims. By creating the new state of Pakistan in the Muslim majority areas of the northwest and northeast of India, the largely Urdu-speaking Muslims of north-central India created new problems for themselves. The bulk of them found themselves left behind in India to face a greater and more hostile Hindu majority than existed before partition.

The Muslims of the Indian state of Uttar Pradesh who migrated to the western wing of Pakistan (the Mohajirs) now find themselves virtually aliens in the country they created. After the creation of Bangladesh, the Mohajirs discovered that what is now Pakistan is essentially a territorial state of four ethnic provinces: West Punjab, Sindh, Balochistan, and the North-West Frontier Province, which is inhabited by Pathans. Ironically, it was not these four provinces (or even Kashmir) that pushed hard for the creation of Pakistan during the independence struggle. For the Muslims of the Indian state of Bihar who migrated to East Pakistan, the state of Pakistan literally vanished from right under their feet, leaving them to face a hostile Muslim Bengali population in the new state of Bangladesh. By arrangement with the Pakistani government, most of them have been repatriated to Pakistan, where as Mohajirs, they now face the hostility of native Sindhis.

Confederal arrangements in South Asia may be attempted to incorporate all of the countries of the South Asian Association for Regional Cooperation (SAARC), a forum that was established in 1983. Essentially, SAARC sought to generate cooperation in noncontroversial socioeconomic and cultural areas. Not only were political and security conflict issues excluded from the deliberations of this organization, but also avoided were contentious bilateral issues in the socioeconomic and cultural fields. This was, in part, to avoid the collapse of SAARC at an early stage and allow the fledgling organization to take root.

However, Pakistan prefers confederal arrangements with the Muslim countries of the ECO bloc to arrangements with the multireligious countries of SAARC. One Pakistani analyst projected the eventual formation of a "United

States of Hilal," a large Muslim confederation that would stretch from Pakistan to Turkey and encompass the newly independent Muslim states that emerged out of the former Soviet Union.[6] In a sense, this would be the logical extension of the concept of "Pakistan" beyond the subcontinent, Pakistan itself having been created as a "homeland" for Indian Muslims within the subcontinent.

But Pakistan's strategy of linking itself with the states of West and Central Asia also carries some weaknesses. Afghanistan needs to be stabilized in order to establish road and rail communications with the Central Asian states, a prospect that remains uncertain despite the overthrow of President Najibullah and the victory of the various factions of the Afghan mujahideen in April 1992. In any case, as in Afghanistan, stability in Tajikistan remained uncertain at the end of 1995.[7]

There are other socioeconomic and demographic problems standing in the way of fostering an Islamic confederation that goes beyond loose economic ties. The 1991 per capita incomes in the Central Asian republics varied between $3,240 in Kazakhstan and $1,460 in Tajikistan, compared to $360 in Pakistan, and the literacy rates are almost 100 percent in all the republics compared to 35 percent in Pakistan.[8] Pakistan's population is 120 million compared to a total population of 60 million in the Central Asian states. Thus, the major population difference and socioeconomic gap that prevails would make integration difficult. Most of the Central Asian states have also expressed a preference for the Turkish democratic secular model over that of Pakistan, Iran, or Saudi Arabia.[9] In the hearts and minds of the Turkish peoples of Central Asia, the concept of a greater Turkestan appears to carry more weight than that of the creation of a greater Pakistan or Muslim confederation.[10] However, it is also important to keep in mind that most of the Central Asian republics are still under the rule of secular ex-Communists turned nationalists, who may be overthrown and replaced by Islamicists. The tide could change.

Even if the ECO were to evolve successfully, there is no reason why Pakistan should not also be a part of SAARC. No doubt, SAARC has been sailing through rough waters since 1987. The armed separatist violence in Kashmir and Punjab in India and among the Tamils in Sri Lanka, as well as the Sindhi-Mohajir conflicts in Pakistan, have all spilled over national boundaries to varying degrees and adversely affected regional relations. However, it is precisely such problems that demonstrate the urgency of promoting SAARC into a confederal organization.

If it is premature to establish a confederation in South Asia, perhaps the countries of South Asia should at least agree on two fundamental principles: that the existing international borders, whether good or bad, legal or illegal, are inviolable; and that none of the states in the region will aid and abet each other's separatist movements. India may find proposals for maintaining the territorial status quo in South Asia more to its liking. Pakistan will surely insist on making an exception of Kashmir, especially since it feels that it had a moral right to Muslim-majority Kashmir at the time of independence. But the reality is that India can enforce the status quo in Kashmir by sheer weight of its military power. It did so in the past and continues to do so during the present crisis. In any case, most Kashmiris want independence that would include Azad Kashmir, which is now under Pakistani control. This would hardly be acceptable to Pakistan. Readjusting the complex ethnic distribution of South Asia through territorial changes could unravel all the countries in the region into several smaller states at a very high human cost, a consequence that should be avoided in the interests of maintaining stability in the region.

PROSPECTS FOR STABILITY IN INDIA

Since the 1980s, perceptions of external threat have been overshadowed by increasing internal violence and armed ethnic separatist movements. Much of the ethnic grievances provoking the rise in internal violence may be traced to rising economic expectations and despair. Indian journalist Prem Shankar Jha summed up the basic problem of India as follows:

> Movements of insurrection are springing up all over the country like toadstools after rain. Most are as yet tiny, but have acquired an importance out of all proportion to the numbers involved because of the AK-47 rifle. The protest is not directed so much at the Indian state as that the state offers the insurrectionists no future within it. For this the very slow growth of the modern industrial and commercial sectors of the economy for 30 years after independence, its inefficient use of capital and the fewness of jobs created are directly to blame. As a result, every insurrectionary group from Punjab to Assam, from Kashmir to Tamil Nadu, is spearheaded by students and the educated unemployed. Slow economic growth has imperilled the polity, but today the opposite is also happening. The increasing weakness of the Center is making it more and more difficult to take harsh economic investment, increase its efficiency, and thereby hasten the rate of job creation in the modern sector.[11]

India's foreign and defense policies and its domestic security and economic policies have become much more interrelated and interdependent than ring past decades. Rapid economic growth and a fair distribution of wealth ll have an important bearing on resolving various domestic ethnic conflicts d separatist movements. Defense programs will need to be cut back substan- lly to redirect more resources, especially foreign exchange, to economic velopment. And India will need to persevere with its economic reforms spite some initial setbacks and failures. The economic dividends that are pected to accrue from the reforms will not be seen in the first year of their plementation, especially in the midst of the present worldwide recession. As ted earlier, the economy had already shown signs of revival by the fall of 1992.

With the end of the Cold War era, closer ties with the United States and e West are perceived as essential for building up India's defense capabilities d for encouraging greater Western investments in India. Military ties with e United States may prove useful given the continuation of old conflict issues South Asia and the continuing arms race in the region and beyond. Military llaboration with the United States may lower India's security risks within the bcontinent and bring about greater stability in the wider region from the orn of Africa to the Strait of Malacca. But the expected payoffs in terms of merican weapons and military technology transfers to India do not appear kely to take place in the short run.

The earlier drive by the Indian Ministry of External Affairs to forge a new do-Russian treaty makes much less sense in the 1990s. Nor do efforts to romote an informal Indo-American military relationship make much sense. gainst whom would this treaty with Russia or military ties with the United tates be directed? Apart from some mutual concerns about the future of the luslim Central Asian republics, India and Russia have few common strategic terests. Russia may still be a useful source for the purchase of cheap weapons, ut these will have to be paid for in hard currency at the maximum price Moscow is able to extract. A treaty will not obtain any special concessions for ndia on the purchase prices. Russian weapons are available to any state, cluding India's current and future adversaries, at whatever price the interna- ional market will fetch. A formal or quasi-military alliance with the United tates will suffer from the same problems that Pakistan experienced during the Cold War. The United States is unlikely to provide any political support, let one military assistance, in the event of military confrontations between India nd Pakistan or China.

This does not mean that India should return to Nehru's nonalignment olicy either. Nonalignment makes little sense in the 1990s. At the meeting of arious Non-Alignment Movement (NAM) leaders in Djakarta in September 992, there was a general lack of purpose and direction. Nonalignment can play ttle part in a world without opposing military blocs primarily characterized by the division between rich and poor nations. Poor states cannot be nonaligned between rich and poor states. India is a poor country and must seek negotiating and bargaining strategies jointly with other developing countries. India cannot be nonaligned between North and South. In the case of regional conflict issues in the former Soviet republics, the former Yugoslavia, the Horn of Africa, and the countries of former French Indochina, the policy option for India is to either become involved or not involved. However, a policy of noninvolvement would not be the same as the old nonalignment policy pursued during the Cold War.

Another hangover from the past is India's nuclear policy, in which there has been little change. Perhaps it is time that India made a choice instead of straddling the fence. India should either overtly embark on a nuclear weapons program and accept the economic sanctions that are likely to be imposed by the Western community, or it should go ahead and sign the Nuclear Non-Proliferation Treaty (NPT). The traditional policy of maintaining the option provides India with no deterrence against China or against a covert nuclear weapons program in Pakistan. Perhaps nuclear weapons are sought after in order to achieve great-power status. Thus, if India cannot obtain the respect of the West because it lacks economic clout, it may obtain such respect through the display of nuclear weapons. But the economic losses that it may suffer from such a policy may not be offset by the dubious intangible gains it may make in international prestige.

Without doubt, the greatest threats that India faces in the 1990s come from within its borders. Armed separatist movements threaten to destroy the integrity of the state and to undermine the country's democratic system, which has survived numerous crises since independence in 1947. After decades of insurgencies in the border states and regions, it should be apparent by now that there can be no purely military solutions to the problems of internal conflict. Only negotiated political solutions may quell armed violence at home and bring about long-term stability. In particular, given the existence of various religious, linguistic, caste, and tribal groups in India, the political structure and process may have to be drastically overhauled. Greater decentralization of political and economic power and a more confederal structural arrangement may prove to be the necessary formula for solving the problems of internal security.

India's perseverance with democracy since independence may not be the only or main reason why the other major states of South Asia turned democratic. Whatever the other reasons, by the early 1990s, all the states of South Asia had democratically elected governments, a situation found elsewhere perhaps only in Western Europe. It may be true that the East and Southeast Asian countries have been able to obtain high and sustained rates of economic growth because of the discipline provided by authoritarian regimes. But democracy has enabled e myriad ethnic groups of India to air their grievances and has thereby relieved ae political pressure on the government. Freedom of expression and the ectoral process have provided outlets for frustration and despair. Democracy as raised the hope that economic conditions can eventually be changed arough the peaceful change of governments and leaders at the ballot box. India more likely to survive as a union if its economy grows at an average of 4 to 8 ercent per year in a democratic capitalist system than at 8 to 12 percent in an uthoritarian capitalist system. Various trade-offs and a measure of balance mong the goals of national security, the maintenance of democracy, and conomic development would appear to be worthwhile.

NOTES

Chapter 1

1. For studies on efforts to create and maintain democracies, see Giuseppe Di Palma, *To Craft Democracies: An Essay on Democratic Transitions*, Berkeley: University of California Press, 1990; and Tatu Vanhanen, *Strategies of Democratization*, Washington, D.C.: Taylor and Francis, 1992.

2. See letter to the editor by Bruce Russett in *The Economist*, April 29–May 5, 1995.

3. Garnham and Tessler noted that democratization need not imply the avoidance of war in the Middle East, especially if the people were to elect radical Islamic leaders determined to spread their beliefs or to confront other religious groups. "More specifically, it will be necessary to specify that democracy leads to pacific international behavior only if citizens do no choose to be governed by regimes with 'fundamentalist' or 'totalitarian' ideologies." See David Garnham and Mark Tessler, Introduction to *Democracies, War and Peace in the Middle East*, ed. David Garnham and Mark Tessler, Bloomington: Indiana University Press, 1995, xix.

4. From "Letters," *The Economist*, April 29–May 5. See footnote 2.

5. See Stuart R. Schram, *The Political Thought of Mao Tse-tung*, New York: Praeger Publishers, 1963, 209.

6. See Thomas S. Axworthy, "Democracy and Development: Luxury or Necessity," in *Development and Democratization in the Third World: Myths, Hopes and Realities*, ed. Kenneth E. Bauzon, Washington, D.C.: Taylor and Francis, 1992, 111-118.

7. For a study of the Pakistani experience, see Ayesha Jalal, *Democracy and Authoritarianism in South Asia*, Cambridge, England: Cambridge University Press, 1995.

8. For a discussion of the 1970 election results and the ensuing rebellion, civil war, and war with India, see Richard Sisson and Leo Rose, *War and Secession: Pakistan, India and the Creation of Bangladesh*, Berkeley: University of California Press, 1990. See also Craig Baxter, Yogendra K. Malik, Charles H. Kennedy, and Robert C. Oberst, *Government and Politics in South Asia*, Boulder: Westview Press, 1991, 257-277.

9. See editorial in the *Christian Science Monitor,* August 9, 1990.

10. See Shahid-ur Rahman, "Pakistan Awaits Elections After Bhutto's Dismissal," *Christian Science Monitor,* August 8, 1990.

11. *New York Times,* August 7, 1990.

12. Figures from *The World Almanac and Book of Facts,* 1992, New York: Pharos Books, 1992, 790.

13. For a discussion of the situation in Sindh, see "Road To Anarchy," *Pakistan Illustrated,* October 1994.

14. For Indian assessments of the political condition in Pakistan, see Aabha Dixit, "Crisis Shows Pakistan is Still a Military State," *India Abroad* (New York) July 30, 1993; and Kuldip Nayar, "No Forgiving in Pakistan Duel," *India Abroad,* July 16, 1993.

15. See Baxter, Malik, Kennedy, and Oberst, *Government and Politics in South Asia,* 257-262.

16. *New York Times,* March 1995.

17. See Thant Myint-U, "Myanmar is Different from Other Lands: The Military Allowed Free Elections and then Ignored the Results," *New York Times,* August 26, 1990.

18. See *New York Times,* July 7, 1993; and *Christian Science Monitor,* July 9, 1993. For an assessment by a Nigerian professor who is a resident of the United States, see Chinua Achebe, "The High Price of Patience," *New York Times,* July 27, 1993.

19. "Most Nigerians Feel Relieved That Coup Failed," letter to the editor by Zubair M. Kazaure, ambassador of Nigeria, *New York Times,* April 8, 1995. See an earlier report regarding the suppressed coup against the Abachi regime in the *New York Times,* March 31, 1995.

20. See *New York Times,* July 3, 1993.

21. See a report entitled, "Living with Islam," in *The Economist,* March 18-24, 1995.

22. See a report entitled, "Why Islam is Turning Violent in Pakistan," in *The Economist,* March 4-19, 1995.

23. See a report entitled, "If Islamists Rule Algeria," in *The Economist,* February 25–March 3, 1995.

24. See a report by Barry Newman, "Democracy is Victim as Tunisia Forestalls Strife like Algeria," *Wall Street Journal,* June 22, 1995.

25. For a recent study, see Roger Daniels, *Prisoners Without Trial: Japanese-Americans in World War II,* New York: Hill & Wang, 1993.

26. See "Civil Liberties in Britain: Are They Under Siege?" *New York Times,* November 1, 1995.

27. See Craig R. Whitney, "Britain Moves to Limit Right of Silence for Ulster Suspects," *New York Times,* October 25, 1995.

28. See the *Independent* (London), November 17, 1991.

29. See David McKittrick, "Internment: The Big Gamble for Both Sides," *Independent*, November 17, 1991.

30. See a report by Sanjay Suri entitled "Treaty Wins Despite Criticism," *India Abroad*, July 30, 1993.

31. For a general study, see Morton H. Halperin and David J. Scheffer, *Self-Determination in the New World Order*, Washington, D.C.: Carnegie Endowment for International Peace, 1992.

32. One of the "Purposes of the United Nations" is stated in Article 1 (2), which reads: "To develop friendly relations among nations based on respect for the principle of equal rights and self-determination of peoples, and to take other appropriate measures to strengthen universal peace." Articles 73 to 91 essentially deal with "Non-Self-Governing Territories" and the "Trusteeship System," but have nothing to do with granting self-determination to peoples within existing sovereign independent states.

33. For various studies of nationalism, see Paul R. Brass, *Ethnicity and Nationalism: Theory and Comparison*, Newbury Park, Calif.: Sage Publications, 1992; James Mayall, *Nationalism and International Society*, Cambridge: Cambridge University Press, 1990; Anthony H. Birch, *Nationalism and National Integration*, London: Unwin Hyman, 1989; John Breuilly, *Nationalism and the State*, Chicago: University of Chicago Press, 1982; Ernest Gellner, *Nations and Nationalism*, Ithaca: Cornell University Press, 1982; Eric J. Hobsbawm, *Nations and Nationalism Since 1780: Programme, Myth and Reality*, Cambridge: Cambridge University Press, 1990; James G. Kellas, *The Politics of Nationalism and Ethnicity*, New York: St. Martin's Press, 1991; Anthony D. Smith, *Ethnicity and Nationalism*, Leiden and New York: E. J. Brill, 1991; Paul R. Brass, *Language, Religion and Politics in North India*, Cambridge: Cambridge University Press, 1974; *Political Dynamics and Crisis in Punjab*, ed. Paul Wallace and Surendra Chopra, Amritsar: Guru Nanak Dev University, 1988.

34. The problem is comprehensively discussed in a book by Ted Robert Gurr, *Minorities at Risk: A Global View of Ethnopolitics*, Washington, D.C.: United States Institute of Peace Press, 1993. See, in particular, the chapter entitled "Why Minorities Rebel: Explaining Ethnopolitical Protest and Rebellion," 123-139.

35. A comprehensive study of the problems caused by internal conflict and state disintegration may be found in Lori Fisler Damrosch, *Enforcing Restraint: Collective Intervention in Internal Conflicts*, New York: Council on Foreign Relations Press, 1993.

36. See Sunil Khilnani, "India's Democratic Career," in *Democracy: The Unfinished Journey, 508 BC to 1993*, ed. John Dunn, Oxford: Oxford University Press, 1992, 189-205.

37. See Hemanta Narzary, "Four Decades of Indian Constitution," *Times of India* (Bombay and New Delhi), January 26, 1990; and Kuldip Nayar, "Binding 59th Amendment Viewed as Excuse to Impose Emergency," *India Abroad,* June 10, 1988.

38. Di Palma, *To Craft Democracies,* 3.

39. Robert A. Dahl, *Democracy and Its Critics,* New Haven: Yale University Press, 1989, 108-114.

Chapter 2

1. See Rajni Kothari, *State against Democracy,* New Delhi: Ajanta Publications, 1988; and Atul Kohli, *Democracy and Discontent: India's Growing Crisis of Government,* Cambridge: Cambridge University Press, 1990.

2. See a study by Dennis Austin, *Democracy and Violence in India and Sri Lanka,* London: Royal Institute of International Affairs, 1995; and New York: Council on Foreign Relations, 1995.

3. For a study of the general problems of promoting democracies in developing countries, see Samuel P. Huntington and Joan M. Nelson, *No Easy Choices: Political Participation in Developing Countries,* Cambridge: Harvard University Press, 1976.

4. *The Economist,* April 22-28, 1995.

5. Robert L. Rothstein, "Democracy in the Third World: Definitional Dilemmas," in *Democracy, War and Peace in the Middle East,* ed. David Garnham and Mark Tessler, Bloomington: Indiana University Press, 1995, 65.

6. From the Constitution of India, Part IV, "Directive Principles of State Policy," Article 39. See S. M. Mehta, *Constitution of India and Amendment Acts,* New Delhi: Deep and Deep, 1990, 14.

7. Cited in Walker Connor, *Ethnonationalism: The Quest for Understanding,* Princeton: Princeton University Press, 1994, 217.

8. See *New York Times,* September 7, 1993.

9. See Nicholas D. Kristof, "China Sees 'Market-Leninism' as Way to Future," *New York Times,* September 6, 1993.

10. The political and economic information for Malaysia and Singapore was obtained from *The 1993 Almanac,* Boston: Houghton Mifflin, 1993, 227, 260.

11. For a discussion of new pressures faced by the secular state, see Mark Juergensmeyer, *The New Cold War: Religious Nationalism Confronts the Secular State,* Berkeley and Los Angeles: University of California Press, 1993.

12. For a study of the erosion of secularism in India and in other democracies, see Juergensmeyer, *The New Cold War.*

13. For studies of similar issues, see Timothy D. Sisk, *Islam and Democracy: Religion, Politics and Power in the Middle East,* Washington, D.C.: United States Institute of Peace Press, 1992; Nazih Ayuli, *Political Islam,* London: Routledge, 1991; *Islam and Politics,* ed. John L. Esposito, Syracuse: Syracuse University Press, 1991; John L. Esposito, *Islam, the Straight Path,* Oxford: Oxford University Press, 1991; Elie Kedouri, *Democracy and Arab Political Culture,* Washington, D.C.: Washington Institute for Near East Policy, 1992; James P. Piscatori, *Islam in the Political Process,* Cambridge: Cambridge University Press, 1983; John Ruedy, *Islamism and Secularism in North Africa,* New York: St. Martin's Press, 1994; John L. Esposito and James P. Piscatori, "Democratization and Islam," *Middle East Journal,* vol. 45, no. 3 (summer 1991), 427-440; and Robin Wright, "Islam, Democracy and the West," *Foreign Affairs,* vol. 71, no. 2 (summer 1992), 131-145.

14. See Shukri B. Abed, "Islam and Democracy," in Garnham and Tessler, ed., *Democracy, War and Peace,* 120.

15. For studies of Hinduism see, K. M. Sen, *Hinduism,* Baltimore: Penguin Books, 1961; *Hinduism Reconsidered,* ed. Gunther Sontheimer and Herman Kulke, Heidelberg: South Asia Institute, 1988; Sarvepalli Radhakrishnan, *Eastern Religions and Western Thought,* New York: Oxford University Press, 1974; Gerald James Larson, *India's Agony over Religion,* Albany: SUNY Press, 1994.

16. See Kushwant Singh, "India, the Hindu State," *New York Times,* August 3, 1993. For studies on Indian secularism, see B. M. Puri, *Secularism in Indian Ethos,* New Delhi: Atma Ram, 1990; and Donald B. Smith, *India as a Secular State,* Princeton: Princeton University Press, 1963.

17. See John L. Esposito, *The Islamic Threat: Myth or Reality,* New York: Oxford University Press, 1992, 126.

Chapter 3

1. According to Dileep Padgaonkar, the editor of India's leading English-language daily, the post–Cold War world could follow two divergent lines. In one, "the affluent North will either exploit or neglect the wretched of the South." In the other, "differences within the Western fold are bound to come out again. . . . They [the poor countries] can exploit the differences to their advantage should they get their own act together." The first is more likely to occur, and therefore, "military preparedness to face any eventuality, a dynamic economy, a stable political and social order: these would appear to be the main elements of India's response to the sweeping changes taking place around us." See Dileep Padgaonkar, "The Post Cold War World: Two Theses on the Emerging Order,"

Times of India (Bombay and New Delhi), February 22, 1992. For an overall assessment of South Asia's strategic environment, see Peter Lyon, "South Asia and the Geostrategics of the 1990s," *Contemporary South Asia*, vol. 1, no. 1, January 1992, 25-39.

2. For a report on the rise of Islamic fundamentalism in Indonesia and Malaysia, see *International Herald Tribune*, June 15, 1992; and *The Observer* (London), June 14, 1992. For an Indian assessment, see Dilip Mukerjee, "Turmoil in Islamic World," *Times of India*, July 14, 1992.

3. For a general assessment of Pakistani options, see Mushahid Hussain, "Pakistan's Foreign Policy Choice," *Nation* (Lahore), October 13, 1991.

4. See *Nation,* October 20, 1992.

5. See the special article entitled, "The Expanded ECO: A New Phenomenon in the Islamic World," *Pakistan Times Overseas Weekly,* June 12, 1992.

6. The *Novdye Vremya* assessment was reported in the *Hindustan Times* (New Delhi), February 7, 1992.

7. This view was expressed to me in a conversation with Naved Iqbal during my visit to Karachi in February 1992. Dr. Iqbal, the editor-in-chief of the Pakistani newsmagazine *The Globe,* was at the time on his way to attend an ECO conference in Teheran. Even if much of this is wishful thinking, there is an influential group of politicians, bureaucrats, and intellectuals who feel that Pakistan's ultimate destiny lies in this direction. This hope, desire, or search for a greater Islamic confederation was expressed to me by a number of Pakistanis during my 1992 visit to Pakistan.

8. There are some skeptics in Pakistan, especially among the Sindhis, who are doubtful about the possibility of forging a larger confederation. However, many Pakistanis who spoke to me seem to think that this would be a desirable objective that would benefit Pakistan politically and economically.

9. A much more optimistic assessment than my own is provided by Dr. Maqbool Ahmad Bhatty, "Prospects for Cooperation with Central Asia," *Nation,* October 8, 1991. Bhatty points out some of same obstacles mentioned here—the instability of Afghanistan and uneven levels of per capita incomes—but feels that these problems can eventually be overcome.

10. See a report by Hugh Pope, "Rudderless Tajikstan Heads for the Rocks," *Independent* (London), June 27, 1992.

11. General V. N. Sharma, "National Security: More Threats from Within," *Hindustan Times,* December 18, 1994.

12. Craig Baxter, Yogendra K. Malik, Charles H. Kennedy, and Robert C. Oberst, *Government and Politics in South Asia,* Boulder: Westview Press, 1991, 48.

13. For reports and analyses on the demand for new states within India, see Ruben Banerjee, "Stoking Ethnic Terror: The Bodo Militants Campaign," *India Today*

(New Delhi), August 31, 1994; Tapas Ray, "Fatal Confusion: Militancy and Growing Worries," and Kalyan Chaudhuri, "Jharkhand Again: A Threat of Direct Action for Statehood," *Frontline* (Madras), September 9, 1994; Charu Lata Joshi, "Uttarkhand: Seeking a Separate Identity," *India Today,* September 30, 1994; August 8, 1994, *Frontline.* See also various reports in the *Statesman* (New Delhi), February 9 and June 16, 1994; the *Telegraph* (Calcutta), September 9, 1994; the *Pioneer* (New Delhi), June 8, August 15 and 25, 1994; and the *Patriot* (Ambala), June 20, 1994.

14. See S. Sahay, "Bihar: Violence a Way of Life," *Hindustan Times,* January 10, 1992; Farzand Ahmed, "Bihar: Harvest of Hatred," *India Today,* November 15, 1990; Ashok Das, "A War of Attrition in Andhra Pradesh," *Hindustan Times,* January 6, 1992; and Sourish Bhattacharyya, "Andhra Pradesh: A Grave Divide," *Times of India,* December 31, 1991. For a report of recent massacres in Bihar, see *Indian Express,* February 14, 1992.

15. See R. Radhakrishnan, "The Mandal Commission Odyssey," in *News India* (New York), October 25, 1991. See also M. N. Buch, "Spreading Inequity," *Hindustan Times,* January 9, 1992; and special report by Harinder Baweja, N. K. Singh, and Kanwar Sandhu entitled, "Mandal Commission Fall-Out: Pyres of Protest," *India Today,* October 31, 1992. For a debate on the caste and quota issue by leading Indian personalities, see the report "Caste Vs. Class" in *India Today,* May 31, 1991.

16. Prabhu Chawla, "Ayodha: Exploiting the Issue," *India Today,* December 31, 1990.

17. See studies by Lieutenant General S. K. Sinha, *Higher Defence Organisation in India,* New Delhi: United Services Institution of India, 1980; and "National Security: Need for a Council," *Hindustan Times,* November 25, 1994.

18. Much of this discussion on security decision making is condensed from Raju G. C. Thomas, *Indian Security Policy,* Princeton: Princeton University Press, 1986, 119-134.

19. From the transcript of the address by Indian Defense Minister C. Subramaniam, entitled, "India's Defence Strategy in the Next Decade," to the National Defence College, New Delhi, October 29, 1979.

20. Lieutenant General S. K. Sinha, *Higher Defence Organization in India,* New Delhi: United Services Institution of India, 1980, 6-9.

21. General Sharma in *Hindustan Times,* December 18, 1994.

22. Lieutenant General S. K. Sinha, *Higher Defence Organization in India,* 10.

23. See Babu Suseelan, "Pseudosecularism, Irrational Tolerance Damaging India," *News India–Times* (New York), August 6, 1993.

24. See the report by I. Gopalkrishnan, "Separating Religion and Politics," in *India Abroad* (New York), August 6, 1993.

25. *News India–Times,* August 20, 1993.

26. See *India Abroad,* July 9, 1993.

Chapter 4

1. For a discussion of the Indian constitution's emergency powers to deal with internal and external security threats, see Raju G. C. Thomas, *Indian Security Policy,* Princeton: Princeton University Press, 1986, 97-105.

2. See Richard L. Park and Bruce Bueno de Mesquito, *India's Political System,* 2n ed., New York: Prentice-Hall, 1979, 76.

3. S. M. Mehta, *Constitution of India and Amendment Acts,* New Delhi: Deep an Deep, 1990, 6-7.

4. See *Indira Gandhi's India,* ed. Henry Hart, Boulder, CO: Westview Press, 1976 16-17.

5. See Robert Frykenberg, "The Last Emergency of the Raj," in Hart, *Indir Gandhi's India,* 37-66.

6. From the *Constituent Assembly Debates,* vol. 7, 196, quoted in M. V. Pylee *Constitutional Government of India,* New Delhi: S. Chand, 1984, 502. For comprehensive study of these issues, see Nishta Jaswal, *Role of the Supreme Cour with Regard to the Right to Life and Personal Liberty,* New Delhi: Ashish Publishing House, 1990.

7. Ibid.

8. See Nishtha Jaswal, *Role of the Supreme Court,* 33.

9. Cited in B. S. Raghavan, "A Constitution Under Strain," *Hindu* (Madras), January 4, 1991.

10. Ibid.

11. See A. H. Hanson and Janet Douglas, *India's Democracy,* New York: Norton, 1972, 36.

12. Jaswal, *Role of the Supreme Court,* 24.

13. Ibid., 25.

14. Hanson and Douglas, *India's Democracy,* 36.

15. The discussions pertaining to the Defense India Rules (1962), the Maintenance of Internal Security Act (1971), the 42nd Amendment (1975), and the National Security Act (1980) are adapted from Raju G. C. Thomas, *Indian Security Policy,* 100-105. The discussions of the 59th Amendment (1988) are derived from news reports in Indian newspapers.

16. See Hart, *Indira Gandhi's India,* 18.

17. See Jaswal, *Role of the Supreme Court,* 76-102.

18. From the Constitution of India, Part III, "Fundamental Rights." See Mehta, *Constitution of India,* 8-9.

19. Hemanta Nazary, "Four Decades of Indian Constitution," *Times of India* (Bombay and New Delhi), January 26, 1989.

20. Mehta, *Constitution of India,* 8.
21. Ibid., 8.
22. *Times of India,* March 9, 1988.
23. See Robert L. Hardgrave, *India: Government and Politics in a Developing Nation,* New York: Harcourt Brace Jovanovich, 1980, 52-54.
24. Statement reported by the Delhi Domestic Service in English and recorded in the *Foreign Broadcast Information Service,* No. 186, September 23, 1980, E3.
25. See *Statesman* (New Delhi), June 23, 1984; and *Indian Express* (New Delhi), June 23, 1984.
26. See *Hindu,* June 23, 1984.
27. Congressman Dan Burton of the U.S. House of Representatives introduced a "Justice in India Act" (H.R. 1519) in 1993 that called for the suspension of U.S. development aid of $143 million to India to protest these Indian measures. The bill did not pass.
28. *Times of India,* March 24, 1988. See also Jaswal, *Role of the Supreme Court,* 91.
29. Kuldip Nayar, "TADA needs to be Scrapped," *Mainstream* (New Delhi), August 20, 1994.
30. See the *Pioneer* (New Delhi and Bombay), September 6 and 9, 1994.
31. See Sunder Raman, *Amending Power Under the Constitution of India: A Politico-Legal Study,* Calcutta and New Delhi: Eastern Law House, 1990, 129.
32. See the Indian Constitution, Part XX, Article 368. One text that may be referred to is S. M. Mehta, *Constitution of India,* 133.
33. See Sunder Raman, *Constitutional Amendments in India,* Calcutta and New Delhi: Eastern Law House, 1989, 5-18.
34. See S. M. Mehta, *Constitution of India,* 5.
35. Sunder Raman, *Amending Power,* 56.
36. Ibid., 124-125.
37. Ibid., 126.
38. Ibid., 96.
39. Ibid., 129.
40. Ibid., 98.
41. See Mehta, *Constitution of India,* 124.
42. For a list of reasons that would justify the declaration of emergency in the states, see S. C. Arora, *President's Rule in Indian States,* New Delhi: Mittal Publications, 1990, 26-28.
43. Figures obtained from Arora, *President's Rule,* 36.
44. Ibid., Appendix 4, 233-235.
45. See the report by Dipankar De Sarkar, "Supporting the Presidential System," *India Abroad* (New York), July 30, 1993.
46. Ibid.

47. For a discussion of the debate in the early 1980s, see, for instance, R. Chakroborty, "Do the People Want Change in the System?" *Statesman,* December 13, 1980; Justice A. K. Das, "Changes to Make the Government Work," *Statesman,* December 18, 1980; Nani A. Palkhivala, "Presidential System: A Question of Timing," *Hindustan Times* (New Delhi), January 7, 1981; and Salman Kurshid, "Palkhivala's Volte Face," *Hindustan Times,* January 13, 1981.

48. The initial part of the second paragraph of the "Statement of Object and Reasons" of the 52nd Amendment Act of 1985 reads as follows:

> The Bill seeks to amend the Constitution to provide that an elected member of Parliament or a State Legislature, who has been elected as a candidate set up by a political party and a nominated member of Parliament or a State Legislature who is a member of a political party at the time he takes his seat or who becomes a member of a political party within six months after he takes his seat would be disqualified on the ground of defection if he voluntarily relinquishes his membership of such political party or votes or abstains from voting in such House contrary to any direction of such party or is expelled from such party. An independent member of Parliament or a State Legislature shall also be disqualified if he joins any political party after his election. . . . The Bill also makes suitable provisions with respect to splits in, and mergers of, political parties.

See Mehta, *Constitution of India,* 355. For a discussion of new problems associated with the implementation of the 52nd Amendment and Tenth Schedule, see V. S. Rama Devi, "The Tenth Schedule of the Constitution," in *Reforming the Constitution,* ed. Subhash C. Kashyap, New Delhi: UBS Publishers Distributors, 1992, 301-306.

49. See *News India–Times* (New York), August 6, 1993.

50. Cited in A. G. Noorani, *The Presidential System: The Indian Debate,* New Delhi and Newbury Park, CA: Sage Publications, 1989, 22-23.

51. Walter Bagehot, *The English Constitution,* World Classics, London: Oxford University Press, 1930, 15.

52. See A. G. Noorani, *The Presidential System,* 69.

53. *Tribune* (Chandigarh), May 4, 1995.

54. For a variety of views on how the Indian constitution should be changed, see Kashyap, ed., *Reforming the Constitution.* See, in particular, the introduction by Subhash Kashyap; and the articles by B. K. Nehru, "A Fresh Look at the Constitution," 128-147; Vasant Sathe, "Democratic Decentralization: Need for Constitutional Reforms," 148-156; and B. S. Raghavan, "A Constitution Under Strain," 208-215.

55. P. G. Mavalankar, "Urgent Need for Amendments: Plea for Constitution Reforms Commission," in Kashyap, ed., *Reforming the Constitution,* 333.

Chapter 5

1. For comparative studies, see S. E. Finer, *The Man on Horseback: The Rise of the Military in Politics,* Baltimore, MD: Peregrine/Penguin Books, 1976; Eric A. Nordlinger, *Soldiers in Politics: Military Coups and Governments,* Englewood Cliffs, NJ: Prentice-Hall, 1977; Amos Perlmutter, *The Military and Politics in Modern Times,* New Haven, CT: Yale University Press, 1977; *The Military and Security in the Third World: Domestic and International Aspects,* ed. Sheldon W. Simon, Boulder, CO: Westview Press, 1978. For a study of the Pakistani case, see Stephen P. Cohen, *The Pakistan Army,* Berkeley and Los Angeles: University of California Press, 1984.

2. For a discussion of the growth and development of the Indian Army until independence, see Stephen P. Cohen, *The Indian Army: Its Contribution to the Development of a Nation,* Berkeley and Los Angeles: University of California Press, 1971. See also Lorne J. Kavic, *India's Quest for Security: Defense Policies, 1945-65,* Berkeley and Los Angeles: University of California Press, 1967. For a later analysis, see Raju G. C. Thomas, *The Defence of India: A Budgetary Perspective of Strategy and Politics,* Delhi: The Macmillan Company of India, 1978, 141-173.

3. See Lieutenant General S. K. Sinha, *Of Matters Military,* New Delhi: Vision Books, 1980, 121.

4. A substantial part of the information in the next two paragraphs was provided to me by Bharat Karnad in 1986, while he was the Washington, D.C., correspondent of the *Hindustan Times.*

5. For a discussion of the sources of Sikh grievances with respect to recruitment to the Indian armed forces, see Stephen P. Cohen, "The Military and Indian Democracy," in *India's Democracy: An Analysis of Changing State-Society Relations,* ed. Atul Kohli, Princeton, NJ: Princeton University Press, 1988, 132-138.

6. Ibid., 133, footnote 50.

7. See *New York Times,* June 11, 1984.

8. Again, I must thank Bharat Karnad, former Washington correspondent of the *Hindustan Times,* for providing the information and insights in this and the next paragraph.

9. Interviews conducted by author in 1973-74 in New Delhi with former Indian Army officers.

10. This is my assessment, and not necessarily that of Bharat Karnad.

11. See Cohen, "The Military and Indian Democracy," 111-113.

12. See Lieutenant General M. L. Thapan, "The Army: How Far to Aid the Civil Authority," *Statesman* (Calcutta), August 3, 1980; Lieutenant General A. M.

Vohra, "Other Tasks of Armed Forces," *Tribune* (Ambala), April 14, 1980; and "Coups and Military Takeovers," *Tribune,* March 28, 1980.

13. Thapan, "The Army."

14. This information and some of the information in the next two paragraphs was provided to me by Bharat Karnad.

15. See various reports in the *New York Times,* June 5, 6, 24, and 29, 1984. See also Rajiv Kapur, *Sikh Separatism: The Politics of Faith,* Winchester, MA: Allen and Unwin, 1986.

16. See Raju G. C. Thomas and Bharat Karnad, "The Military and National Integration in India," in *Ethnicity, Integration and the Military,* ed. Henry Dietz and Jerrold Elkin, Boulder, CO: Westview Press, 1990, 127-150.

17. Interviews conducted by author in 1992 in Sri Lanka with various Tamil and Sinhalese political analysts and journalists.

18. Interview with former Minister of Defense (and earlier of Home Affairs) Jagjivan Ram.

19. General V. N. Sharma, "National Security: More Threats from Within," *Hindustan Times* (New Delhi), December 18, 1994.

20. See Raju G. C. Thomas, "The Armed Services and the Indian Defense Budget," *Asian Survey,* vol. 20, no. 3 (March 1980), 280-297.

21. See Lieutenant General A. M. Vohra (Retired), "More Paramilitary Forces Are Needed," *Times of India* (Bombay and New Delhi), July 14, 1992.

22. See Shankar Bhaduri, "Paramilitary has Become a Generalist Force," *Asian Age* (New Delhi), October 27, 1994; and Amar Zutshi, "Counter-Insurgency: Dilemma of the Forces," *Hindustan Times,* June 26, 1995.

23. *India Weekly* (London), June 17, 1992.

24. See Raju G. C. Thomas, *Indian Security Policy,* Princeton, NJ: Princeton University Press, 1986, 72-77.

25. See Manoj Joshi, "Rashtriya Rifles Battalions to East Army's Burden," *Times of India,* August 11, 1994; Pravin Sawhney, "RR: Army by Another Name but with More Problems," *Asian Age,* October 8, 1994; Mohan Guruswamy, "Rashtriya Rifles: Force for a Different War," *Hindustan Times,* November 21, 1994; and Zutshi, "Counter-Insurgency: Dilemma of the Forces."

Chapter 6

1. See Barrington Moore, Jr., *Social Origins of Dictatorship and Democracy,* Boston: Beacon Press, 1966.

2. For a study of the tension of development between the city and the countryside in India, see Ashutosh Varshney, *Democracy, Development, and the Countryside:*

Urban-Rural Struggles in India, Cambridge: Cambridge University Press, 1995. For other studies contrasting India and China, see George Rosen, *Contrasting Styles of Industrial Revolution: China and India in the 1980s,* Chicago: University of Chicago Press, 1992; and T. N. Srinivasan, *Agriculture and Trade in China and India,* San Francisco: ICS Press, 1994.

3. Edward Friedman, "Development, Democracy and Dictatorship: China Versus India." Paper presented at the conference "Comparative Reforms in China and India," Center for International Studies, Marquette University, May 13-14, 1995.

4. Karen E. House, "Two Asian Giants, China and India, Growing Apart," *Wall Street Journal,* February 24, 1995.

5. Shalendra D. Sharma, "Neo-Classical Political Economy and the Lessons from East Asia," *International Studies Notes* (International Studies Association), vol. 20, no. 2 (spring 1995) 22-24.

6. K. Subrahmanyam, "India Need Not Fear Domination by the U.S.," *India Abroad* (New York), March 3, 1995.

7. See Raju G. C. Thomas, "Indo-U.S. Security Ties," *Orbis,* vol. 27, no. 2 (summer 1983), 371-392.

8. G. C. Katoch, "Defence Expenditure: Some Issues," *Indian Defence Review,* January 1992, 35.

9. Much of the discussion here is drawn from Raju G. C. Thomas, *Indian Security Policy,* Princeton, NJ: Princeton University Press, 1986, 211-233. For a comprehensive Indian study undertaken in the early 1990s, see D. D. Khanna and P. N. Mehrotra, *Defence Versus Development: A Case Study of India,* New Delhi: Indus Publishing Company, 1993.

10. Emile Benoit, *Defense and Economic Growth in Developing Countries,* Lexington, Mass.: Lexington Books, 1973.

11. Ibid., 162-164.

12. Ibid., 164.

13. Robert E. Looney and David Winterford, *Economic Causes and Consequences of Defense Expenditures in the Middle East and South Asia,* Boulder, CO: Westview Press, 1995, 61.

14. Ibid., 216.

15. See K. Subrahmanyam, *Defence and Development,* Calcutta: Minerva Associates, 1973; David K. Whynes, *The Economics of Third World Military Expenditure,* London: Macmillan, 1979; and P. Terhal, "Guns or Grain: Macro-Economic Cost of Indian Defence, 1960-70," *Economic and Political Weekly* (Bombay), vol. 16, no. 49, December 5, 1981.

16. Nicole Ball, *The Military in the Development Process,* Claremont, CA: Regina Books, 1981, 7-8. A more comprehensive study of the problem is provided in

Nicole Ball, *Security and Economy in the Third World,* Princeton, NJ: Princeton University Press, 1988.

17. D. D. Khanna and P. N. Mehrotra, *Defence Versus Development,* 158-166.

18. Air Marshal Vir Narain (Retired), "Military Expenditure and the Poor," *Indian Defence Review,* January 1992, 43, 44.

19. Figures obtained from Raj Krishna, "The Economic Development of India," *Scientific American,* 243, no. 3, September 1980, 172. See also Raju G. C. Thomas, *The Defence of India: A Budgetary Perspective of Strategy and Politics,* Delhi: The Macmillan Company of India, 1978, 134.

20. See Khanna and Mehrotra, *Defence Versus Development,* 161.

21. I have highlighted and elaborated on a view suggested by Prem Shankar Jha in his article, "The Perilous Politics of Economic Reforms," *India Abroad,* July 17, 1992.

22. See Jayshree Sengupta, "Policy-Makers Debate the Road after Dabhol," *India Abroad,* August 25, 1995.

23. Rashmi Mayur, "Maharashtra was Right to have Scrapped Enron," *India Abroad,* August 25, 1995.

24. See I. Gopalakrishnan, "Thirteen Economists Attack Liberalization," *India Abroad,* March 10, 1995.

25. See Alan Heston, "India's Economic Reforms: The Real Thing?" *Current History,* vol. 91, no. 563, 113-116.

26. Ibid., 115.

27. From Finance Minister Manmohan Singh's interview with *India Today* (New Delhi), July 31, 1992.

28. *Hindustan Times* (New Delhi), January 14, 1992.

29. See *India Abroad,* September 27, 1991, and July 3, 1992.

30. *India Abroad,* March 8, 1993.

31. Ibid.

32. See *India News* (Embassy of India, Washington, D.C.), April 1, 1994.

33. *Financial Times* (London), November 19 and 21, 1991.

34. *India Abroad,* October 2, 1992.

35. *Daily News* (Colombo), January 21, 1992.

36. *Times of India* (Bombay and New Delhi), May 23, 1992.

37. *India News,* June 1, 1994.

38. For Indian assessments, see Subir Roy, "Future of Reforms," *Times of India,* July 20, 1992; and Prem Shankar Jha, "The Perilous Politics of Economic Reforms," *India Abroad,* July 17, 1992.

39. *Times of India,* July 14, 1992.

40. See I. Gopalkrishnan, "Doubts Raised on Reform's Pace," *India Abroad,* July 10, 1992.

41. See Suman Dubey, "Indian Economy Shows Signs of Recovery," *Wall Street Journal,* September 8, 1992.
42. Statement by Finance Minister Dr. Manmohan Singh, entitled, "Investing in India," in the advertising supplement to *The Washington Post National Weekly Edition,* June 26–July 2, 1995.
43. See *Financial Times,* November 21, 1991; and *India Abroad,* June 26, 1992.
44. *India Abroad,* July 23, 1993.
45. See Rajendra Bajpai, "India's Reform Keeps Bumping Along," *International Herald Tribune,* July 23, 1992; and special report in *India Today,* May 31, 1992.
46. *India Abroad,* July 30, 1993.
47. *India Abroad,* August 6, 1993.
48. *India Today,* July 31, 1992.
49. See *Ethnic Conflict in South Asia* (Special Issue), ed. Ashgar Ali Engineer, *Islamic Perspective,* July 1987; Paul R. Brass, *Language, Religion and Politics in North India,* Cambridge: Cambridge University Press, 1974.; Lt. Gen. V. K. Nayar, *The Threat from Within: India's Internal Security Environment,* New Delhi: Lancer Publishers, 1992; P. R. Rajagopal, *Communal Violence in India,* New Delhi: Uppal Publishing House, 1987; and Govind Narain, *Internal Threats and National Security,* New Delhi: United Services Institution of India, 1986.
50. See the special supplement, "Survey of India," in *The Economist* (London), January 21, 1995.

Chapter 7

1. See Madhu Limaye, "Will the Indian State Degenerate Into a Coercive One," *Times of India* (Bombay and New Delhi), October 12, 1989.
2. See M. V. Pylee, *Constitutional Government in India,* New Delhi: S. Chand Company, 1984, 444-448.
3. Ibid., 444.
4. Ibid., 449.
5. For a further discussion of this point, see Raju G. C. Thomas, "Wrestling with India's Sikh Crisis," *Christian Science Monitor,* June 7, 1988.
6. This view was expressed to me during a conversation with Naved Iqbal during my visit to Karachi in February 1992. Dr. Iqbal, the editor-in-chief of the Pakistani newsmagazine *The Globe,* was at the time on his way to attend the ECO conference in Teheran. Even if much of this is wishful thinking, there is an influential group of politicians, bureaucrats, and intellectuals who feel that Pakistan's ultimate destiny lies in this direction.

7. A much more optimistic assessment than my own is provided by Dr. Maqbool Ahmad Bhatty, in "Prospects for Cooperation with Central Asia," *Nation* (Lahore), October 8, 1991. Bhatty points out some of same obstacles mentioned here—the instability of Afghanistan and uneven levels of per capita incomes—but feels that these problems can be overcome eventually. See also the report by Hugh Pope, "Rudderless Tajikstan Heads for the Rocks," *Independent* (London), June 27, 1992.

8. These figures were obtained from the economic research section at the International Institute for Strategic Studies. The comparable per capita income for Turkmenistan is $3,020; for Kyrghystan, $2,043; for Azerbaijan, $1,850; and for Uzbekistan, $1,630. See also Maqbool Ahmad Bhatty, "Prospects for Cooperation with Central Asia," *Nation*, October 8, 1991. According to Bhatty, "the Central Asian republics have relatively advanced economies, compared to ours [Pakistan's], with an average per capita income 6 to 7 times higher than that of Pakistan."

9. Some Indian reports, confirmed by Pakistani analysts I met in Islamabad, indicate that initial Pakistani overtures for Islamic ties were rebuffed by the Central Asian republics, who indicated their preference for the secular ideology that they had become accustomed to when they were part of the Soviet Union. They also insisted that they did not wish to see an Islamic fundamentalist regime replace the Najibullah regime in Kabul. See the report by Vinod Sharma entitled, "Afghan Stalemate May Turn Republics Hostile to Pakistan," *Hindustan Times* (New Delhi), January 10, 1992.

10. See reports in the *International Herald Tribune,* November 26, 1991; and the *Independent,* April 27, 1992.

11. Prem Shankar Jha, "The Perilous Politics of Economic Reforms," *India Abroad* (New York), July 17, 1992.

ABOUT THE AUTHOR

RAJU G. C. THOMAS is Professor of Political Science at Marquette University in Milwaukee, Wisconsin. He is the Co-Director of the joint Center for International Studies of the University of Wisconsin–Milwaukee and Marquette University, one of 16 National Resource Centers set up by the U.S. Department of Education. Professor Thomas was a Visiting Scholar/Research Fellow at Harvard University (1980-81, 1988-89); UCLA (1982-83); the Massachusetts Institute of Technology (1988-89); the International Institute for Strategic Studies–London (1991-92); and the University of Wisconsin–Madison (summer 1994). Between 1965 and 1969, he worked for British multinational companies in India.

His books include *The Defence of India: A Budgetary Perspective* (Macmillan of India, 1978); *Indian Security Policy* (Princeton University Press, 1986); *South Asian Security in the 1990s* (Brassey's/IISS-London, 1993). He is the contributing editor of *The Great Power Triangle and Asian Security* (Lexington Books, 1983); with Bennett Ramberg, *Energy and Security in the Industrializing World* (University Press of Kentucky, 1990); *Perspectives on Kashmir* (Westview Press, 1992); and, with Richard Friman, *The South Slav Conflict: Religion, Ethnicity, and Nationalism* (Garland Publishing Inc., January 1996). He is currently editing a volume entitled *The Nuclear Non-Proliferation Regime: The Next Phase* and working on a research project with Barrett McCormick entitled *Comparative Reforms in China and India*. Raju Thomas has published extensively in professional journals, edited collections, and leading newspapers.

Professor Thomas was educated at Bombay University; the London School of Economics; and UCLA, where he obtained his Ph.D. in political science.

INDEX

Abachi, Sani, 12
Abed, Shukri B., 43
Abiola, Moshood, 12
Abkhazia, 19
Advani, L. K., 67, 133
Afghanistan (Afghans), 7, 18, 53-55, 59, 63, 141, 155
Ahmedi, A. M., 85
Akali Dal, 90, 104
Albania (Albanians), 19, 48
Algeria, 4, 13, 46
Allen, Graham, 17
Allende, Salvador, 122
Ambedkar, B. R., 78, 95
Amnesty International, 17, 70
Andhra Pradesh, 59, 90, 97, 108
Aquino, Benigno, 40
Aquino, Corazon, 5, 12, 40
Arab-Israeli Wars, 15
Argentina, 4, 14, 100, 145
Aristide, Jean-Bertrand, 13
Arunachal Pradesh, 90, 152
Asia Watch, 70
Assam (Assamese), 10, 20-21, 29, 34-35, 47, 56-58, 69, 75, 91, 93, 109-111, 113, 115-117, 120, 141-142, 150, 152-153, 156
Australian, 78, 140
Awami League, 7, 10
Azerbaijan, 54

Babangida, Ibrahim, 12
Bagehot, Walter, 96
Ball, Nicole, 130
Balochistan (Balochis), 7, 9, 18, 20, 32, 47-48, 56, 71, 109, 111, 153-154
Bangladesh, 6-7, 9-12, 18-19, 32, 34, 44, 49, 56-59, 64, 66, 75, 80-81, 99-101, 109, 115, 141-142, 151, 154
Bangladesh National Party, 10
Basques, 47-48
Basu, Jyoti, 133
Beg, Mirza Aslam, 8, 10
Belgium, 143
Bengal, 34-35, 152; East Bengal, 66
Bengalis, 9, 18, 27, 48, 71, 91, 111, 118, 142, 153-154
Benoit, Emile, 129-130
Bhagwati, Jagdish, 137
Bharatiya Janata Party (BJP), 60, 64, 67-68, 93, 96, 106, 133-134, 140-141
Bhargava, Thakurdas, 77
Bhutan 6-7, 11

Bhutto, Benazir, 7-10, 109, 148
Bhutto, Zulfiqar Ali, 7, 9, 148
Biafra, 47, 49
Bihar, 59, 84, 91, 105, 146, 154
Bihari Muslims, 48, 66
Bodoland (Bodos), 21, 58
Bosnia-Herzegovina, 19, 35, 48-49, 71
Brazil, 4, 14, 100, 145
Britain, 12-13, 15-17, 19, 35, 39, 55, 64, 79, 103, 130, 134
British, 5, 15-16, 21, 36, 45, 52, 77-78, 94-97, 100-104, 109, 111, 119, 123, 135, 140, 152, 154
Buddhists (Buddhism), 22, 43-44, 64
Burkina Faso, 143
Burma (Myanmar), 4, 12, 30, 47, 58, 115
Burton Dan, 70

Cabinet Committee on Political Affairs (CCPA), 61, 63
Cabinet Mission Plan, 34-35, 152
Canada (Canadian), 48, 78-79, 94
Cariappa, K. M., 114
Carter, Jimmy, 13
Castes, 22
Cedras, Raoul, 13
Central Treaty Organization (CENTO), 53, 106
Chakmas, 58
Chandrashekhar, 94, 96
Chatterjee, Somnath, 68
Chavan, S. B., 85
Chiefs of Staff Committee (CSC), 61-62
Chile, 14, 100, 122, 124, 145
China (Chinese), 4, 7 14, 17, 21, 30, 38-39, 41-42, 47-48, 55, 61, 70, 80, 107-108, 110, 114-115, 122-123, 125-127, 137, 143, 147, 157-158
Christians, 15, 22, 43-49, 56-57, 63-65, 107, 154
Cold War, 2-3, 17-18, 26, 52-53, 124-127, 136, 153, 157-158
Commonwealth of Independent States (CIS), 34-35, 152
Communist Party of India (CPI), 68, 108, 140
Communist Party-Marxist (CPM), 68, 90, 93, 108, 133, 140
Congress Party (government), 8, 33, 36-37, 41, 68, 75, 83-86, 88, 91, 93-95, 106, 108, 112, 132-134, 138, 140-141, 148
Constitutent Assembly, 33, 77-79, 95
Croatia (Croatians), 19-20, 35, 48-49, 71, 152

Cuba, 30
Cyprus, 18-19
Czechoslovakia, 19

Dahl, Robert A., 22
Daman and Diu, 90
Dayal, Rajeshwar Singh, 110-111
D'Azelio, Massimo, 35
De, Niren, 88
Defamation Bill, 21, 118
Defense and Development, 126-132
Defense Committee of the Cabinet (DCC), 61
Defense of India Act (1939), 77
Defense of India Act (1962), 80
Defense of India Rules (DIR), 17, 21, 55, 80-83, 108
Defense Minister's Committee (DMC), 61-62
Defense Planning Committee (DPC), 61-62
Desai, Morarji, 83, 96
Di Palma, Giuseppe, 22
Dogras, 104
Dravida Munnetra Kazagham (DMK), 56
Dubashi, Jay, 140
Duncan, Emma, 143
Economic Cooperation Organization (ECO), 54-55, 154-155
Egypt, 13, 46, 131
Eighth Amendment (Pakistan), 8
Eightieth (80th) Amendment, 67-68
Elizabeth, Queen, 39
Eritrea, 49
Ershad, H. M., 10, 64
Ethiopia, 49
European Community (Union), 34, 153

Fernandes, George, 68
Fifty-Second (52nd) Amendment, 95
Fifty-Ninth (59th) Amendment, 21, 80, 84-85, 118
First (1st) Amendment, 87
Forty-Fourth (44th) Amendment, 82, 84, 88
Forty-Second (42nd) Amendment, 21, 70, 73, 80-81, 83-85, 88, 118
France (French), 14, 92, 94-97
Friedman, Edward, 122

Gandhi, Indira, 8, 10, 17, 20, 25, 29, 38, 70, 74-75, 77, 80, 83, 85, 88, 90-91, 94, 96, 108, 119, 136, 148
Gandhi, Mohandas K. (Mahatma), 32, 44, 79, 152
Gandhi, Rajiv, 80, 84-86, 93-96, 108, 136
Gandhi, Ved, 130
Garwahlis, 104
Georgia, 19, 48

Germany (Germans), 18, 77, 137, 153
Gerschenkron, Alexander, 124
Gharos, 56, 63, 69
Ghosh, Arun, 134
Goa, 65, 90
Golaknath Case, 87-88
Government of India Act (1935), 77
Governor's Rule, 91
Greece, 18
Guatemala, 4
Gujerat (Gujeratis), 33, 36, 84, 141, 150
Gulati, L. S., 134
Gulf War (1991), 53, 71
Gupta, Indrajit, 68
Gurkhaland (Gurkhas), 21, 58, 103-104, 110-111

Habibullah, Enayat E., 107
Haiti, 4, 13, 30
Hamid, Abdul, 107
Haq, Zia-ul, 8-9, 13, 29, 40, 148
Harijans, 22, 57, 59
Haryana, 66, 91-92
Hazaras, 32
Hidayatullah, Mohammed, 88
Hindus, 22, 36, 41, 43-49, 52, 56-60, 63-68, 79, 91, 103, 106-108, 111, 115, 125, 133-134, 141, 152-154
House, Karen E., 123
Hungarians, 48
Hussain, Altaf, 9
Hussain, Saddam, 71
Hyderabad, 79

India, 2, 4-6, 9-10, 16, 18-23, 26-27, 29, 35-36, 38, 41-42, 44-45, 47, 49, 52-71, 73, 79-89, 92, 94; civil-military relations, 60-63, 99-102, 112-114, 118-120; constitution, 21, 73-97, 148-149; economic conditions, 133-144; ethnicity and society, 22, 102-107; external threats, 52-55, 107-109; federalism, 148-152; human rights, 68-71; internal threats, 55-60, 109-111, 146; secularism, 43-46, 63-68
Indian Air Force, 103, 107; Royal Indian Air Force, 103, 106
Indian Army, 62, 101, 103-114, 118-120; British Indian Army, 102-103, 106, 110
Indian National Congress, 34, 36
Indian Navy, 103, 107; Royal Indian Navy, 103, 106
Indonesia, 12, 14, 39-40, 47-48, 53, 70, 121, 157
Indo-Pakistani Wars, 7, 11, 20-21, 25, 55, 61-62, 64, 80, 94, 106-107, 116, 126, 128

Indo-U.S. cooperation, 124-126
International Convention on Human Rights, 69
International Monetary Fund (IMF), 136, 140
Iran (Iranian), 18-19, 43, 53-55, 63, 155
Iraq, 47-48, 71
Ireland (Irish), 16, 78-79
Irish Republican Army (IRA), 15-16
Islami Jamhoori Ittehad (IJI), 7-8
Islamic Salvation Front, 13
Israel, 15, 19
Israeli, 5
Italy, 14, 35, 45

Jains, 22, 44, 67
Jamaat-i-Islami, 45
Jammu and Kashmir. See Kashmir.
Jana Sangh, 67, 83
Janata Dal (and government), 60, 68, 93-95,
    105, 108, 133, 140
Janata Party (and government), 41, 61, 82-83,
    88, 93, 105, 112
Janatha Vimukthi Peramuna (JVP), 11
Japan, 2, 39, 42, 77, 121-124, 127, 137, 143
Japanese-Americans, 14
Jatoi, Ghulam Mustafa, 8
Jayawardene, Julius, 96
Jews, 22
Jha, Prem Shankar, 156
Jharkand, 58, 65
Jinnah, Mohammed Ali, 34, 45, 47, 63, 152
Johnson administration, 14
Joshi, Murli Manohar, 133
Joshi, P. C., 134

Kachins, 47, 58
Kamath, H. V., 77
Karnataka, 150
Kashmir (Kashmiri Muslims), 8, 10-11, 16, 18-
    21, 26, 29, 32, 34, 47-48, 52-53, 56-58,
    63-66, 68-71, 75, 84, 89, 91, 108-109,
    111, 113, 115-117, 120, 125, 141-142,
    146, 150, 152-156
Katoch, G. C., 126
Kazakhstan, 54, 15
Kazaure, Zubair, 13
Kerala, 65, 67, 75, 90-91, 108, 150
Kesavananda Bharati Case, 87-88
Khalistan, 20, 85, 92, 119, 153
Khan, Ayub, 9, 29, 40, 92
Khan, Sahabzada Yaqub, 107
Khan, Shami, 107
Khan, Sikander Hayyat, 110
Khan, Yahya, 7, 9, 26
Khan, Ghulam Ishaq, 8, 109, 148
Khanna, D. D., 130-131

Khomeini, Ayatollah, 53
Koirala, Giriga Prasad, 11
Koreans, 18
Kosovo, 19
Kristof, Nicholas, 39
Kurds, 47-48, 71
Kurian, C. T., 134
Kyrgystan, 54

Latvia, 19
Lebanon, 15
Liberation Tigers of Tamil Ealam (LTTE), 11,
    69, 111
Limaye, Madhu, 146-147
Looney, Robert E., 130

Mahars, 104
Marathas, 103-104, 111
Macedonia, 48
Madhya Pradesh, 65, 146
Maharashtra, 84, 105, 134, 141, 150
Mahbubani, Kishore, 31
Maintenance of Internal Security Act (MISA),
    17, 21, 55, 68, 80-83
Malayasia, 12, 14, 39, 53
Maldives, 6-7, 11
Malkani, B. R., 133
Mandal Commission Report, 60
Manipur, 21, 58, 91
Marcos, Ferdinand, 12, 39-40
Market-Leninism, 39
Marwaris, 33
Marx, Karl, 33
Mathai, John, 150
Maudling, Reginald, 16
Mavalankar, P. G., 97
Mawdudi, Maulana Abul Ala, 45
Mayur, Rashmi, 134
Meghalaya, 21, 58, 65
Mehrotra, P. N., 130-131
Mitra, Ashok, 134
Mizoram (Mizos), 21, 56, 58, 65, 69, 90, 110,
    113
Mohajir Qaumi Movement (MQM), 9
Mohajirs, 7, 9, 32, 66, 154-155
Moldova, 19
Moore, Barrington, 122, 124
Moors (Sri Lanka), 111
Morocco, 54
Moros, 48
Mosque-Temple dispute, 59-60
Mubarak, Muhammed Hosni, 13
Mukhopadhyay, Ajoy, 140
Muslim Brotherhood, 13
Muslim League (pre-partition), 34, 45,

Muslim League, 67-68
Muslims (Islam), 5, 13, 22, 36, 43-49, 52-59, 63-68, 79-80, 84, 91, 193, 106-108, 110-111, 115, 141-142, 152-156
Myanmar. See Burma.

Nabiyev, Rakhmon, 55
Nagaland (Nagas), 20-21, 47-48, 56, 63, 69, 75, 110, 113, 153
Najibullah, 55, 155
Narain, Vir, 130
Nasser, Gamel Abdel, 13
National Conference (Kashmir), 90, 108
National Emergency, 17, 20-21, 25, 29, 70, 73-75, 81, 84, 91, 94, 117
National Front, 93
National Security Act (NSA, 1980), 21, 83-84, 118
Naxalites, 59
Nayar, Deepak, 134
Nayar, Kuldip, 85
Nehru, Jawaharlal, 32, 34-36, 38, 42, 44-45, 65, 67, 75, 86, 94, 135, 146, 150, 152, 157
Nepal, 6, 11-12, 18
Nigeria, 4, 12, 47, 49, 100
Nixon administration, 14
Non-Alignment Movement (NAM), 157
Northern Ireland, 5, 15-16
North Korea, 30, 42
North-West Frontier Province, 7, 20, 111, 154
Nuclear Non-Proliferation Treaty (NPT), 158

Official Secrets Act, 21
Organization of African Unity (OAU), 49
Organization of American States (OAS), 13
Orissa, 91, 146

Pakistan, 2, 6-13, 17-21, 26, 29, 32, 34-35, 44-49, 53-57, 59, 63-67, 69, 71, 79-80, 92, 99-101, 105, 107-111, 115, 119, 126, 130-131, 137, 141, 145, 150-152, 154-158; East Pakistan 7, 34, 48, 56, 66, 69, 107, 109, 118, 152-154; West Pakistan, 34, 66, 107, 111, 154
Pakistan Army, 69, 111
Pakistan People's Party (PPP), 7-8
Palestinians, 53
Palestine Liberation Organization (PLO), 15
Paramilitary forces, 115-120
Parsees, 33, 36, 67
Pashtuns (Pashtunistan), 7, 9, 18, 32, 47, 153-154
Patel, Vallabhai, 65, 146
Patil, Shivraj, 97
Philippines, 4-5, 12, 39-40, 48

Pickering, Thomas, 137
Pinochet, Augusto, 122
Poland, 138
Pondicherry, 90
President's Rule, 75, 78, 89-92, 148
Punjab (India), 8, 16, 20-21, 29, 34-36, 48, 56-58, 66-68, 70-71, 75, 79, 84, 89-92, 101, 108-111, 113, 115-117, 120, 141-142, 146-147, 150, 152, 155-156; Punjab (Pakistan), 45, 66, 79, 110, 154; Punjab (pre-partition), 110, 152
Punjabis (Pakistan), 7, 9, 32, 111, 153
Pylee, M. V., 149

Quebecois, 48

Raghavan, B. R., 78
Rahman, Sheikh Mujibur, 7, 10
Rahman, Ziaur, 10
Raj, K. N., 134
Raju, Krishna, 134
Rajasthan, 105, 108, 152
Rajputs, 104, 106, 111
Ram, Jagjivan, 112, 116
Ramos, Fidel, 12
Rao, N. T. Rama, 90
Rao, P. V. Narasimha, 34, 75, 91-92, 94-96, 136-138
Rashtriya Swayamsevak Sangh (RSS), 64
Rau, B. N., 79
Regional Cooperation for Development (RCD), 53-54
Regional integration, 153-156
Republican Party (U.S.), 41
Rodrigues, S. F., 118
Rothstein, Robert L., 31
Russett, Bruce, 3
Russia (Russian), 19, 39, 48, 53-55, 138, 143, 157

Sachs, Jeffrey, 138
Sadat, Anwar, 13
Sahai, Subodh Kant, 93
Sait, Ibrahim Suleiman, 67
Sajjan Singh Case, 87-88
Sanjay Dutt Case, 85
Saudi Arabia, 145, 155
Serbia (Serbs), 19, 35, 48, 152
Shah of Iran, 19, 53
Shah, Sultan Azian Muhibuddin, 39
Seventeenth (17th) Amendment, 87
Shankari Prasad Case, 87-88
Shans, 47, 58
Sharif, Mian Nawaz, 8, 10, 53
Sharma, Shalendra, 123

Sharma, V. N., 56, 62, 112
Shiv Sena, 64, 134, 141
Sikhs, 10, 16, 18. 20, 27, 47, 52, 56-57, 63,
    65-66, 70, 79, 83-84, 91-92, 101, 103-
    105, 107, 110-111, 115, 119, 142, 150,
    152
Sikri, S. M., 88
Sindh (Sindhis), 7, 9, 32, 45, 48, 57, 66, 71, 111,
    141, 151, 154-155
Sindhudesh, 7, 153
Singapore, 12, 14, 39, 121, 145
Singh, Ajit, 95, 140
Singh, Beant, 91
Singh, Jaswant, 68
Singh, Manmohan, 140
Singh, V. P., 36-37, 60, 94, 96, 108
Singh, Zail, 83, 104
Sinha, S. K., 61-62, 103
Sinhalese, 8, 34, 69, 111, 153
Sino-Indian War, 20-21, 25-26, 55, 80, 108,
    126-129
Siraikis, 32
Slovenia, 20, 35, 48-49, 71, 152
Socialist Party, 83
South Africa, 110
South Asian Association for Regional Coopera-
    tion (SAARC), 6, 154-155
Southeast Asian Treaty Organization (SEATO),
    106
South Korea, 4, 12, 14, 30, 32, 39-40, 100, 121,
    124, 145
Soviet Union (Soviet), 2, 18-20, 35, 42, 48-49,
    54, 57, 63, 108, 122, 124-125, 127, 136,
    152-153, 155
Spain, 48
Sri Lanka, 4, 6, 8-11, 18, 20, 26, 32, 34-35, 44,
    47-49, 56-57, 64, 69-71, 105, 111-112,
    141
Subrahmanyam, K., 125, 130
Sudan, 143
Supreme Court of India, 73-74, 80, 85-89, 92
Suseelan, Babu, 64
Suu Kyi, Aung Sang, 7
Sweden, 32
Switzerland, 137

Taiwan, 12, 14, 30, 39-40, 100, 121, 124, 145
Tajikistan (Tajiks), 54-55
Tamil Ealam, 153
Tamil Nadu, 56-57, 96, 156
Tamils, 10-11, 18-19, 26, 34, 47, 56-57, 70-71,
    104, 111-112, 141, 153, 155
Telugu Desam, 90
Terrorist Affected Areas Special Courts Act
    (1984), 21, 84, 118

Terrorist and Disruptive Activities Prevention
    Act (TADA, 1987), 21, 84-85, 118
Thailand, 4, 12, 14, 30, 40, 100, 121, 124, 145
Thapan, M. L., 109, 113
Thatcher, Margaret, 15
Tibetans, 47-48
Timorese (East), 47-48
Tofa, Bashir, 12
Tripura, 21, 58, 105, 108
Tunisia, 13
Turkey (Turkish), 18, 19, 45, 47-48, 53-54, 71
Turkish Republic of Northern Cyprus, 19
Turkmenistan, 54
Twenty-Fourth (24th) Amendment, 87
Twenty-Fifth (25th) Amendment, 87
Twenty-Ninth (29th) Amendment, 87

Ukraine, 19
Ulster Loyalists, 15
United Liberation Front of Assam (ULFA), 69,
    115,
    142
United National Party, 96
United Nations, 13, 20; Charter, 17
United States, 2, 13-14, 17-18, 25-26, 31, 40-
    41, 46, 48, 71, 97, 124-125, 127, 132,
    137, 140, 143, 150-151, 157; Congress,
    52, 70; political system, 15, 78, 92, 94-97
Uruguay, 14
Uttarkhand, 58
Uttar Pradesh, 59-60, 65, 84, 91, 115, 152
Uzbekistan (Uzbeks), 54-55

Vajpayee, A. B., 133
Vietnam, 3, 14, 42; Vietnam War, 26
Vishwa Hindu Parishad (VHP), 64
Vohra, A. M., 109, 113

West Bengal, 59, 90-91, 108, 133, 142, 146
    150
Whynes, David, 130
Winterford, David, 130
World Bank, 136, 140, 143
World Wars, 3, 14, 18-19, 25, 103

Xiaoping, Deng, 39

Yew, Lee Kuan, 39
Yugoslavia, 18-20, 35, 48-49, 57, 71, 152-153,
    158

Zaki, Mohammed Abdullah, 111
Zedong, Mao, 4, 108, 122
Zia, Begum Khaleda, 10
Zoroastrians, 22, 44